References for the Rest of Us!®

COMPUTER BOOK SERIES FROM IDG

Are you intimidated and confused by computers? Do you find that traditional manuals are overloaded with technical details you'll never use? Do your friends and family always call you to fix simple problems on their PCs? Then the... *For Dummies*® computer book series from IDG Books Worldwide is for you.

... *For Dummies* books are written for those frustrated computer users who know they aren't really dumb but find that PC hardware, software, and indeed the unique vocabulary of computing make them feel helpless. ... *For Dummies* books use a lighthearted approach, a down-to-earth style, and even cartoons and humorous icons to diffuse computer novices' fears and build their confidence. Lighthearted but not lightweight, these books are a perfect survival guide for anyone forced to use a computer.

> *"I like my copy so much I told friends; now they bought copies."*
>
> **Irene C., Orwell, Ohio**

> *"Quick, concise, nontechnical, and humorous."*
>
> **Jay A., Elburn, Illinois**

> *"Thanks, I needed this book. Now I can sleep at night."*
>
> **Robin F., British Columbia, Canada**

Already, hundreds of thousands of satisfied readers agree. They have made ... *For Dummies* books the #1 introductory level computer book series and have written asking for more. So, if you're looking for the most fun and easy way to learn about computers, look to ... *For Dummies* books to give you a helping hand.

IDG BOOKS WORLDWIDE

COMPUTER
BOOK SERIES
FROM IDG

OLE For Dummies®

Cheat Sheet

Application OLE Specific Menu Commands

Command	Purpose
Insert⇨Object	Use this command to create new objects. You can also use it to create a link to an existing file or embed it in a compound document.
Edit⇨Paste Special	This command allows you to embed or link an object that you copied to the clipboard. You don't need to link or embed an entire file when using this command.
Edit⇨Links	You will normally see a list of the links in the current compound document when using this command. Some applications allow you to change the links. Most applications will allow you to update the links.
Edit⇨Object	Displays a list of actions associated with a particular object
Context Menu	Right clicking on an object displays its Context Menu. This menu contains a list of actions associated with the object along with some editing commands.

OLE File Names

Filename	Purpose
OLE2.DLL	This dynamic link library (DLL) provides some base OLE 2 functions. (A DLL is a special Windows program.)
OLECLI.DLL	This file contains all the basic client code that your application needs.
OLESRV.DLL	This file contains all the basic server code that your application needs.
OLE2CONV.DLL	This file provides the generic routines that a program needs to uses to convert an object to the client program's native format.
OLE2DISP.DLL	Every OLE client application uses this program to help it display the objects it contains.
OLE2NLS.DLL	This program helps OLE keep pace with the rest of Windows in providing support for other languages.
OLE2.REG	A registry file. You can import this file into your registry to install OLE 2 support.
MCIOLE.DLL	This special DLL provides the support an application needs to handle a sound object.
OLE32.DLL	A whole group of OLE files in the SYSTEM directory have "32" somewhere in their file names. These files provide the same services as their 16-bit counterparts except to 32-bit applications.
MFCOLEUI.DLL	C programmers need every bit of help they can get. This file (and any with similar names) provides the Microsoft Foundation Class C interface to OLE.
*.VBX	A special form of DLL (also known as a custom control) that allows you to expand the capability of Visual BASIC and other languages that support VBXs.
*.OCX	An extension of the VBX custom control with an OLE emphasis that allows you to expand the capability of Visual BASIC and other languages that support OCXs.

... For Dummies: #1 Computer Book Series for Beginners

COMPUTER
BOOK SERIES
FROM IDG

OLE For Dummies®

Cheat Sheet

Standard OLE Actions

Action	Meaning
Convert	Changes the object format into another format.
Edit	The edit option changes the menu and tool bar of the client application to match the configuration of the application used to create the object.
Open	The server opens the original version of the object in a new window and allows the user to edit it.
Play	The play action allows the user to hear or see what the object contains.
Undo/Redo	The Undo action allows the user to reverse any changes they made to the object. The Redo action undoes your undo.
Text Properties	This menu entry tells the server to change the text properties as needed since embedded objects will not let you adjust their text properties directly.
Copy	This command allows you to copy an object from a compound document instead of opening the original document.
Cut	This command allows you to cut an object from a compound document.
Paste/Paste Special	The paste command performs a standard paste within the current object. The paste special command allows you to link or embed another object into the current object.

OLE Linking versus Embedding

	Pros	Cons
Linking	Keeps files separate and small in size	Difficult to share multiple linked files with other users
Embedding	Stores all embedded objects in a single file	A file containing embedded objects can get very large

... For Dummies: #1 Computer Book Series for Beginners

OLE

FOR

DUMMIES®

OLE FOR DUMMIES®

by John Paul Mueller
and
Wallace Wang

IDG Books Worldwide, Inc.
An International Data Group Company

Foster City, CA ♦ Chicago, IL ♦ Indianapolis, IN ♦ Braintree, MA ♦ Dallas, TX

OLE For Dummies®

Published by
IDG Books Worldwide, Inc.
An International Data Group Company
919 E. Hillsdale Blvd.
Suite 400
Foster City, CA 94404

Library of Congress Catalog Card No.: 95-79561

ISBN: 1-56884-338-0

Printed in the United States of America

10 9 8 7 6 5 4 3 2 1

1B/TQ/RR/ZV

Distributed in the United States by IDG Books Worldwide, Inc.

Distributed by Macmillan Canada for Canada; by Computer and Technical Books for the Caribbean Basin; by Contemporanea de Ediciones for Venezuela; by Distribuidora Cuspide for Argentina; by CITEC for Brazil; by Ediciones ZETA S.C.R. Ltda. for Peru; by Editorial Limusa SA for Mexico; by Transworld Publishers Limited in the United Kingdom and Europe; by Al-Maiman Publishers & Distributors for Saudi Arabia; by Simron Pty. Ltd. for South Africa; by IDG Communications (HK) Ltd. for Hong Kong; by Toppan Company Ltd. for Japan; by Addison Wesley Publishing Company for Korea; by Longman Singapore Publishers Ltd. for Singapore, Malaysia, Thailand, and Indonesia; by Unalis Corporation for Taiwan; by WS Computer Publishing Company, Inc. for the Philippines; by WoodsLane Pty. Ltd. for Australia; by WoodsLane Enterprises Ltd. for New Zealand.

For general information on IDG Books Worldwide's books in the U.S., please call our Consumer Customer Service department at 800-762-2974. For reseller information, including discounts and premium sales, please call our Reseller Customer Service department at 800-434-3422.

For information on where to purchase IDG Books Worldwide's books outside the U.S., contact IDG Books Worldwide at 415-655-3021 or fax 415-655-3295.

For information on translations, contact Marc Jeffrey Mikulich, Director, Foreign & Subsidiary Rights, at IDG Books Worldwide, 415-655-3018 or fax 415-655-3295.

For sales inquiries and special prices for bulk quantities, write to the address above or call IDG Books Worldwide at 415-655-3200.

For information on using IDG Books Worldwide's books in the classroom, or ordering examination copies, contact Jim Kelly at 800-434-2086.

For authorization to photocopy items for corporate, personal, or educational use, please contact Copyright Clearance Center, 222 Rosewood Drive, Danvers, MA 01923, or fax 508-750-4470.

About the Authors

John Mueller

John Mueller is a freelance author and technical editor. He has writing in his blood, having produced 26 books and almost 200 articles to date. The topics range from networking to artificial intelligence and from database management to heads-down programming. His technical editing skills have helped over 22 authors refine the content of their manuscripts. In addition to book projects, John has provided technical editing services to both *Data Based Advisor* and *Coast Compute* magazines. You can reach John on CompuServe at 71570,641.

Wallace Wang

Wallace Wang has written over a dozen computer books, including IDG's *Visual Basic 4 For Dummies*, *CompuServe For Dummies*, and *PROCOMM PLUS 2 For Dummies*. When not writing books, he writes a monthly column for *Boardwatch Magazine* and also performs stand-up comedy in the San Diego area. He can be reached on CompuServe at 70334,3672.

ABOUT IDG BOOKS WORLDWIDE

Welcome to the world of IDG Books Worldwide.

IDG Books Worldwide, Inc., is a subsidiary of International Data Group, the world's largest publisher of computer-related information and the leading global provider of information services on information technology. IDG was founded more than 25 years ago and now employs more than 7,700 people worldwide. IDG publishes more than 250 computer publications in 67 countries (see listing below). More than 70 million people read one or more IDG publications each month.

Launched in 1990, IDG Books Worldwide is today the #1 publisher of best-selling computer books in the United States. We are proud to have received 8 awards from the Computer Press Association in recognition of editorial excellence and three from Computer Currents' First Annual Readers' Choice Awards, and our best-selling *...For Dummies®* series has more than 19 million copies in print with translations in 28 languages. IDG Books Worldwide, through a joint venture with IDG's Hi-Tech Beijing, became the first U.S. publisher to publish a computer book in the People's Republic of China. In record time, IDG Books Worldwide has become the first choice for millions of readers around the world who want to learn how to better manage their businesses.

Our mission is simple: Every one of our books is designed to bring extra value and skill-building instructions to the reader. Our books are written by experts who understand and care about our readers. The knowledge base of our editorial staff comes from years of experience in publishing, education, and journalism — experience which we use to produce books for the '90s. In short, we care about books, so we attract the best people. We devote special attention to details such as audience, interior design, use of icons, and illustrations. And because we use an efficient process of authoring, editing, and desktop publishing our books electronically, we can spend more time ensuring superior content and spend less time on the technicalities of making books.

You can count on our commitment to deliver high-quality books at competitive prices on topics you want to read about. At IDG Books Worldwide, we continue in the IDG tradition of delivering quality for more than 25 years. You'll find no better book on a subject than one from IDG Books Worldwide.

John J. Kilcullen

John Kilcullen
President and CEO
IDG Books Worldwide, Inc.

WINNER
Eighth Annual
Computer Press
Awards 1992

WINNER
Ninth Annual
Computer Press
Awards 1993

IDG Books Worldwide, Inc., is a subsidiary of International Data Group, the world's largest publisher of computer-related information and the leading global provider of information services on information technology. International Data Group publishes over 250 computer publications in 67 countries. Seventy million people read one or more International Data Group publications each month. International Data Group's publications include: **ARGENTINA:** Computerworld Argentina, GamePro, Infoworld, PC World Argentina; **AUSTRALIA:** Australian Macworld, Client/Server Journal, Computer Living, Computerworld, Digital News, Network World, PC World, Publishing Essentials, Reseller; **AUSTRIA:** Computerwelt, PC TEST; **BELARUS:** PC World Belarus; **BELGIUM:** Data News; **BRAZIL:** Annuário de Informática, Computerworld Brazil, Connections, Super Game Power, Macworld, PC World Brazil, Publish Brazil, SUPERGAME; **BULGARIA:** Computerworld Bulgaria, Networkworld/Bulgaria, PC & MacWorld Bulgaria; **CANADA:** CIO Canada, ComputerWorld Canada, InfoCanada, Network World Canada, Reseller World; **CHILE:** Computerworld Chile, GamePro, PC World Chile; **COLUMBIA:** Computerworld Colombia, GamePro, PC World Colombia; **COSTA RICA:** PC World Costa Rica/Nicaragua; **THE CZECH AND SLOVAK REPUBLICS:** Computerworld Czechoslovakia, Elektronika Czechoslovakia, PC World Czechoslovakia; **DENMARK:** Communications World, Computerworld Danmark, Macworld Danmark, PC World Danmark, PC World Danmark Supplements, TECH World; **DOMINICAN REPUBLIC:** PC World Republica Dominicana; **ECUADOR:** PC World Ecuador, GamePro; **EGYPT:** Computerworld Middle East, PC World Middle East; **EL SALVADOR:** PC World Centro America; **FINLAND:** MikroPC, Tietoverkko, Tietoviikko; **FRANCE:** Distribuique, Golden, Info PC, Le Guide du Monde Informatique, Le Monde Informatique, Reseaux & Telecoms; **GERMANY:** Computer Business, Computerwoche, Computerwoche Extra, Computerwoche Focus, Electronic Entertainment, GamePro, I/M Information Management, Macwelt, PC Welt; **GREECE:** GamePro, Macworld & Publish; **GUATEMALA:** PC World Centro America; **HONDURAS:** PC World Centro America; **HONG KONG:** Computerworld Hong Kong, PCWorld Hong Kong, Publish in Asia; **HUNGARY:** ABCD CD-ROM, Computerworld Szamitastechnika, PC & Mac World Hungary, PC-X Magazine; **INDIA:** Computerworld India, PC World India, Publish in Asia; **INDONESIA:** InfoKomputer PC World, Komputek Computerworld, Publish in Asia; **IRELAND:** ComputerScope, PC Live!; **ISRAEL:** PC World 32 BIT, People & Computers; **ITALY:** Computerworld Italia, Computerworld Italia Special Editions, Lotus Italia, Macworld Italia, Networking Italia, PC Shopping, PC World Italia, PC World/Walt Disney; **JAPAN:** Macworld Japan, Nikkei Personal Computing, SunWorld Japan, Windows World Japan; **KENYA:** East African Computer News; **KOREA:** Hi-Tech Information/Computerworld, Macworld Korea, PC World Korea; **MACEDONIA:** PC World Macedonia; **MALAYSIA:** Computerworld Malaysia, PC World Malaysia, Publish in Asia; **MEXICO:** Computerworld Mexico, GamePro, Macworld, PC World Mexico; **MYANMAR:** PC World Myanmar; **NETHERLANDS:** Computable, Computer! Totaal, LAN Magazine, Macworld, Net Magazine; **NEW ZEALAND:** Computer Buyer, Computerworld New Zealand, MTB, Network World, PC World New Zealand; **NICARAGUA:** PC World Costa Rica/Nicaragua; **NIGERIA:** PC World Africa; **NORWAY:** Computerworld Norge, Computerworld Privat, CW Rapport Klient/Tjener, CW Rapport Nettverk & Telecom, CW Rapport Offentlig Sektor, IDG's KURSGUIDE, Macworld Norge, Multimedia World, PC World Ekspress, PC World Nettverk, PC World Norge, PC World's Produktguide, Windows Spesial; **PAKISTAN:** Computerworld Pakistan, PC World Pakistan; **PANAMA:** GamePro, PC World Panama; **PARAGUAY:** GamePro, PC World Paraguay; **P. R. OF CHINA:** China Computerworld, China Infoworld, Computer & Communication, Electronic Product World, Electronics Today, Game Camp, PC World China, Popular Computer Week, Software World, Telecom Product World; **PERU:** Computerworld Peru, GamePro, PC World Profesional Peru, PC World Peru; **POLAND:** Computerworld Poland, Computerworld Special Report, Macworld, Networld, PC World Komputer; **PHILIPPINES:** Computerworld Philippines, PC Digest, Publish in Asia; **PORTUGAL:** Cerebro/PC World, Correio Informático/Computerworld, Mac•In/PC•In Portugal; **PUERTO RICO:** PC World Puerto Rico; **ROMANIA:** Computerworld Romania, PC World Romania, Telecom Romania; **RUSSIA:** Computerworld Rossiya, Network World Russia, PC World Russia; **SINGAPORE:** Computerworld Singapore, PC World Singapore, Publish in Asia; **SLOVENIA:** MONITOR; **SOUTH AFRICA:** Computing S.A., Network World S.A., Software World; **SPAIN:** Computerworld España, COMUNICACIONES WORLD, Dealer World, Macworld España, PC World España; **SWEDEN:** CAP&Design, Computer Sweden, Corporate Computing, MacWorld, Maxi Data, MikroDatorn, Nätverk & Kommunikation, PC/Aktiv, PC World, Windows World; **SWITZERLAND:** Computerworld Schweiz, Macworld Schweiz, PCtip; **TAIWAN:** Computerworld Taiwan, Macworld Taiwan, PC World Taiwan, Windows World; **THAILAND:** Thai Computerworld, Publish in Asia; **TURKEY:** Computerworld Monitör, MACWORLD Turkiye, PC WORLD Turkiye; **UKRAINE:** Computerworld Kiev, Computers & Software Magazine, PC World Ukraine; **UNITED KINGDOM:** Acorn User, Amiga Action, Amiga Computing, Amiga, Appletalk, CD Powerplay, CD-ROM Now, Computing, Connexion, GamePro, Lotus Magazine, Macaction, Macworld, Open Computing, Parents and Computers, PC Home, PC Works, The WEB; **UNITED STATES:** Cable in the Classroom, CD Review, CIO Magazine, Computerworld, Computerworld Client/Server Journal, Digital Video Magazine, DOS World, Electronic, InfoWorld, I-Way, Macworld, Maximize, MULTIMEDIA WORLD, Network World, PC World, PUBLISH, SWATPro Magazine, Video Event, WebMaster; **URUGUAY:** PC World Uruguay; **VENEZUELA:** Computerworld Venezuela, GamePro, PC World Venezuela; and **VIETNAM:** PC World Vietnam   10/17/95

Dedication

This book is dedicated to those poor souls who still think OLE is something you yell at a bullfight. It's also dedicated to our family members, who had to listen to endless streams of bullfight jokes while we wrote this text.

Acknowledgments

Thanks to Rebecca Mueller for gathering the information for Chapter 20. She also came up with the terms (and many of the definitions) for the Glossary and performed a final proofread of the manuscript.

Matt Wagner, our agent, deserves credit for helping us get the contract for this book in the first place and for taking care of business details that most authors don't really think about.

John Pont deserves a special mention for his superior editing skills, and many thanks to Ron Dippold, our superb technical editor.

We would also like to thank the IDG Books staff, especially Mary Corder and Amy Pederson, for their efforts in producing this final text.

Finally, we wish to extend our thanks to all our cats. They had absolutely nothing to do with the publication or creation of this book, but without their existence, our lives would be filled with much less mirth, joy, and general happiness (as well as less cat hair, fur balls, and kitty litter).

(The Publisher would like to give special thanks to Patrick J. McGovern, without whom this book would not have been possible.)

Credits

Senior Vice President and Publisher
Milissa L. Koloski

Associate Publisher
Diane Graves Steele

Brand Manager
Judith A. Taylor

Editorial Managers
Kristin A. Cocks
Mary C. Corder

Product Development Manager
Mary Bednarek

Editorial Executive Assistant
Richard Graves

Editorial Assistants
Constance Carlisle
Chris Collins
Stacey Holden Prince
Kevin Spencer

Acquisitions Assistant
Gareth Hancock

Production Director
Beth Jenkins

Production Assistant
Jacalyn L. Pennywell

Supervisor of Project Coordination
Cindy L. Phipps

Supervisor of Page Layout
Kathie S. Schnorr

Production Systems Specialist
Steve Peake

Pre-Press Coordination
Tony Augsburger
Patricia R. Reynolds
Theresa Sánchez-Baker

Media/Archive Coordination
Leslie Popplewell
Kerri Cornell
Michael Wilkey

Project Editor
John W. Pont

Technical Reviewer
Ron Dippold

Project Coordinator
Valery Bourke

Graphics Coordination
Shelley Lea
Gina Scott
Carla Radzikinas

Production Page Layout
Shawn Aylsworth
Brett Black
Dominique DeFelice
Todd Klemme
Jill Lyttle
Jane Martin
Drew R. Moore
Elizabeth Cárdenas-Nelson
Kate Snell

Proofreaders
Betty Kish
Christine Meloy Beck
Gwenette Gaddis
Dwight Ramsey
Carl Saff
Robert Springer

Indexer
Liz Cunningham

Cover Design
Kavish + Kavish

Contents at a Glance

Introduction *1*

Part I: What the Heck Is OLE? *7*
Chapter 1: Understanding OLE 9
Chapter 2: All About Clients and Servers 19
Chapter 3: The Limitations of OLE 27

Part II: Using OLE *35*
Chapter 4: Why Use OLE? 37
Chapter 5: Identifying Your Application's OLE Capabilities 45
Chapter 6: Putting OLE to Work 57

Part III: Developing with OLE *69*
Chapter 7: An Introduction to OLE Automation 71
Chapter 8: OLE for Graphics 81
Chapter 9: Advanced OLE for Graphics 99
Chapter 10: OLE for Spreadsheets 109
Chapter 11: OLE for Database Managers 123
Chapter 12: OLE for Word Processors 145

Part IV: Programming OLE with Application Programs *167*
Chapter 13: Why Program? 169
Chapter 14: OLE Programming Principles 175
Chapter 15: Writing OLE Programs with Access BASIC 191
Chapter 16: Writing OLE Programs with Visual BASIC 207
Chapter 17: Writing OLE Programs with Delphi 223
Chapter 18: Testing Your Application 235
Chapter 19: What to Do When Things Go Wrong 247

Part V: The Part of Tens *257*
Chapter 20: Ten OLE Add-Ins for Visual BASIC 259
Chapter 21: Ten OLE Topics that Didn't Fit Anywhere Else 271

Glossary 295

Index 301

Reader Response Card .... Back of Book

Cartoons at a Glance

By Rich Tennant

page 246

page 69

page 166

page 257

page 167

page 7

page 44

page 35

page 55

page 98

Table of Contents

Introduction **1**

    About This Book 2
    Foolish Assumptions 2
    How This Book Is Organized 3
        Part I: What the Heck Is OLE? 3
        Part II: Using OLE 3
        Part III: Developing with OLE 3
        Part IV: Programming OLE with Application Programs 3
        Part V: The Part of Tens 4
    Icons Used in This Book 4
    Where to Go from Here 5

Part I: What the Heck Is OLE? **7**

    Chapter 1: Understanding OLE **9**

        Where OLE Came From and Why It Exists 10
            Integrated programs to the rescue (sort of) 10
            Microsoft Windows sets a new standard 10
        Why OLE Exists 12
            Sharing data 12
                Linking 12
                Embedding 13
            In-place editing 14
            Creating custom applications through OLE automation 15
        The Future of OLE 16

    Chapter 2: All About Clients and Servers **19**

        The Wonderful World of Objects 19
        Linking and Embedding 20
        What Is a Client? 20
        What Is a Server? 22
        How Clients and Servers Work Together 24
            Cutting, copying, and pasting data 24
            Linking objects 24
            Embedding and editing objects 25

Chapter 3: The Limitations of OLE **27**

The System Resource Problem 27
RAM cram 28
The incredible shrinking hard disk 28
The Lack of Complete OLE Acceptance 30
The slow migration to OLE 30
The domino effect 31
The Problems of a Single-User Standard 31
No network support 31
No multiplatform (Mac and Windows) support 32
Is OLE Worth Learning? 32

Part II: Using OLE *35*

Chapter 4: Why Use OLE? **37**

Sharing Data Between Applications 37
Storing data in a single file (or, putting all your eggs in one basket) 38
Updating multiple files simultaneously 38
Customizing Applications 40
Shrinking applications to a manageable size 40
Making your own applications 41
Ensuring Compatibility with Other Applications 42
Because Microsoft Says So 43

Chapter 5: Identifying Your Application's OLE Capabilities **45**

Types of OLE Capabilities 46
Checking for OLE Client Capabilities 47
Checking for OLE Server Capabilities 50
Checking for OLE 1 and OLE 2 Features 51

Chapter 6: Putting OLE to Work **57**

Practicing with Windows 3.1 57
OLE embedding 57
OLE linking 60
Practicing with Windows 95 60
OLE embedding 61
OLE linking 63
Using OLE with Microsoft Office 65
OLE embedding 65
OLE linking 67

Part III: Developing with OLE *69*

Chapter 7: An Introduction to OLE Automation 71

OLE and Applications 72
Using Macros to Speed OLE 72
Planning Your Macro 77
The OLE Cast of Characters 78

Chapter 8: OLE for Graphics 81

Graphics Applications and OLE 82
Using paint programs with OLE 83
Can your paint program handle the job? 83
Putting your paint program to work 86
Using drawing programs with OLE 91
CorelShow: The other macro 92
Using CorelDRAW! with VBA 92
Special OLE capabilities in drawing programs 93

Chapter 9: Advanced OLE for Graphics 99

Specialized Server Methods 99
CAD Programs and OLE Scripts 103
OLE and Chart Programs 104

Chapter 10: OLE for Spreadsheets 109

Spreadsheets and OLE 110
Objects Within a Spreadsheet 112
Linking data in spreadsheets 112
Embedding data in spreadsheets 115
Spreadsheets and OLE Macros 118
Spreadsheets and OLE Automation 120

Chapter 11: OLE for Database Managers 123

DBMSs and OLE 124
Objects Within a DBMS 125
Using OLE in DBMS Forms and Reports 128
Using OLE in DBMS Macros 131
Object properties 131
Creating a simple form macro 133
Creating some tables 134
Designing a form 137
Programming a macro 140
Creating a simple object macro 142

Chapter 12: OLE for Word Processors **145**

Word Processors and OLE 145
Objects Within a Document 146
OLE as Part of Documents 150
  Inserting pictures 150
  Inserting databases 151
Using OLE in Word Processing Macros 158
  Creating the initial macro 159
  Adding a dialog box 161

Part IV: Programming OLE with Application Programs *167*

Chapter 13: Why Program? **169**

All About Programming and OLE 170
Types of OLE Programs 171
  Macros 171
  High-level languages 171
  Low-level languages 172
Macros Versus Programming Languages 172

Chapter 14: OLE Programming Principles **175**

Deciding What to Program 175
  Is it a client or a server? 176
  Using the command line interface 177
Things Every OLE Program Needs 178
  The four OLE programming modes 178
  Actions that OLE programs perform 180
  Inside-out or outside-in? 183
  Registering your application 185
Writing the OLE Portion of Your Program 187

Chapter 15: Writing OLE Programs with Access BASIC **191**

Programming, Macros, Forms, or Queries 193
Changing the Contents of a Table 194
  Modifying OLE objects 194
  Adding OLE objects 198
Using Forms to Their Full Potential 202

Chapter 16: Writing OLE Programs with Visual BASIC **207**

Using the Insert Object Dialog Box 207
  Testing OLE embedding 209
  Testing OLE linking 211

Using the Paste Special Dialog Box..212
    Testing OLE embedding 213
    Testing OLE linking 213
Adding In-Place Activation 214
Creating OLE Servers 217
    Writing an OLE server 217
    Testing your OLE server 219

Chapter 17: Writing OLE Programs with Delphi **223**

Using the Insert Object Dialog Box...223
    Testing OLE embedding 226
    Testing OLE linking 226
Using the Paste Special Dialog Box..228
    Testing OLE embedding 230
    Testing OLE linking 231
Using In-Place Activation 232

Chapter 18: Testing Your Application **235**

Initial Testing Makes Stronger Applications 236
    Subsystem testing 237
    System integration 238
    Unexpected events 239
Broken Applications 240
    Feature-related errors 240
    OLE 1 and other compatibility problems 241
    Interactions with other applications 241
    INI file gotchas 241
    Memory-related errors 242
Fixing Broken Applications 243
Bug Hunting 244

Chapter 19: What to Do When Things Go Wrong **247**

Register that Application 247
Fixing a Broken Windows 95 Registry 252
Repairing Broken OLE Links 253

Part V: The Part of Tens *257*

Chapter 20: Ten OLE Add-Ins for Visual BASIC **259**

Graphics and OLE 260
    ImageKnife/VBX 261
    Graphics Server SDK 261
Communicating with OLE 262
    Communications Library 3 262
    FaxMan 263
    App-Link 263

Graphs and OLE 264
    Visio 264
OLE-Equipped Hypertext Tools 265
    Hypertext Manager 265
    ALLText HT/Pro 265
Creating OLE-Supported Reports 266
    Crystal Reports Pro 266
Squashing OLE Bugs 267
    PinPoint VB 267
Just in Case You Haven't Seen Enough 268
    Custom Control Factory 268
    Rocket 269
    NetPak Professional 269
    justButtons 270

Chapter 21: Ten OLE Topics that Didn't Fit Anywhere Else 271

Getting Even Deeper into OLE Programming 271
    C and C++ compilers 272
    The Microsoft OLE SDK 272
    The Microsoft Windows SDK 272
    A book that explains how to use OLE with C and C++ ... 273
Peering Inside the Windows 95 Registry 273
    Learning the registry lingo 274
    Adding the Registry Editor to the Start menu 275
    An overview of the registry 277
        File association and OLE entries 279
        Current user configuration and environment settings 279
        Hardware configuration entries 280
        Permanent user configuration and environment settings 280
        Graphics device interface (GDI) settings 280
        System status and performance settings 281
        In a nutshell 281
    Taking a closer look at the registry and OLE 282
    Special shell extension subkeys 286
    OLE 1 entries in the registry 287
    OLE 2 entries in the registry 289
Future Shock — OLE and VBA 293

Glossary *295*

Index *301*

Reader Response Card .... *Back of Book*

Introduction

· ·

*1*f you've ever written a report in your favorite word processor, created a graph in your favorite graphics program, and calculated a list of numbers in your favorite spreadsheet, you know the problems you face when trying to organize this information into one place. Although Windows lets you copy your spreadsheet data into your word processing document, what happens if you change your spreadsheet data at a later date? You have to make identical changes to the spreadsheet data you copied into your word processor report. Clumsy? Yes. Avoidable? Of course.

You could go crazy trying to keep track of information stored in different files created by different programs from different software developers. To help you keep your sanity, Microsoft created a universal standard called Object Linking and Embedding (or OLE, which has the same pronunciation as the cheer a crowd might yell when a raging bull rushes past a matador).

With OLE, you can forge links between files created by separate programs. When you update data stored in one file, OLE can automatically update the data stored in other files as well.

Although OLE has been around for several years, it's one of those little-known tools that most people tend to ignore. They don't realize that it makes computers easier to use and keeps you from going mad in the process.

But if OLE is so great, why aren't more people using it? Maybe it's because nobody has ever explained OLE in terms that make sense to regular folks. Take a look at most books about OLE, and you'll find that they weigh several pounds, offer terse descriptions that only technical wizards can understand, and focus primarily on teaching C++ programmers how to use OLE. So, what about the rest of us?

That's where this book, *OLE For Dummies*, comes in. Although this book won't teach you how to create OLE-compliant programs in C++ (plenty of other books do that), it will teach you what the heck OLE is (and why Microsoft is so excited about it), how to use OLE in practical applications, and how to create OLE-compliant programs in Visual BASIC and other languages that normal people can understand.

Armed with this knowledge, beginners can finally tap the power of OLE and make their computers a lot easier to use. Intermediate users can also pick up a few tips for using OLE, while advanced users can learn about creating their own programs which include OLE features. If you want to learn about OLE but could care less about learning C++, this book is for you.

About This Book

Think of this book as a friendly introduction and guide to using and programming in OLE. Now, before the word *programming* gets you into a frenzy, relax. Because this book explains OLE for beginners as well as intermediate and advanced users, you can pick the sections that make sense to you and ignore the rest. Beginners can avoid the programming sections of this book, while advanced users can skip the introductory stuff and jump right into the programming parts.

The book is broken into parts which make it easy for you to find just the material you need without wading through a lot of stuff you don't want to know. Parts I through IV progress through increasing levels of difficulty from novice to advanced user. Part V includes a bit of information for everyone; beginners can easily avoid the OLE deep waters in these chapters by bypassing the sections marked with a Technical Stuff icon.

This book provides three types of information about OLE:

- Explanations of what the heck OLE is and why would anyone want to use it.
- Tips for using OLE effectively to make your computer easier to use.
- Advice for using a programming language to create your own programs that can use OLE.

Foolish Assumptions

To use OLE, you have to know how to use your programs' cut, copy, and paste features. In addition, you need one or more programs that actually use OLE. (Not all programs can use OLE, but this book explains how to tell which of your programs can do so.)

In addition, this book assumes you're using the latest copy of Microsoft Windows. You can still use the information in this book if you're using Windows 3.1 or 3.0, but the bulk of this book applies specifically to Windows 95.

Other than knowing how to use your computer and having a program that uses OLE, you just need a desire to goof around with your computer and see what happens next. Don't worry, OLE can't screw up your computer, so feel free to experiment.

How This Book Is Organized

This book is divided into five parts, each of which contains several chapters. You don't have to read each part in order, though you can if you want. Feel free to flip through the book and learn at your own pace. Despite the intimidating nature of other books about OLE, you'll find that using or programming OLE really isn't that complicated after all.

Here is a rundown of the different parts in this book:

Part I: What the Heck is OLE?

In Part I, you'll learn the reasons for OLE's existence, what it can (and cannot) do, and what part it may play in the future of the software industry. You'll also learn the difference between OLE client and server programs, and other fancy stuff like that.

Part II: Using OLE

Part II describes how to use OLE among different programs. Most important, this part of the book explains how to determine which of your current programs use OLE and how much of the OLE specification they support.

Part III: Using OLE in Applications

If you want to know how to assemble useful applications with OLE, you should read Part III. This is where you'll find tips for using OLE to actually do something important.

Part IV: Developing with OLE

For those hard-core techies who want to work with OLE in Visual BASIC and other programming languages, Part IV explains what OLE can do and how to use OLE with your favorite programming language.

Part V: The Part of Tens

In addition to helping you figure out what to do when things go wrong, the chapters in Part V provide lots of useful information that just didn't fit anywhere else in the book.

Icons Used in This Book

This icon signals technical details that may be nice to know but are totally unnecessary. However, if you really want to impress your friends, you can memorize this information and share your knowledge at the next (and probably last) cocktail party you're invited to.

This icon points out helpful information that can make you a happier computer user.

This icon highlights important information that you should commit to memory — or at least read.

This icon highlights information you need to know or else you'll risk messing up something important, but not critical.

This icon highlights information about Windows 3.1 or 3.0.

This icon highlights information about Windows 95.

Be careful! This icon waves a red warning flag to let you know of things that could totally screw up your computer and ruin your whole day. (You can ignore this icon if you're using someone else's computer and don't care if you wreck it.)

Step-by-step instructions and explanations follow this icon.

You will see remarks or amplifying information follow this icon. A note usually provides background information you need to know to understand the rest of the section.

Deep, dark secrets about OLE or Windows follow this icon. Only the privileged few know about this information, and even they're afraid to say much (Microsoft has spies everywhere, you know). Normally, this icon tells you about undocumented details that only a programmer would love to know.

Where to Go from Here

OLE may seem mysterious, but this book will help you understand it, use it, and, most importantly, take full advantage of its features. So, relax and get ready to learn more about OLE than you ever thought possible. OLE is easy to learn and extremely useful, but only when you know what you're doing, which is what this book is all about.

Part I

What the Heck Is OLE?

"Now, when someone rings my doorbell, the current goes to a scanner that digitizes the audio impulses and sends the image to the PC where it's converted to a Pict file. The image is then animated, compressed, and sent via high-speed modem to an automated phone service that sends an e-mail message back to tell me someone was at my door 40 minutes ago."

In This Part...

Despite the fact that OLE has been around for several years, it's been ignored by most people except for dedicated computer enthusiasts who like tinkering around with their computers, just to see what might happen next.

However, OLE offers tremendous advantages that are slowly starting to appear in mainstream programs. Microsoft uses OLE extensively in the new Microsoft Office 95 suite of programs — Word, Excel, PowerPoint, and Access — to make these programs easier to use. As OLE finally seeps into the public consciousness (sort of like the environmental and peace movements of the 1960s), you'll find more and more programs using OLE to make your computer easier and simpler to use.

Of course, before you can use OLE, you have to know what it can do, and before you know what OLE can do, it's a good idea to learn how it works. In this part of the book, you'll learn where OLE came from, where it may be heading, and how it works so you can use it effectively.

Chapter 1

Understanding OLE

● ●

In This Chapter

▶ The evolution of OLE

▶ Why OLE exists

▶ The future of OLE

● ●

OLE is a fancy acronym that stands of Object Linking and Embedding. Of course, that long-winded term means nothing if you don't know what OLE is for or how to use it.

The one thing you need to know about OLE is that OLE manipulates objects. An object can be any piece of information, such as a graphics file or a sound file. OLE lets you copy, delete, move, view, or hear an object.

For example, suppose you've created a graph using a spreadsheet, and you need to write a report explaining what the graph really means. Before the miracle of OLE, you would have to store the graph in one file and your report in a second file. If you wanted to change your report and your graph, you would first have to load a word processor to edit your report, and then load a spreadsheet to edit your graph. Clumsy and cumbersome? You bet.

With OLE, you can store your report and your graph in the same file (known as *embedding*) or in separate files (known as *linking*). With embedding, you can store data from multiple programs — for example, a spreadsheet, a word processor, and a database — in a single file, known as a *compound document*. By storing data in a compound document, you can easily organize your information by its use, rather than by the program that created it.

As a second alternative to embedding, you can link files. Linking files lets multiple files display information from another file. For example, you might have three different reports linked to the same graph. If you view any of the three reports, you'll see the same graph. The moment you edit the file containing the graph, the graph changes simultaneously in any files linked to that file. By linking data in separate files, you can make sure changing your data in one file will automatically update other files.

Where OLE Came From and Why It Exists

Back in the early days of personal computers, programs didn't follow any standards. To save a file in one word processor, you had to press Ctrl+K+D, while to save a file in another word processor, you had to press F10.

Besides using wildly differing commands to perform identical tasks, each program also stored information in its own peculiar file format. For example, letters written in WordPerfect couldn't be used in Microsoft Word, and spreadsheets created in Excel couldn't be used by Lotus 1-2-3.

Integrated programs to the rescue (sort of)

Integrated programs were the first, feeble attempt to solve the dual problems of differing program commands and file formats. An integrated program combines the features of a word processor, a spreadsheet, and a database in a single program. Common integrated programs include Microsoft Works, ClarisWorks, and virtually any other program that manages to incorporate *Works* into its name.

In addition to using a consistent set of commands for saving, copying, and deleting data, an integrated program is designed to share data easily among its separate parts. For example, if you created a graph using the integrated program's spreadsheet, you could easily copy that graph into a letter you wrote using the integrated program's word processor.

Integrated programs worked, up to a point. Unfortunately, because an integrated program tried to do everything, it typically did everything poorly. Even worse, files created by one integrated program (such as Microsoft Works) wouldn't work with another integrated program (such as ClarisWorks), which essentially defeated the purpose of integrated programs in the first place.

Microsoft Windows sets a new standard

Following these ineffective integrated programs, the next evolutionary step occurred when Microsoft introduced Windows. Windows provided a graphical user interface (GUI) that encouraged developers of different programs to provide a common set of commands for performing identical tasks, such as saving a file or deleting data.

Microsoft Windows also introduced a new feature called Dynamic Data Exchange (DDE), which let different Windows programs share data with one another through links. For example, you could link a spreadsheet file to a word processor document. If you changed the numbers in the spreadsheet, those changes would automatically appear in your word processor document, as shown in Figure 1-1.

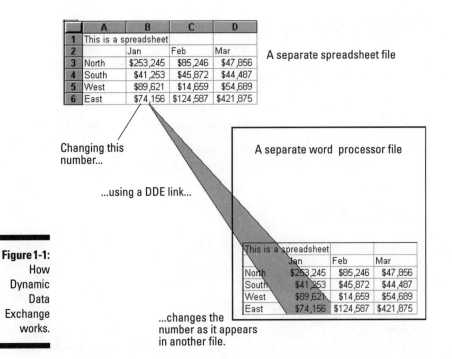

A separate spreadsheet file

Changing this
number...

...using a DDE link...

A separate word processor file

...changes the
number as it appears
in another file.

Figure 1-1:
How
Dynamic
Data
Exchange
works.

Although DDE worked, it also had its limitations. DDE allowed only a one-way
transfer of information, from the program that created the data (known as the
server) to the program receiving the data (known as the client). In addition,
DDE links were very feeble. Any change in either linked file could break the link.
Although linking a spreadsheet file to a word processor document using DDE
was easy enough, problems arose when you tried to edit the client end of a link.
If you wanted to edit the spreadsheet file, you had to run your spreadsheet
program. Then, if you wanted to see the changes the spreadsheet made in your
word processor document through its DDE link, you had to start your word
processor program and perform a manual update.

Switching back and forth between multiple programs was clumsy and time-
consuming. That's why Microsoft eventually created OLE.

Why OLE Exists

Basically, the whole purpose of OLE is to make computers easier to use by providing three key advantages:

- ✔ Data can be shared among different programs.
- ✔ Data can be edited without having to exit and load a second (or third) program.
- ✔ Programs (for example, word processors and spreadsheets) can be automated to create custom applications.

Sharing data

OLE lets programs share data in two ways:

- ✔ Linking
- ✔ Embedding

Linking

Linking lets you tell your computer, "See these two files? I want the data stored in this file to appear in this other file." For example, you could link a spreadsheet graph to a word processor document. Although the spreadsheet graph appears inside the word processor document, it actually exists as a separate file, as shown in Figure 1-2.

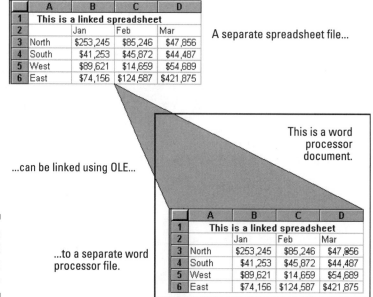

A separate spreadsheet file...

...can be linked using OLE...

This is a word processor document.

Figure 1-2: How OLE linking works.

...to a separate word processor file.

Although linking is simple, it does have its drawbacks. If you want to share your linked files with another user, you have to give that person every linked file. If you have two linked files but only give someone one of those files, guess what? OLE displays an empty space where the linked file is supposed to appear, as shown in Figure 1-3.

Embedding

Embedding lets you tell the computer, "See that object over there? Cram it into this other file over here." For example, you could embed a spreadsheet graph into a word processor document. Unlike linking, which consists of two or more separate files, embedding creates a single file, as shown in Figure 1-4.

The drawback of embedding is that the more objects you embed in a single file, the fatter that file becomes. The advantage is that sharing a file containing embedded objects is easy; you just have to give people one file.

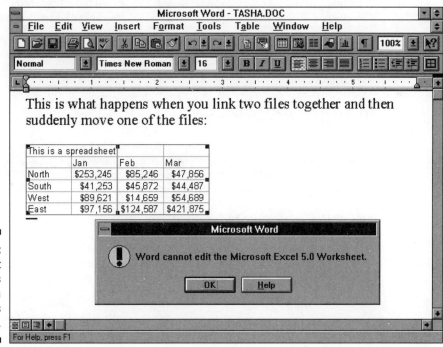

Figure 1-3: Here's what happens when a linked file is missing.

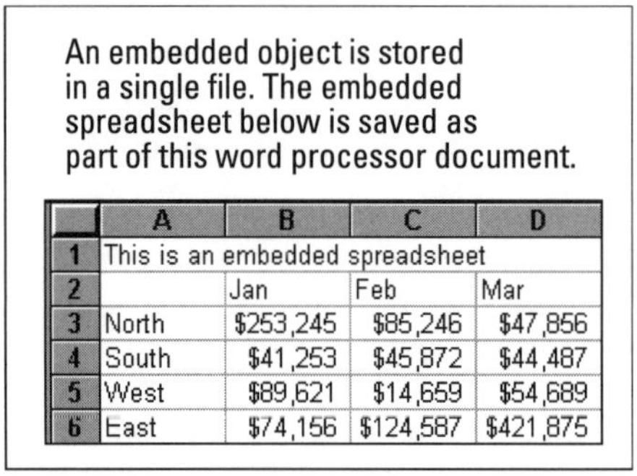

An embedded object is stored
in a single file. The embedded
spreadsheet below is saved as
part of this word processor document.

	A	B	C	D
1	This is an embedded spreadsheet			
2		Jan	Feb	Mar
3	North	$253,245	$85,246	$47,856
4	South	$41,253	$45,872	$44,487
5	West	$89,621	$14,659	$54,689
6	East	$74,156	$124,587	$421,875

Figure 1-4:
How OLE
embedding
works.

Table 1-1	The pros and cons of linking and embedding	
	Pros	*Cons*
Linking	Keeps files separate and small in size.	Difficult to share multiple linked files with other users.
Embedding	Stores all embedded objects in a single file.	A file containing embedded objects can get very large.

In-place editing

Suppose you embedded a spreadsheet graph inside a word processor document and then decided you need to edit the graph. Without OLE, if you wanted to edit the spreadsheet graph, you would have to load your spreadsheet, edit the graph, and then switch back to your word processor.

But with OLE, you can just click on the spreadsheet graph that's embedded in your word processor document. Your spreadsheet's menus magically appear, letting you modify the spreadsheet graph without exiting your word processor. This magical process is known as *in-place editing*. See Figure 1-5 to get a better idea how it works.

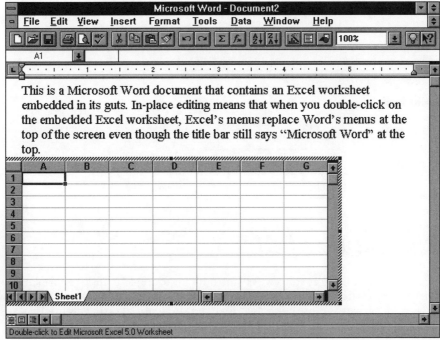

Figure 1-5:
How in-
place
editing
works.

Once you're done editing your spreadsheet graph, just click on your word processor document, and your word processor's menus reappear.

The first version of OLE (version 1.0) didn't allow in-place editing. The second version of OLE (version 2.0) fixed that problem. So, if you happen to be using a program that only supports OLE 1.0, you won't be able to use in-place editing.

Creating custom applications through OLE automation

Perhaps the most powerful feature of OLE is its capability to create custom programs. A single word processor, spreadsheet, or database usually won't offer all the features you need. However, your word processor may provide one feature you need, and your spreadsheet may provide another useful feature. OLE can connect the features of these two programs, essentially letting you create your own, custom-made program without having to develop a word processor and a spreadsheet from scratch with a weird programming language such as C++. Figure 1-6 shows how OLE will eventually let you create custom applications.

OLE lets you create a custom
application by bundling
separate OLE objects together.

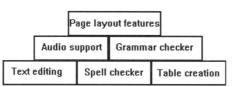

Figure 1-6:
Creating a
custom
application
with OLE.

The Future of OLE

OLE is Microsoft's way of introducing a long-sought-for goal in personal computers dubbed *document-centric* computing. This means that the document you create is more important than the application(s) that created it.

OLE's rivals

Because Microsoft created the OLE standard, it's no surprise that rival companies have proposed alternate standards to make OLE look stupid. IBM created a standard called System Object Model (SOM), which they use in their much-overlooked operating system, OS/2. In fact, the OS/2 Workplace Shell was actually created using SOM, showing you a real-life example of something from IBM that actually works.

Unfortunately, SOM and OLE are two completely different standards. Rather than bet on which standard is going to dominate the computer industry (Microsoft versus IBM, who would you put your money on?), several companies — including Apple, Novell, Lotus, and Borland International — have proposed a rival standard called OpenDoc.

OpenDoc is a superset of OLE, which means that most anything that OLE can do, OpenDoc can do as well. Although Apple is heavily promoting OpenDoc for the Macintosh, the OpenDoc standard hasn't yet been implemented in many Windows programs.

Because OpenDoc offers the same features as OLE, you might as well learn about OLE first. Then, if OpenDoc becomes the new standard, you'll be able to use what you've learned about OLE in any programs that use OpenDoc.

The new document-centric approach lets you focus on getting a task done, rather than on deciding which application is needed. This means you can pick and choose the best features from different applications. For example, if you like writing and editing in Microsoft Word but you prefer the spell-checker and grammar checker found in WordPerfect, just use the features of both to write all your word processor documents.

OLE also has a bright future for networks. Today, programs and documents may be scattered among any number of computers connected to a network. How can you find them all? Easy, you can't.

The current version of OLE (version 2.0) provides Lightweight Remote Procedure Call (LRPC). LRPC allows OLE to find any file or program on your desktop computer, even if you don't remember where the file is stored. Future versions of OLE will use something called Remote Procedure Call (RPC), which essentially tells your computer, "If you don't find the file or program you need on my computer, look for it on the other computers connected to the network."

Eventually, OLE will make computers not only easier to use, but more powerful as well. Then again, that's what the computer industry has been promising us for years. We're seeing progress all the time, but using computers is still so confusing.

Test your newfound knowledge

1. Why did Microsoft invent OLE?

  a. So they could make more money and continue their worldwide domination of the computer industry.

  b. To make computers easier to use by letting you share information between different programs.

  c. To invent yet another acronym that keeps computers as confusing as ever to the uninitiated.

  d. OLE? I thought this was a book about batch file programming for DOS.

2. Name the three advantages of OLE.

  a. Sharing data, in-place editing, and creating custom programs.

  b. OLE makes your computer slower, more confusing, and more error-prone than ever before.

  c. See no evil, hear no evil, speak no evil.

  d. There is no advantage to using OLE. Microsoft created OLE to keep rival software companies busy adding OLE features to their programs that nobody will use anyway.

Chapter 2

All About Clients and Servers

. . . .

In This Chapter

▶ The wonderful world of objects

▶ What is a client?

▶ What is a server?

▶ How clients and servers work together

. . . .

*O*LE doesn't define a single program. Instead, OLE defines the communication between two or more programs. At the bare minimum, OLE requires at least two programs sharing information with one another — although it's possible to have multiple programs sharing information.

Of course, getting two programs to cooperate with one another can be troublesome, especially when they're written by different companies. To overcome these obstacles, OLE defines specific ways in which programs must communicate so they can work together.

The Wonderful World of Objects

When two or more programs share information, they don't just share raw data such as numbers or letters. Instead, they share objects.

Objects are self-contained, autonomous units (much like unruly teenagers). An object has five key parts:

- ✔ The data — such as text, numbers, or graphs.
- ✔ The format of that data, which controls how it appears on the screen.
- ✔ The name of the program that created the data (so you can edit it later).
- ✔ Identifying information, such as the object's author and anything unique about the object.
- ✔ A list of things you can do with the object. For example, does the originating application allow you to print the object? If so, a print entry would be provided as part of the object.

Any OLE object exists as an independent entity, but can be programmed using commands such as you might find in a macro language. OLE defines two parts of every object:

- *Methods* perform actions on an object. For example, a Document object might provide a Print method.
- *Properties* define the state of an object. For example, a Drawing object might have a Color property.

Each OLE object contains a great many details about that object — everything that makes the object unique and identifiable. By using an object's methods, you can make that object do something to itself. By using an object's properties, you can modify the object.

The power of OLE lies in its simplicity; with OLE, you can easily create large applications by combining different objects. Objects act like building blocks for assembling applications. Without OLE, plain old data is more like raw material such as sand and gravel — it's not particularly useful unless you have the right tools for using it to build something.

Linking and Embedding

OLE programs can share objects by either linking or embedding. With linking, one program creates an object and tells a second program, "Here's the information you need, but I'm keeping it with me." The second program has only a pointer to the information. A pointer is like a mailing address; it tells you where something can be found.

With embedding, one program creates an object and gives it to the second program, essentially telling the second program, "Here's the information you need, it's yours to keep." When asked by the second program, the first application still modifies the object.

OLE programs must behave differently, depending on whether they're receiving objects from other programs or sharing objects with other programs. To help identify the role each OLE program is playing, OLE classifies programs as clients or servers.

What Is a Client?

OLE always considers one program as the client. Any files created by the client program contain embedded objects or pointers to linked objects created by other programs, such as graphs, charts, or numbers from a spreadsheet package or a presentation graphics program.

Because files created by client programs can gather objects from a wide variety of programs, client programs typically offer features for displaying data and making it pretty. For that reason, word processors, graphics applications, and desktop publishing programs are often used as clients, as shown in Figure 2-1.

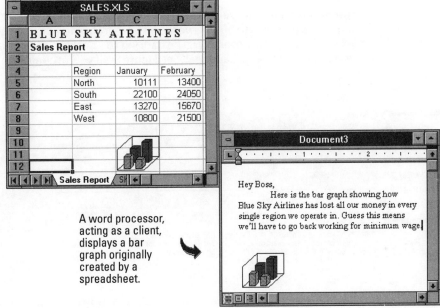

Figure 2-1: A client program contains information from other programs.

A word processor, acting as a client, displays a bar graph originally created by a spreadsheet.

Because a file created by a client program holds data from other programs, clients are sometimes called *containers*. (So, the next time you meet with clients at work, call them containers and see what happens.)

Basically, client programs need to know how to do two things:

✔ Store and display data created by any OLE-compatible program.

✔ Ask the server program to manipulate the data.

An OLE object can contain methods — that is, instructions — for performing a wide variety of tasks. For example, there is absolutely no reason why a telephone number object in a database couldn't contain a method that tells how to dial itself. Reality is a bit different, though. Most programmers provide methods only for editing, printing, and displaying the data. Some programmers also provide a method for converting the data from its original format to the native format of the client application. OLE is capable of doing a lot more than most programmers are allowing it to; few programs take full advantage of OLE's capabilities.

What Is a Server?

At the simplest level, a server sends (serves) an object to a client, much like a tennis player serves a tennis ball. Servers create objects; clients organize and display objects.

Any program can be a server, such as a database or a spreadsheet. It's even possible for a program to be a server to one program and a client to another. For example, a word processor can be a server to a desktop publishing program, and a client to a spreadsheet. See Figure 2-2 if you're confused.

Figure 2-2:
A program
can be a
server and a
client at the
same time.

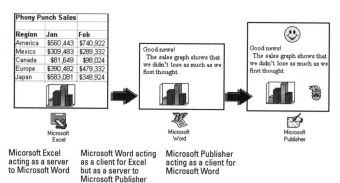

Micorsoft Excel
acting as a server
to Microsoft Word

Microsoft Word acting
as a client for Excel
but as a server to
Microsoft Publisher

Microsoft Publisher
acting as a client for
Microsoft Word

In addition to sending objects to a file created by a client program, a server must communicate with that client program. For example, if the user tries to edit an object embedded in a file, the client program that created that file has no idea how to edit that data. Instead, the client must ask the server for help. As shown in Figure 2-3, the server then rushes over to help the user edit the object that the server originally created.

Although this two-program communication process is invisible to the user, it's a fairly complicated process of coordination. Without OLE defining this standard for coordination, getting two programs to work together would be nearly impossible. (Getting two programs to agree on anything is almost as difficult as getting two people to agree on anything. That's why this book was originally called *OLE For Politicians*, but we decided that *OLE For Dummies* was more truthful and accurate.)

Basically, server programs need to know how to

 ✔ Send data to any file created by an OLE-compatible program.

 ✔ Edit data stored in a file created by another OLE-compatible program.

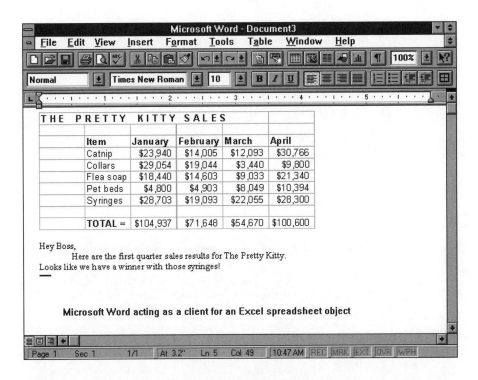

Microsoft Word acting as a client for an Excel spreadsheet object

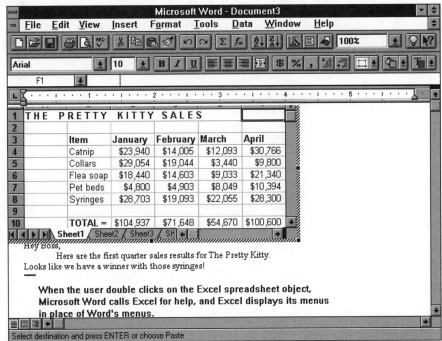

When the user double clicks on the Excel spreadsheet object,
Microsoft Word calls Excel for help, and Excel displays its menus
in place of Word's menus.

Figure 2-3:
How a
server
works with
data
embedded
in a client.

How Clients and Servers Work Together

Clients and servers can work together in various ways, depending on whether you're using OLE to

- Link objects
- Embed objects
- Edit objects
- Print objects
- Perform other object-specific tasks

Cutting, copying, and pasting data

When you cut, copy, and paste an object between two OLE programs, you're essentially stripping the data — for example, text, numbers, graphics — out of the object and plopping it into another program.

Raw data is fairly dumb in the sense that any changes you make to the data don't affect the original location of the data. For example, you might copy a graph from a spreadsheet and paste it into a document created with your word processor. If you go back to your spreadsheet and modify the graph, you must copy that same graph and paste it into your word processor document all over again. As far as the computer is concerned, the graph in your spreadsheet and the graph in your word processor are two entirely different sets of data, even though they look identical.

Linking objects

With linking, the server program creates and stores an object in a separate file. The client program simply displays that object.

The client doesn't actually contain linked data. Instead, it contains information (known as a pointer) identifying the location of the file that contains the data.

That's what makes linked objects so convenient to use. If you create a graph with a spreadsheet program and link it to a document created with your word processor, any changes you make to the graph are automatically reflected in your word processor document.

When you move a file containing a linked object, guess what? You have to reestablish the link so the client program can find the linked object again. This process isn't difficult, just annoying. So, if you frequently link objects, try to avoid moving files around too often or you'll have to reestablish links over and over again.

Although this may look like magic, it's not. All you're really doing is changing a single object (within your server program). This is like touching your face while standing in a funhouse hall of mirrors, and then marveling that all your reflections are touching their faces at the same time.

You can always convert linked objects into embedded ones. That way, you won't have to worry about moving files around and accidentally breaking links. In some cases, you can also convert linked data to the client application's native format. Of course, that means you can no longer use the original application to edit the object.

Embedding and editing objects

With embedding, the server program creates an object but the client program physically contains that object. An embedded object contains the data as well as the name of the program that created it.

When you click on an embedded object, the object asks itself, "Hey, which program created me?" Within the blink of an eye, the object searches for its creator and runs that particular program.

For example, you might embed a graph from a spreadsheet into a word processor document. The moment you click on the graph to edit it, the graph (as an object) rushes off and loads the spreadsheet (the server) that created it.

Your word processor (as the client) is still running, but the spreadsheet (the server) is temporarily running at the same time. The moment you click any part of the word processor document, the spreadsheet (server) quits running and hands control back to the word processor (client).

With embedded objects, the client is always running but the servers are constantly loading and unloading each time the user clicks and edits their objects.

Computers with limited memory (4MB or less) may have trouble with embedded objects. Your computer needs enough memory not only for loading the client program, but for constantly loading and unloading server programs. If your computer doesn't have enough memory, it may not be able to load the server program.

Test your newfound knowledge

1. What's the purpose of a client and a server?

   a. *The Client* is the name of a best-selling novel by John Grisham, which tells the highly implausible story of a lawyer actually willing to work for $1. A server is someone who plays tennis and hits the ball first.

   b. A client works in direct opposition to the server. Anything the server gives to the client, the client immediately destroys.

   c. A client contains and displays objects created by other programs known as servers.

   d. A client is someone able to pay the outrageous fees charged by today's doctors and lawyers. A server is someone who charges an outrageous fee for doing practically nothing at all.

2. What is an object?

   a. An object is a self-contained entity consisting of data, methods, and properties.

   b. An object is what trial lawyers use to keep competing lawyers from saying something misleading — as in, "Your honor, I object."

   c. Objects can be both unidentified and flying, and are otherwise known as Unidentified Flying Objects, or UFOs.

   d. An object is something that you can hit your head on if you're not careful.

Chapter 3
The Limitations of OLE

· ·

In This Chapter

▶ The system resource problem

▶ The lack of complete OLE acceptance

▶ The problems of a single-user standard

▶ Is OLE worth learning?

· ·

*H*aving learned about the wonderful features of OLE in the previous two chapters, you might want to know what drawbacks OLE has. After all, nothing is perfect, and anything as complicated as getting two programs to cooperate with one another has plenty of room for error.

Basically, OLE suffers from three types of limitations:

⮕ It requires massive amounts of system resources.

⮕ It lacks complete acceptance by the computer industry.

⮕ The current standard is designed only for single-user applications.

The System Resource Problem

Even if OLE worked perfectly in every program you could buy (keep dreaming), OLE still needs to work on every computer that uses Windows. However, computers come with different microprocessors (80386, 80486, Pentium), different amounts of memory (4MB, 8MB, or 16MB of RAM), and different hard disk sizes (540MB, 730MB, 1.2GB, and so on).

So, if you're using Microsoft Word and Lotus 1-2-3, OLE might work perfectly fine on your computer. But the moment you try doing the exact same thing on a different computer, OLE might suddenly refuse to work. The problem isn't that you're doing anything wrong; the second computer might not have enough memory or hard disk space.

How can you solve this problem? You can't, at least not through OLE. You just have to use computers of equal capabilities, use fewer OLE features, or simply resign yourself to the fact that OLE works on your computer but never works on your coworkers' computers (or vice versa).

RAM cram

Because OLE depends on the specific applications you're using (for example, WordPerfect, Excel, Paradox), OLE is always limited by the memory constraints of each program. For example, Microsoft Word and Microsoft Excel require different amounts of memory than WordPerfect and Quattro Pro. If your computer doesn't have enough memory to load all your programs, you may not be able to use OLE.

Even if you jam your computer with 32MB of RAM, it's possible that some company will release an application that requires all 32MB, which means you still may not be able to use all of OLE's features with your other programs.

The incredible shrinking hard disk

Like memory, hard disk space seems to rapidly disappear on today's computers. Just when 540MB of hard disk space seemed to be enough, each program you buy suddenly requires 30MB, and 1.2GB hard disks have become the norm.

The biggest problems with hard disk space come when you share OLE compound documents with other users. As we've mentioned, these compound documents gobble up hard disk space. What's more, if you want other users to edit the compound documents, they each need their own copy of the programs you used.

For example, you might create a WordPerfect document in which you embed a Lotus 1-2-3 spreadsheet chart. If you share this compound document with your coworkers, they must also have their own copies of WordPerfect and Lotus 1-2-3. If they don't have Lotus 1-2-3, they won't be able to edit the embedded 1-2-3 spreadsheet chart in the WordPerfect document.

Sharing compound documents can only work if everyone uses the same programs. If one person suddenly updates a program to version 7.0 and starts embedding objects from that program, guess what? Everyone else must update their programs to that version as well.

All about system resources

If you can't run several programs simultaneously because your computer doesn't have enough memory, you could install more memory and still not solve the problem. The reason for this is because Windows allocates memory to three different programs to run an application:

- ✔ KRNL386.EXE, which loads Windows applications and manages memory.

- ✔ GDI.EXE, which controls each application's graphics and printing.

- ✔ USER.EXE, which controls the keyboard, the mouse, sound, communication ports, and windows management.

GDI.EXE uses memory to hold graphics such as icons. USER.EXE uses memory to hold pushbuttons (the picture of a pushbutton you see on the screen) and other controls. Unfortunately, the GDI.EXE and USER.EXE programs each use only 64K of memory for data storage. In other words, every computer effectively has only 128K of memory for storing this special Windows data. That's why your computer could have 32MB of RAM and still run out of system resources.

Every program you load gobbles up some system resources. In addition, some programs greedily hold on to system resources even after you've exited them. This is like the miser who plans to hold on to his money even after he's dead. He doesn't need it, but he's not going to let others have it either.

To get the most out of your computer's system resources, try reducing the number of on-screen colors from 256 to 16. Also, consider removing any wallpaper, screen savers, and other Windows frills that chew up memory.

Use permanent (not temporary) swap files. If that still doesn't help, increase the size of the swap file. (If you have no idea what a swap file is, get someone to change it for you.)

Finally, try replacing a memory-hungry application with a smaller one. For example, WordPad supports the Word for Windows file format. Because it uses a lot less memory, you could substitute WordPad for Word for Windows and still use OLE.

To maintain compatibility with everyone, you should link and embed objects using the earliest version of a program. For example, if some people use Word for Windows version 2.0 and others use Word for Windows version 6.0, everyone can share compound documents as long as embedded objects use the Word for Windows version 2.0 format.

OLE embedding versus file converting

When you link or embed an object created by another program, that object retains its original format. For example, if you embed a Quattro Pro chart in a WordPerfect document, the Quattro Pro chart appears inside WordPerfect, but it's not stored in a WordPerfect file format.

OLE linking or embedding is different from file conversion. With file conversion, you physically change a file from one program format to another, such as from Lotus 1-2-3 to WordPerfect. With OLE linking or embedding, no file conversion takes place.

The Lack of Complete OLE Acceptance

Microsoft created the OLE standard, and the rest of the computer industry grudgingly follows its lead. Competing companies never like adopting a standard created by a rival, especially when that rival is Microsoft.

The slow migration to OLE

To take full advantage of OLE, you obviously need programs that follow the OLE standard. Unfortunately, this isn't as easy as it sounds.

Programs from all the major software publishers (including Microsoft, which created OLE in the first place) offer varying degrees of OLE support. Some programs offer full OLE client and server capabilities. Others only offer client or server capabilities, and still other programs simply ignore OLE altogether. Many smaller software publishers and nearly all shareware publishers are either ignoring OLE altogether or following the simpler OLE version 1.0 standard.

So, if you want to use OLE with your favorite applications, you must first make sure those applications know how to use OLE. Then, you have to determine which OLE features your applications support. After this tedious exercise, you'll finally be able to use OLE.

Because few people enjoy determining each program's OLE capabilities (for that matter, not many people even know how to do it), it's not surprising that the vast majority of people never use OLE, or use only a fraction of OLE's capabilities.

The domino effect

Even if all your applications work perfectly with OLE, there's still another pitfall to avoid. OLE simply defines a way for multiple applications to work together; it does nothing to ensure that they work the way you want.

OLE gives you the tools; it's up to you to use them correctly. If you don't keep track of your OLE links and any embedded objects, changing one file might have a rippling, domino effect on other linked or embedded files somewhere else on your hard disk.

For example, you might link a chart from Microsoft Excel into a WordPerfect document. In turn, this WordPerfect document might be embedded in a PageMaker file, which is linked to a Microsoft Word document, which is embedded in a PowerPoint presentation.... By making one seemingly minor change in a single file, OLE can change multiple files simultaneously, causing a ripple effect of change throughout your hard disk files.

Make sure you know the consequences of changing a file. It's possible that a single file can be linked to two or more separate files. Changing one file can ultimately change multiple files at the same time. If that's what you want, great; but if not, have fun untangling the web of multiple links and embedded objects.

Although some programs can list all your OLE links in a convenient dialog box, many more programs won't do anything at all to help you. Now aren't you glad you bought a computer to make you more productive?

The Problems of a Single-User Standard

The current incarnation of OLE (version 2.0) is a single-user standard. That means if you want to share and edit compound documents with other users, you better make sure everyone's using the exact same programs you're using. If one person uses Lotus 1-2-3 and another uses Excel, not everyone will be able to edit linked or embedded compound documents.

No network support

The current version of OLE can only interact with programs stored on a single computer, using a long-winded term called Lightweight Remote Procedure Call (LRPC). If you have a Freelance Graphics chart embedded in a WordPerfect document and you double-click the Freelance Graphics chart, OLE looks for a copy of Freelance Graphics on your computer.

If you don't have a copy of Freelance Graphics, OLE gets dumbfounded and won't let you edit the embedded Freelance Graphics chart — even if your coworker has a copy of Freelance Graphics and your computers are connected on a network.

Future versions of OLE promise to use Remote Procedure Call (RPC) technology, which means that OLE will be able to hunt for the programs it needs across a network. But until that version of OLE arrives with full RPC support, you're stuck within the confines of your own computer and the programs squeezed onto its hard disk.

No multiplatform (Mac and Windows) support

Another problem facing OLE is the lack of multiplatform support. Microsoft is having a hard enough time getting other companies to support OLE on Windows, let alone on the Macintosh.

To be truly useful for the many companies that have both IBM and Macintosh computers connected on a network, OLE needs multiplatform support. With this capability, you could embed an object created with the Macintosh version of Microsoft Word into a file created with the Windows version of WordPerfect, with the two files stored on separate computers connected across a network.

But don't expect this feature to appear any time soon (if ever). Apple Computer is feverishly supporting a rival standard called OpenDoc for the Macintosh, as well as trying to impose this standard on the Windows world. For now, if you have a Macintosh and an IBM-compatible computer, forget about using OLE to share your data across a network.

Is OLE Worth Learning?

Given the limitations we've just described, should you consider using OLE, let alone developing applications that support OLE? In a word, yes.

The entire computer industry agrees that if OLE actually works, its features will truly make computers easier to use and more powerful. What the computer industry can't agree on is whether to use OLE, the rival OpenDoc standard, or an altogether new standard.

So, while the computer industry fumbles around, Microsoft will continue to make OLE easier to use and more powerful. Eventually (perhaps after the third or fourth version), OLE will become as commonplace as the concept of graphical user interfaces, and by then all your hard-won knowledge about OLE will finally pay off.

Until then, you might as well learn and use OLE, because mighty Microsoft says that if you don't, you'll be left behind in the computer Dark Ages.

Test your newfound knowledge

1. What are OLE's three biggest flaws?

   a. It costs too much; it's too hard to use; and it's incompatible with the computers that most people own, which means it should sell a million copies a month.

   b. It was developed by Microsoft; it's supported by Microsoft; and it's being used by Microsoft.

   c. Nobody knows what the acronym OLE really stands for.

   d. It gobbles up system resources; it hasn't gained widespread support; and it's limited to single-user applications.

2. What problem might result from linking files?

   a. A change in one file could accidentally change two or more linked files.

   b. It's impossible to link files with the current version of OLE. If you want to link files, you'll have to wait for Windows 99 and OLE version 27.5.

   c. Files do not like being linked together; they try to break their links whenever you're not looking.

   d. There are no problems. Computers are always perfect. If anything goes wrong, it's the user's fault.

Part II
Using OLE

In This Part...

*N*ow that you have a basic understanding of what OLE can do, where it came from, and what it might do for you, it's time to see for yourself the magic of OLE. This part of the book gives you reasons for using OLE (so you can justify taking the cost of this book as a business expense) along with step-by-step examples that show you how OLE works.

Once you get some practical experience using OLE, you'll be able to experiment with your favorite programs. The more you know about OLE, the more you'll be able to identify situations in which you can use it to work more efficiently and productively, which is what the makers of personal computers have been promising to help us do for years.

Chapter 4

Why Use OLE?

In This Chapter

▶ It lets you share data between applications

▶ You can customize applications

▶ It helps ensure compatibility among different applications

▶ Because Microsoft says so

*O*LE may be a powerful standard that uses objects to increase productivity, but so what? No matter how brilliant technology may be, people won't use it unless it offers tremendous advantages over other currently available solutions.

That's why hardly anyone uses video telephones, trash compactors, or nuclear-powered home air conditioners that science fiction promised us years ago. The technology is available, it's just that nobody really wants to use it.

So, this chapter is all about convincing you that learning and mastering OLE is worth your time and effort. Ideally, OLE will become an industry-wide standard that makes computers easier to use. Either that, or OLE will soon fade into obscurity, just like CP/M-86, UCSD Pascal, and the MS-DOS operating system.

Although OLE might seem like something new that Microsoft just introduced, the idea of sharing data between different programs has been around for quite a while. When Microsoft introduced Windows version 2.0, it included a technology called Dynamic Data Exchange (DDE). With the introduction of Windows 3.0, Microsoft created a better version of DDE, called OLE version 1.0. Finally, when Microsoft introduced Windows 95 and Windows NT, it enhanced OLE to its present form in version 2.0.

Sharing Data between Applications

The most compelling reason for using OLE is for your own convenience in sharing data between different applications. At the simplest level, the capability to share data means you won't have to worry about loading different programs or converting between specific file formats again. At a more complex level, sharing data means having the capability to automatically update multiple files simultaneously.

Storing data in a single file (or, putting all your eggs in one basket)

Suppose you need to create a report that explains why your company is going bankrupt. You could start by writing your report using any word processor that supports OLE — such as Microsoft Word or WordPerfect. Then, you might create a graph using a spreadsheet program such as Lotus 1-2-3 or Microsoft Excel, or a presentation graphics program such as Harvard Graphics or Microsoft PowerPoint.

Finally, you can use OLE to combine your word processor report and your graph in a single file. Now, your data appears in one location instead of two or more separate files.

Not only does this reduce the risk of losing a crucial file, it eliminates the problem of converting data between multiple file formats. As long as you use an application that supports OLE, you can share your data with anyone else who also uses an application that supports OLE.

Updating multiple files simultaneously

In addition to avoiding the problems of converting among different file formats, OLE makes it easy to update multiple files. For example, you might create a spreadsheet chart in Lotus 1-2-3 that you need to share with a coworker who is writing a report in WordPerfect and another colleague who is creating a presentation using Harvard Graphics.

Without OLE, you could just copy your Lotus 1-2-3 chart into your coworkers' WordPerfect document and Harvard Graphics presentation. But what happens if you change just one number in your Lotus 1-2-3 chart? Now, your coworkers have to recopy your chart.

However, if you use OLE, your computer does all the hard work for you, and you can daydream when you should be working. If you change your spreadsheet chart, OLE can automatically change that data stored in your coworkers' WordPerfect document and Harvard Graphics presentation. By automatically updating data used in multiple files, OLE ensures that everyone always has the latest copy of data they need.

(If you've ever changed addresses, you know how tiresome it can be to notify everyone of your new address. But if all your friends used OLE, you could just type your new address once, and OLE would automatically update everyone's database with your new address. See how much simpler life would be if the whole world used OLE?)

OLE can only share data between programs stored on the same computer or on computers connected to the same network. If your computer isn't connected to a network, there's no way OLE can magically update files stored on other computers to match any data you change on your computer. Figure 4-1 shows the differences between the two ways (linking and embedding) in which programs can share data using OLE.

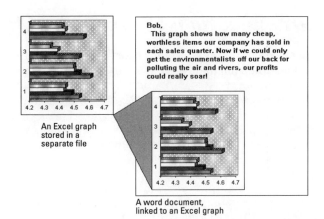

An Excel graph
stored in a
separate file

A word document,
linked to an Excel graph

Figure 4-1:
The
differences
between
linking and
embedding.

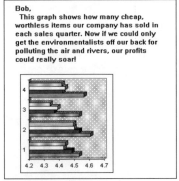

An Excel graph embedded
in a Word document
(saved as a single file)

Customizing Applications

Whether we like it or not, software development is increasingly focusing on objects. An *object* is simply a self-contained chunk of data, such as text, graphics, or a video clip. As the theory of objects gains more followers and support for OLE becomes more widespread, you'll be able to use OLE to create your own custom applications.

Why would anyone want to bother creating custom applications when they have enough trouble just installing programs such as Windows 95 or Microsoft Word? The answer is simple.

Shrinking applications to a manageable size

In the old days, a program such as WordPerfect or Lotus 1-2-3 could fit on a single floppy disk. As companies added new features that 90 percent of the population didn't even know existed, programs gradually bloated in size to the point at which it now takes 20 or more floppy disks to contain a single program.

In addition to gobbling up 20 or more megabytes of hard disk space, today's programs have so many features that almost nobody uses all of them (or even understands any of them).

Such multifeatured programs are known as *fatware*. If the trend toward fatware continues, programs will become larger, more complicated, and more likely to contain minor (or major) bugs that keep them from working 100 percent correctly.

Objects are an effort to reverse this trend, and OLE represents the first concerted effort to provide a standard for managing objects. Rather than create a single, monolithic program, software companies can use OLE to create smaller, specialized, and (we hope) more reliable objects that you can assemble like building blocks. The difference between today's fatware programs and tomorrow's promise of object-oriented programs is like the difference between carving a skyscraper out of a single piece of granite and constructing it piece by piece.

As a result of objects and the OLE standard, more software companies will create programs out of several separate OLE objects. Instead of buying a single program such as WordPerfect, you'll buy several OLE objects that, when combined, create WordPerfect.

So, what happens if you don't like part of WordPerfect? With today's monolithic programs, you just have to suffer. But with tomorrow's programs, created using separate OLE objects, you'll have the option of unbundling one or more objects.

By unbundling portions of a program, you can keep only those features you want and need, while keeping the program to a manageable size on your hard disk.

Making your own applications

Even better, if you like a feature found in Microsoft Word, guess what? You could unbundle that Microsoft Word feature and add it to WordPerfect. If you want to get really bizarre, you could even add features from Microsoft Excel to WordPerfect, creating a hybrid spreadsheet/word processor specially designed for writing financial reports.

Best of all, smaller companies are likely to sell their own OLE objects that you can combine with other OLE objects. For example, a company might sell an OLE object for stock market analysis or one for real estate management. That way, you can create your own word processor designed for producing financial reports, or your own spreadsheet for creating real estate listings. Figure 4-2 shows how OLE can help you create your own custom applications.

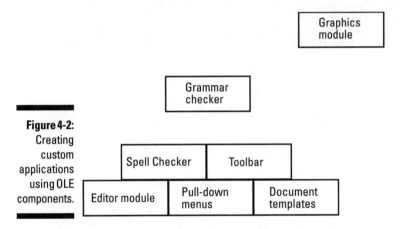

Figure 4-2:
Creating
custom
applications
using OLE
components.

(In today's software market, stock market or real estate programs are specialized applications that don't integrate well with mainstream programs such as word processors and spreadsheets. In tomorrow's world of objects, specialized applications will integrate smoothly with all your other programs, giving you the best of all worlds.)

Of course, customizing applications with OLE is just speculation at this point, but it definitely represents the future of the software industry. After all, you really don't want to buy a 25GB hard disk just to store a single copy of WordPerfect version 25.91, do you?

The world of objects as they exist today

The era of third-party component software has already begun, with companies selling VBX (Visual BASIC eXtension) and OCX (OLE Custom eXtension) components. VBX and OCX components are designed to act as building blocks that help programmers create new programs quickly and easily. By using the right VBX or OCX components, you can quickly create a new program with very little programming.

Originally, only Visual BASIC programmers could use VBX components. However, every language — including C++, Delphi, dBASE, and PowerBuilder — soon began supporting VBX components.

Unfortunately, VBX components were designed for the 16-bit operating system of Windows 3.1.

With the introduction of Windows 95, Microsoft developed a new standard, OCXs. OCXs often come in two varieties: a 16-bit version (for Windows 3.1) and a 32-bit version (for Windows 95).

(Dynamic link library — or DLL — files are similar to VBX and OCX components. The main difference is that a DLL contains only code while a VBX or an OCX can contain its own user interface as well as code.)

As more developers adopt the OLE standard and allow you to combine their programs with additional OLE objects, expect to see more third-party developers selling OCX components directly to users of programs such as Microsoft Word and WordPerfect.

Ensuring Compatibility with Other Applications

Perhaps the most compelling reason for using OLE (or at least understanding it) stems from compatibility issues. The majority of personal computers use Microsoft Windows, so most programs require Microsoft Windows.

Because Microsoft defined the OLE standard, it's also implemented it as part of its Windows operating system and in all of its applications, including Word, Excel, Access, PowerPoint, and Schedule. All of this means that the dominant force in the software industry (Microsoft) is using OLE, and the rest of the software industry is likely to follow—perhaps out of blindness, if nothing else.

As the advantages of OLE become apparent, more companies will be forced to adopt OLE in their own programs, just to remain competitive and take full advantage of the Windows operating system. Eventually, people using programs that don't support OLE won't be able to share data with users of other programs, which is like buying an eight-track cartridge or a beta format videocassette and then wondering why you can't share your tapes with other people.

By taking the time to understand how OLE works today and how it may affect the software industry in the future, you won't be left behind when the change comes faster than anyone expected. Just think of all those programmers who thought that MS-DOS would always be the dominant operating system. You can find most of them feverishly trying to catch up and learn Windows programming before they wind up standing in the unemployment line.

Many programs are already billed as being Microsoft Office compatible, which means they use similar menu commands and can easily share data with all the Microsoft Office programs. As Microsoft pushes the OLE standard in its own programs, it's only a matter of time before other companies start advertising their programs as being OLE compliant or OLE compatible as well.

Because Microsoft Says So

Microsoft created history's youngest billionaire and the wealthiest person on the planet Earth, so it's no surprise that when Microsoft sets out in one direction, the rest of the computer industry eagerly follows, hoping to capitalize on whatever trend Microsoft might be setting.

Most of the world ignored Windows when it was first released. However, when Windows suddenly soared in popularity, many companies rushed to develop Windows versions of their popular DOS applications. Many of these same companies lost millions of dollars and market share because their Windows programs arrived too late in the marketplace.

For that reason, the computer industry is leery of straying too far from any standard that Microsoft sets. Companies have a legitimate fear of getting stuck with a small market while their competitors march toward greater profits, right behind Microsoft.

Think of all those companies that developed OS/2 programs. Sure, they have less competition, but they also have fewer customers than a company selling similar Windows software.

Now that Microsoft has announced that OLE will be the object-orientation standard of the future, you can bet that a vast majority of other companies will follow, grudgingly perhaps, but following nevertheless.

Even though today's OLE standard is still primitive, limited in its capabilities, complicated, and confusing for the average person to use, don't worry. The more you know about OLE now, the more comfortable you'll be when OLE finally becomes accepted by the rest of the world. That may take another few years and another few versions of the OLE standard, but as long as Microsoft backs it, the OLE standard will be around for a long time.

Test your newfound knowledge

1. Name two advantages of using OLE to share data between applications.

   a. There is no advantage to using OLE, but I'm going to read the rest of this book anyway, just in case I might be wrong.

   b. OLE gives you twice as many chances to ruin your data than ever before.

   c. OLE lets you store data, created by multiple programs, in a single file. In addition, OLE can automatically update multiple files that share the same data stored in another file.

   d. OLE? I thought this book was *DOS For Dummies*.

2. How will OLE help create smaller, specialized, and more reliable programs?

   a. Programs are never reliable. Haven't you been using computers long enough to know this yet?

   b. OLE can divide a single program into smaller objects that you can combine to create more complex programs.

   c. It won't, because OLE is destined to become the next obsolete technology that Microsoft abandons in midstride, just like OS/2.

   d. OLE can do all that? Wow, where can I learn more about this fascinating technology?

The 5th Wave

By Rich Tennant

"We're concerned—Kyle doesn't seem to be able to hot key between apps like all the other children."

Chapter 5

Identifying Your Application's OLE Capabilities

In This Chapter

▶ Types of OLE capabilities

▶ Checking for OLE client capabilities

▶ Checking for OLE server capabilities

▶ Checking for OLE 1 and OLE 2 features

Although OLE has been around for years, not all programs (or users) know how to use it. Some programs (such as all DOS-based programs and many older Windows 3.1 programs) don't know how to use OLE at all. Some programs can only contain an OLE object; some can only provide OLE objects to other programs; and some can handle both tasks.

If a company wants to use that all-important *Designed for Microsoft Windows 95* logo, its programs must follow the OLE 2 standard. Although it's possible that someone (for example, a shareware programmer) will write a Windows 95 program that doesn't support OLE 2 at all, most major programs designed for Windows 95 will support OLE 2.

With such varying OLE capabilities available, it's no surprise that few people even know about OLE, let alone use it on a regular basis. Before you can use OLE, you need to determine the level of OLE compatibility your programs provide. If one program supports OLE as a client program but another doesn't support OLE at all, guess what? You won't be able to use all the wonderful technology behind OLE, no matter how hard you cry, whine, or complain.

If you're using a program that displays the official Microsoft Windows 95 logo on its box or in its manual, you can be certain that program supports some form of OLE. If you're using programs designed for Windows 3.1, those programs may not support OLE.

Types of OLE Capabilities

Each program you use may offer varying degrees of OLE compliance:

- ✔ No OLE capabilities
- ✔ OLE client capabilities
- ✔ OLE server capabilities
- ✔ OLE client or server capabilities

An *OLE client* is a program that can store and display OLE objects, which may be either linked or embedded. Any file that contains OLE objects is called a *container*. Containers are typically compound documents that consist of linked or embedded objects.

An OLE server is a program that can create and edit OLE objects for other programs to display and store. OLE servers provide objects (either linked or embedded) that OLE clients can display.

Many programs can act as both OLE clients and servers. If you use a program to display OLE objects, it is acting as an OLE server. If you use it to create OLE objects, it is acting as an OLE client. It's even possible for a single program to act as an OLE client for one program and as an OLE server to another program.

Some programs may follow the older OLE 1 standard instead of the newer OLE 2 standard. If one program follows the OLE 1 standard but another follows the OLE 2 standard, the two programs will only be able to share data using the OLE 1 standard.

Table 5-1 provides some general guidelines for determining your program's OLE capabilities. Most of the major programs — for example, Microsoft Word and Lotus 1-2-3 — support some form of OLE. However, you might not find any OLE support in little-known, niche programs — for example, shareware programs, programs from companies you've never heard of, or specialized programs such as medical office-management or educational programs.

Table 5-1 Determining your program's likely OLE capabilities

Type of program	Likely OLE capabilities
DOS	No OLE capabilities
Windows 3.1	No OLE capabilities
	OLE client
	OLE server
	Both OLE client and server

Type of program	Likely OLE capabilities
Windows 95 and Windows NT	OLE client
	OLE server
	Both OLE client and server

As a quick way to check whether your program offers any OLE capabilities, look for the following index entries in your program's manual:

- ✔ Creating links
- ✔ Inserting objects
- ✔ Linking
- ✔ Object linking and embedding
- ✔ Objects
- ✔ OLE
- ✔ Sharing data with other applications

If you don't find any of these entries (or similar ones) in the manual's index, your program probably doesn't support OLE in any form.

Checking for OLE Client Capabilities

The programs that most commonly offer only OLE client capabilities are those that specialize in presenting information, such as presentation graphics programs, word processors, and desktop publishing programs. An OLE client may support OLE in two ways:

- ✔ Linking
- ✔ Embedding

Linking stores data in separate files, but can display the data in multiple files. Embedding stores data from multiple programs in a single file.

To check for OLE linking or embedding capabilities, look for the following commands in your program:

- ✔ Edit⇨Paste Special (see Figure 5-1)
- ✔ Edit⇨Paste Link (see Figure 5-2)

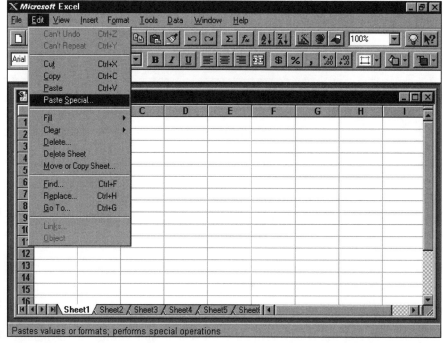

Figure 5-1:
A typical
Paste
Special
command in
the Edit
menu.

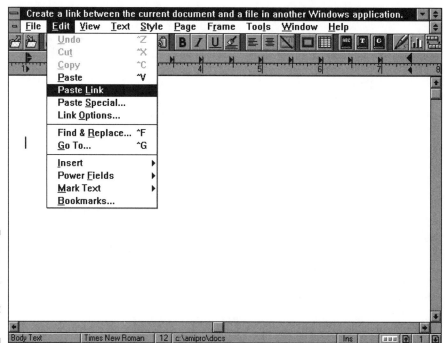

Figure 5-2:
A typical
Paste Link
command in
the Edit
menu.

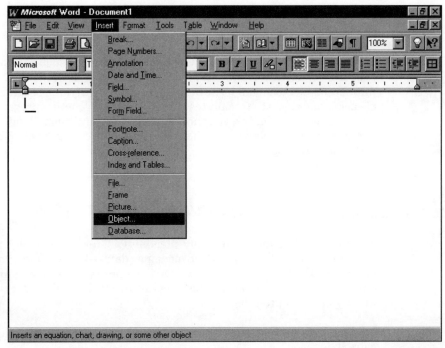

Figure 5-3:
A typical
Object
command in
the Insert
menu.

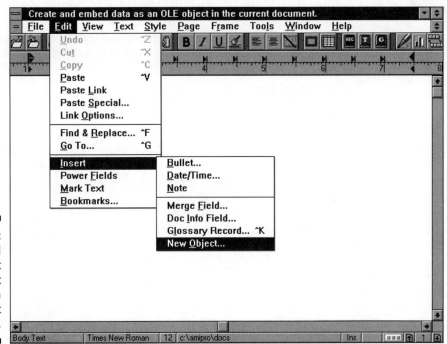

Figure 5-4:
A typical
Insert
Object
command in
the Edit
menu.

 ✔ Insert⇨Object (see Figure 5-3)

 ✔ Edit⇨Insert Object (see Figure 5-4)

Most programs that support OLE will display commands such as Paste Special or Insert Object. However, some programs that support OLE may not display these common commands. The best method for identifying a program's OLE client capabilities is to actually test the program with another program you know can act as an OLE server, such as Microsoft Paintbrush (Windows 3.1) or Microsoft Paint (Windows 95). Chapter 6 explains how to use both Paintbrush and Paint as OLE servers.

Checking for OLE Server Capabilities

The programs that most commonly offer only OLE server capabilities are those that specialize in manipulating and managing data—for example, spreadsheets and databases. Once you've determined that one of your programs offers OLE client capabilities, you can use that program to check for OLE server capabilities in your other programs.

Use the following steps to determine which of your programs offer OLE server capabilities:

1. Load a program that you know has OLE client capabilities.

2. Depending on your program's particular menu structure, choose one of the following commands (or a similar command). Note that before you can choose the Edit⇨Paste Special command, you must first copy or cut an object.

   • Insert⇨Object

   • Edit⇨Insert Object

   • Edit⇨Paste Special

   As shown in Figure 5-5, an Insert New Object dialog box is displayed. (If you chose the Paste Special command, a Paste Special dialog box appears instead.)

3. To see which of your programs can be used as an OLE server, scroll through the Object Type scroll box. For example, Figure 5-5 identifies Lotus Approach, Delrina WinComm PRO, HiJaak Image, HyperACCESS, Microsoft Excel, and Microsoft Word as OLE servers.

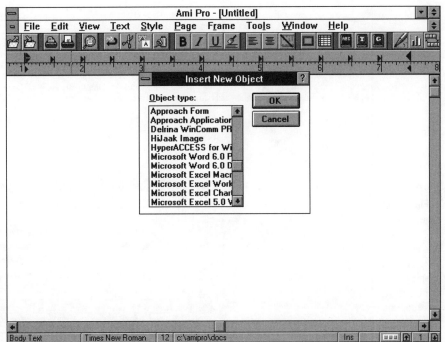

Figure 5-5:
The Insert
New Object
dialog box.

Checking for OLE 1 and OLE 2 Features

The major user-related difference between OLE 1 and OLE 2 occurs when you try to edit an embedded object. In a program that supports OLE 1, if you double-click an embedded object, that object is displayed in a separate window, which is running the program that created the embedded object.

For example, you might embed a Windows 3.1 Paintbrush object in the Write program. Because these programs support only OLE 1, double-clicking the embedded Paintbrush object displays Paintbrush as a separate window, as shown in Figure 5-6.

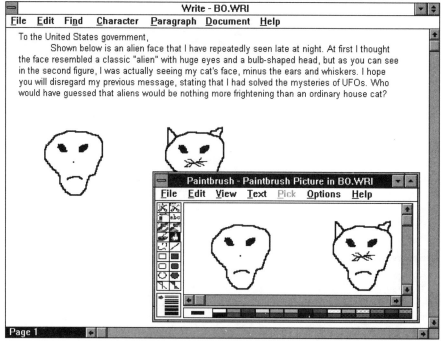

Figure 5-6:
Editing an
OLE 1
embedded
object
displays that
object in a
separate
window.

If a program supports OLE 2, double-clicking an embedded object invokes something called *in-place editing*. Instead of displaying the embedded object in a separate window, in-place editing displays the menus of the program within the window of the program you're using right now.

For example, you can embed an Excel spreadsheet object in a Word document. If you double-click the embedded Excel spreadsheet object, the Word menus disappear and are replaced by the Excel menus, as shown in Figures 5-7 and 5-8.

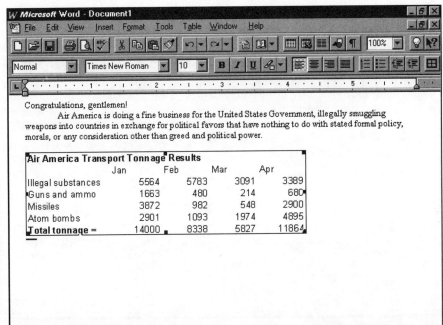

Figure 5-7:
Word's menus are displayed before you double-click an embedded Excel object.

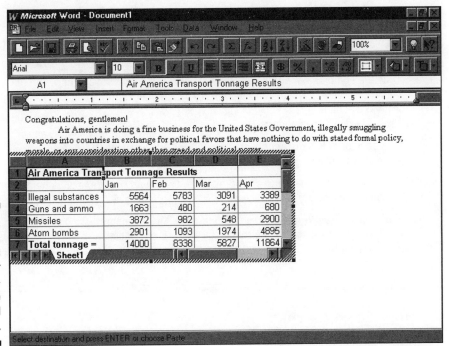

Figure 5-8:
Excel's menus appear after you double-click the embedded Excel object.

Technical differences between OLE 1 and OLE 2

OLE 1 simply allows you to link or embed objects. OLE 2 includes basic linking and embedding features as well as in-place activation, nested object support, drag-and-drop support, OLE automation, and object conversion.

✔ *In-place activation* means that double-clicking an embedded object lets you edit that object without opening a separate window.

✔ *Nested object support* means you can embed objects within other objects.

✔ *Drag-and-drop support* means if you have two windows open, you can drag an object from one window and drop it inside the other window. By using drag and drop, you can avoid using clumsy menu commands and dialog boxes to link or embed OLE objects.

✔ *OLE automation* lets one program control another, such as a word processor that automatically calculates a result in a spreadsheet.

✔ *Object conversion* means you can convert an object created by one program (such as WordPerfect) into a format that can be edited by another program (such as Microsoft Word).

Test your newfound knowledge

1. Name two methods for determining whether your program offers OLE client capabilities.

   a. Check the Edit menu and look for a Paste Special or a Paste Link command, or look in the index of your program's manual for OLE or object linking and embedding.

   b. Flip a coin, or call your friendly neighborhood psychic hotline.

   c. There's no way to determine a program's OLE capabilities, so don't bother even trying.

   d. Whenever you really need to use OLE in a specific program, you can be certain that it won't be supported.

2. Name three differences between OLE 1 and OLE 2.

   a. OLE 1 uses the number 1, but OLE 2 uses the number 2.

   b. OLE 1 is completely incompatible with OLE 2, and will actually destroy any programs that try to use the OLE 2 standard.

   c. OLE 2 means that Microsoft is giving OLE a second chance to work before completely giving up on this technology.

   d. OLE 1 supports linking and embedding. OLE 2 is compatible with OLE 1, and offers in-place activation, drag-and-drop support, and OLE automation.

Chapter 6
Putting OLE to Work

● ●

In This Chapter

▶ Practicing with Windows 3.1

▶ Practicing with Windows 95

▶ Using OLE with Microsoft Office

● ●

*O*nce you understand why Microsoft invented OLE in the first place, the best way to learn about OLE is by using it with your own programs. This chapter provides three examples you can try, using OLE with Windows 3.1, Windows 95, and the Microsoft Office programs.

Practicing with Windows 3.1

To practice using OLE under Windows 3.1, you'll need Microsoft Paintbrush and Microsoft Write. These programs are usually stored in the Accessories group. If neither of these programs are stored on your computer, you may have to install them from your Windows 3.1 master disks.

OLE embedding

This exercise shows you how to embed an object. In this case, you'll embed a Paintbrush drawing in a Microsoft Write document.

1. Open Microsoft Write. You'll be using Microsoft Write as the client program.

2. Move the cursor to the location at which you want to embed the object.

3. Choose Edit⇨Insert Object. As shown in Figure 6-1, the Insert Object dialog box is displayed.

4. In the Object Type list box, choose Paintbrush Picture. Click OK. As shown in Figure 6-2, the Paintbrush window is displayed, allowing you to create the object you'll embed in your Write document.

5. Draw your picture in the Paintbrush window.

6. Choose File⇨Update. The Update command embeds your Paintbrush drawing in your Write document.

7. Choose File⇨Exit & Return to. Your picture is now embedded in the Write document, as shown in Figure 6-3.

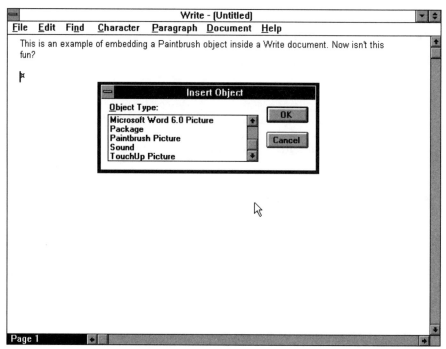

Figure 6-1:
The Insert
Object
dialog box.

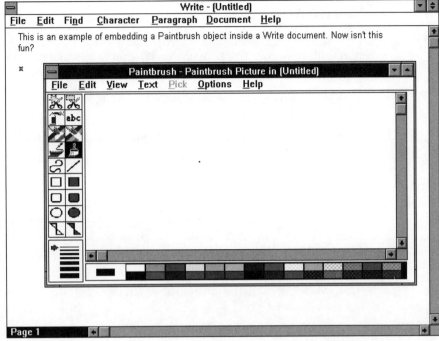

Figure 6-2:
The
Paintbrush
window
inside the
Write
window.

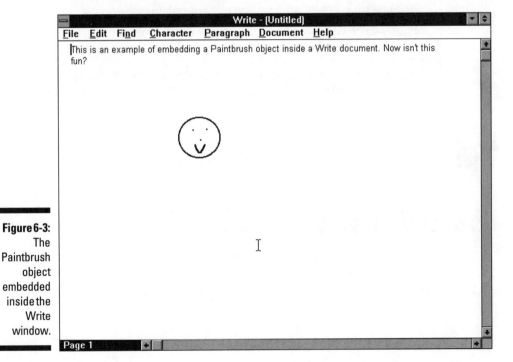

Figure 6-3:
The
Paintbrush
object
embedded
inside the
Write
window.

OLE linking

In this exercise, OLE linking lets you create and store a Paintbrush picture in a separate file from your Write document. Whenever you change the Paintbrush file, the OLE link automatically updates the image displayed in the Write file.

1. Open Microsoft Paintbrush. You'll be using Microsoft Paintbrush as the server program.

2. Draw your picture that you want to link to a client program.

3. Choose File⇨Save, or press Ctrl+S. Paintbrush displays a Save As dialog box.

4. Type a filename and click OK.

5. Use the Scissors tool to select the picture, and then choose Edit⇨Copy (or press Ctrl+C).

6. Open Microsoft Write. You'll be using Microsoft Write as the client program.

7. Move the cursor to the location at which you want to display the Paintbrush picture.

8. Choose Edit⇨Paste Link. Your Paintbrush picture is displayed in your Write document.

9. Switch back to Paintbrush and edit your picture.

10. Return to Write and verify that the changes you made to your Paintbrush picture also appear within the Write document.

Suppose you close Microsoft Write and then modify the OLE-linked picture in Microsoft Paintbrush. The next time you open the OLE-linked Write file, Windows will display the dialog box shown in Figure 6-4, asking if you want to update the OLE link.

For some odd reason known only to their programmers, some programs display the update dialog box regardless of whether the linked file has been changed.

Practicing with Windows 95

To practice using OLE under Windows 95, you'll need two programs: Microsoft Paint and WordPad. The programs are usually stored in the Accessories group. If neither of these programs are stored on your computer, you may have to install them from your Windows 95 master disks.

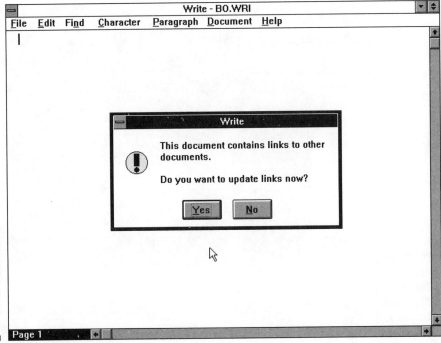

Figure 6-4:
This dialog
box asks if
you want to
update an
OLE link.

OLE embedding

This exercise shows you how to embed an object. In this case, you'll be embedding a Paint drawing in a Microsoft WordPad document.

1. Open Microsoft WordPad. You'll be using WordPad as the client program.

2. Move the cursor to the location at which you want to embed the object.

3. Choose Insert⇨Object. As shown in Figure 6-5, the Insert Object dialog box is displayed.

4. In the Object Type list box, choose either Bitmap Image or Paintbrush Picture, and then click OK. As shown in Figure 6-6, the Paint window is displayed, which lets you create a picture to embed in your WordPad document.

5. Draw your picture inside the Paint window.

6. Click anywhere outside the Paint window to see your drawing as it appears in your WordPad document.

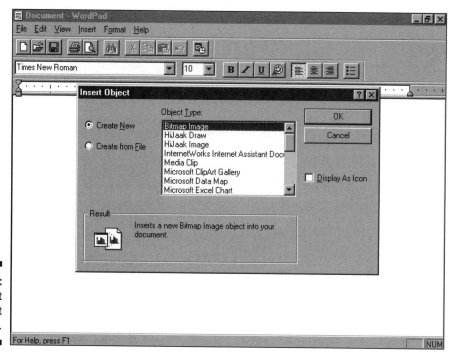

Figure 6-5:
The Insert
Object
dialog box.

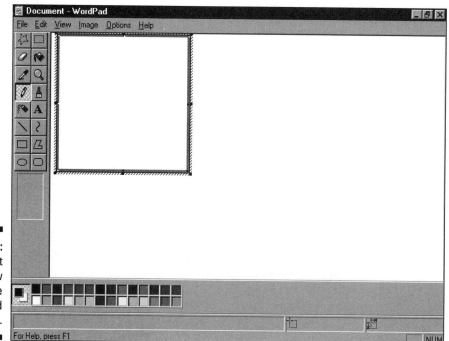

Figure 6-6:
The Paint
window
inside the
WordPad
document.

OLE linking

In this exercise, OLE linking lets you create and store a Paint picture in a separate file from your WordPad document. Whenever you change the Paint file, the OLE link automatically updates the image displayed in the WordPad file.

1. Open Microsoft Paint. You'll be using Microsoft Paint as a server program.

2. Draw your picture.

3. Choose File⇨Save, or press Ctrl+S. Paint displays a Save As dialog box.

4. Type a filename, and click the Save button.

5. Use the Select tool to encompass the picture, and choose Edit⇨Copy (or press Ctrl+C).

6. Open Microsoft WordPad. You'll be using Microsoft WordPad as the client program.

7. Move the cursor to the location at which you want to display the Paint picture.

8. Choose Insert⇨Object. WordPad displays the Insert Object dialog box.

9. Click the Create from File radio button. The Insert Object dialog box changes its appearance as shown in Figure 6-7.

10. Click the Link check box.

11. Click the Browse button. A Browse dialog box is displayed.

12. Select the Paint file that you want to link, and click the Insert button. The Insert Object dialog box appears again.

13. Click OK. Your Paint picture appears in the WordPad document, showing that OLE successfully linked your Paint picture to your WordPad document.

14. Click on the Paint picture.

15. Click the right mouse button to open the pop-up menu shown in Figure 6-8.

16. Choose Linked Bitmap Image Object, and then Open. The Paint window appears.

17. Edit your Paint picture. Notice that any changes you make automatically appear within the WordPad document.

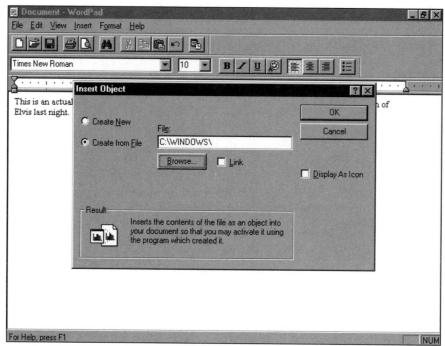

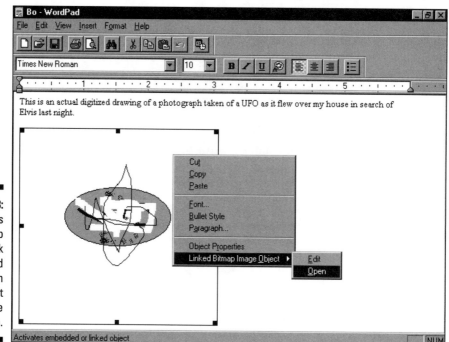

Using OLE with Microsoft Office

The standard version of Microsoft Office includes Microsoft Word, Excel, and PowerPoint; the professional version also includes Microsoft Access. (Microsoft Office 95 also includes a personal information manager program called Microsoft Schedule+.)

As a software suite, the programs making up Microsoft Office are designed to share data with one another through both OLE linking and embedding.

OLE embedding

This exercise shows you how to embed an object. In this case, you'll embed an Excel spreadsheet in a Word document.

1. Open Microsoft Word. You'll be using Microsoft Word as the client program.

2. Move the cursor to the location at which you want to embed the object.

3. Choose Insert⇨Object. As shown in Figure 6-9, Word displays the Object dialog box.

4. Click the Create New tab to create a new object to embed in your Microsoft Word document.

5. In the Object Type list box, choose Microsoft Excel Worksheet. Then, click OK. The Excel spreadsheet appears, as shown in Figure 6-10.

6. Enter any numbers, formulas, and labels in the Excel spreadsheet.

7. To see your Excel spreadsheet as it appears in your Word document, click anywhere outside the spreadsheet.

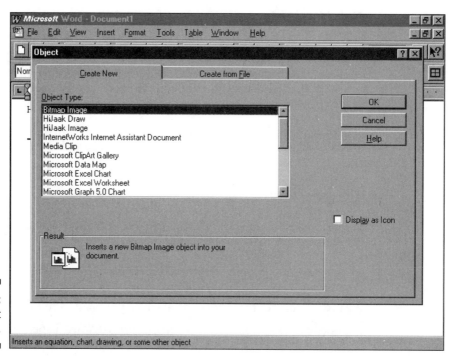

Figure 6-9:
The Object
dialog box.

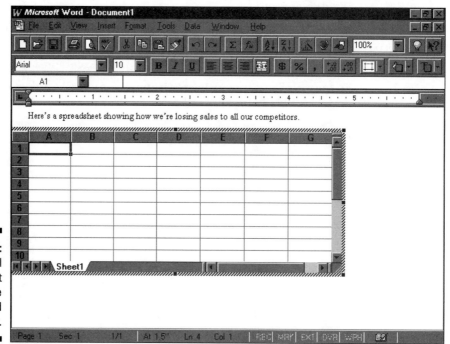

Figure 6-10:
The Excel
spreadsheet
inside the
Word
document.

OLE linking

In this exercise, OLE linking lets you create and store an Excel spreadsheet as a separate file from a Word file. Whenever you change the Excel file, the OLE link automatically updates the image displayed in the Word document.

1. Open Microsoft Excel. You'll be using Microsoft Excel as the server program.

2. Enter some numbers, formulas, or labels in the spreadsheet.

3. Choose File⇨Save, or press Ctrl+S. Excel displays a Save As dialog box.

4. Type a filename, and click Save.

5. Highlight the part of your spreadsheet that you want to link into another file.

6. Choose Edit⇨Copy, or press Ctrl+C.

7. Open Microsoft Word. You'll be using Microsoft Word as the client program.

8. Move the cursor to the location at which you want to display the Excel spreadsheet.

9. Choose Edit⇨Paste Special. As shown in Figure 6-11, Word displays the Paste Special dialog box.

10. Click the Paste Link radio button.

11. In the As list box, select Microsoft Excel Worksheet Object, and click OK. Your Excel spreadsheet appears in the Word document.

12. Switch to Excel and change some numbers.

13. Switch back to Word and verify that the changes you made in your Excel spreadsheet also appear within the Write document.

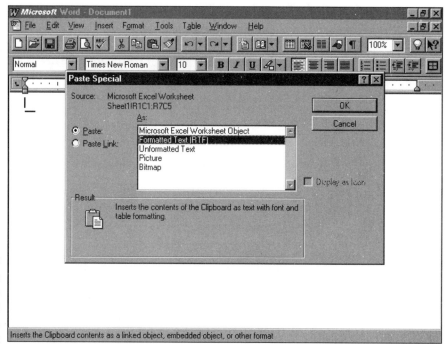

Figure 6-11:
The Paste
Special
dialog box.

Test your newfound knowledge

1. What's the main reason for using OLE linking?

a. OLE linking lets you build chain link fences quickly and easily.

b. OLE linking is Microsoft's latest plan for dominating the industry and making Bill Gates owner of Planet Earth.

c. OLE linking lets you run Macintosh programs on an IBM and share data between DOS, Windows, the Macintosh, and OS/2.

d. OLE linking lets you change one file and automatically update multiple files simultaneously.

2. What is the main difference between OLE linking and OLE embedding?

a. OLE linking stores data in separate files, while OLE embedding stores data in a single file.

b. OLE linking is spelled differently from OLE embedding.

c. OLE embedding only works if you're using Windows 95. OLE linking only works if you refuse to use Windows at all.

d. There's no difference. OLE linking and OLE embedding do exactly the same thing but use different procedures and techniques, and produce entirely different results.

Part III
Using OLE in
Applications

The 5th Wave   By Rich Tennant

"WELL, SYSTEMS INTEGRATION ISN'T PERFECT. SOME DEPARTMENTS STILL
SEEM TO GET MORE INFORMATION THAN OTHERS."

In This Part...

*T*he best way to learn about OLE is by seeing how different vendors add it to the applications sitting on your machine. Each class of application — for example, spreadsheet, word processor, or database manager — has different requirements when it comes to sharing data. These differences show up in the way these applications implement OLE.

You'll especially want to read through this section if you plan to develop applications, because it contains a wealth of ideas about what is possible. Looking at what other programmers have done will give you some ideas about what you can add to your own programs.

Whether you are a user or a programmer, this section will help you use the OLE capabilities of your existing applications to their full potential. After all, what good is a tool if you don't know how to use it?

Chapter 7

An Introduction to OLE Automation

··

In This Chapter

▶ Using OLE within applications

▶ Macros, the fast way to program

▶ Diagramming your macro

▶ A look at the OLE players

··

*E*ver notice how some people try to put a label on everyone and everything? They try to cram the whole world into a few categories, such as baby boomers and generation X, or programmers and users. These people will try to tell you that OLE falls into two levels: user and programmer. Don't fall into this trap. You're unique! Don't allow some moron to pigeonhole you.

This chapter presents a special view of OLE. We'll look at how you can use OLE within an application without performing the same steps over and over again. This is a third level of OLE interaction — macros — and you need to know about it.

A computer can usually do any repetitious task you can do with an application, only faster. Because of this, many applications allow you to automate the tasks they perform. A macro is a way of recording your keystrokes so that you can play them back later, sort of like a tape recording.

The computer stores the keystrokes you record in the current document or in a file on disk. Every time you ask the computer to run the macro, it automatically follows the keystrokes you recorded one by one. Using a macro allows you to perform a repetitious task over and over again with exactly the same result every time.

It takes time to tell the computer how to perform a task automatically, so it's usually more efficient to perform simple, nonrepetitive tasks yourself. Repetitious tasks — for example, adding objects to your documents with OLE — are always good candidates for automation with macros. The more often you perform a task, the greater the payback for converting it to a macro.

OLE and Applications

In previous chapters, we've shown you some of the basics of using OLE manually within an application. However, we haven't looked at any specific applications. Chapters 8 through 12 will give you those specifics.

These chapters will also introduce you to the specifics of macro languages. Macros started out as a way to automate repetitive tasks. For example, if you always follow the same steps to create a new document in your word processor, you can automate those steps by having the computer perform them. When the computer executes your macro, it uses the same menu commands you would use if you were performing the task manually.

Macros can offer more than simple keystroke repetition. Even the earliest applications allowed you to create equations for solving math problems with a macro. Modern applications aren't any different; with a macro, you can perform a variety of tasks that you couldn't ordinarily do manually.

Some applications even provide a pseudo programming language. For example, most Microsoft products offer Visual BASIC for Applications (VBA). Other vendor products offer similar application-based languages. These languages can't replace the general-purpose languages used by programmers, but they will allow you to automate your application tasks to the point that you barely notice which application is actually running.

Using Macros to Speed OLE

So, how do you automate an OLE task? It can be as simple as turning on the macro recorder for your application and running through the same steps you normally complete to perform that task. Although we'll soon see that it isn't always quite so simple, the procedure for automating an OLE task doesn't have to be difficult.

What kinds of OLE tasks can you automate? Well, you might need to grab one of several company logos for the top of a letter. The logo you use might depend on whom you're sending the letter to and the type of letter you're creating, so there isn't any easy way to create a letter template. This is a perfect situation for using a macro. All you would need to do is tell your word processor whom you're sending a letter to and the type of letter you want to create, and it would take care of embedding the proper logo for you.

Why use application-based languages?

Many people refuse to become programmers. They figure the only important issues are that they know how to use an application, and they need to make it do some work. Macros originally provided all the automation users needed for simple applications. However, as applications and user needs became more complex, macros couldn't do the job by themselves. An application-based language is one solution to this problem. It is designed to work with the application's macros to give the user a little more flexibility.

Unfortunately, this solution to a user need gives rise to additional problems. For one thing, the BASIC used in Access won't work with the BASIC used in Word, even though both products come from the same vendor, Microsoft.

The reason for this incompatibility is twofold. First, these products were created by different design teams. The two teams didn't coordinate their efforts, so even though both teams started with BASIC as the basis for their language, they ended up with incompatible dialects. Other vendors have the same problem, but it's more noticeable when you look at Microsoft's long list of products.

Visual BASIC for Applications (VBA) is Microsoft's attempt to fix this problem. Now, you can use the same language for all Microsoft applications. This means the little routine you wrote for Access will also work with Word. VBA won't replace the macros you use, but it will make it easier to write macro add-ons that you can use with more than one application.

Lotus is already following suit with LotusScript, a BASIC-like language. You can probably count on Borland coming up with a mini version of Delphi (Borland's Pascal derivative) for its products. Of course, other vendors, such as Novell, will also get in on the standardization act. (Rumor has it that Novell is working on a C-like language.)

Even with these new languages, your problems as a user are not completely solved. Any modules you write for one product can be used with another product, as long as both products come from the same vendor. But what happens if you use Microsoft Word and Lotus 1-2-3? Well, perhaps someday vendors will get together and come up with a common language for applications, but we aren't holding our breath.

It pays to browse through your application's help file or manual when you're learning to write macros. Most applications provide macro functions that many people don't know exist. Often, these are the functions that prove most useful when you're writing the complex macros that some OLE automation tasks require. For example, the DDE-Execute command provided by most spreadsheet and some word-processing applications allows you to tell another application to perform some task. We demonstrate this command in Chapter 10.

The following example uses Microsoft Word and Microsoft Paint to show you how to automate a task with a macro. We'll do something simple like insert an MS Paint bitmap object into a Word document. You could use any applications on your machine to do the same thing. The precise steps vary from application to application, but the principles are the same. Follow along with the example even if you don't use Microsoft Word. The intent of this example is to show you a simple OLE macro.

1. Open Word, and create a new document. The first thing you need to do is define a macro and start the macro recorder.

2. Choose Tools⇨Macro. Word displays the Macro dialog box shown in Figure 7-1.

3. Click the Record pushbutton, and fill out the Record Macro dialog box that's displayed, as shown in Figure 7-2.

4. Click OK to start recording your macro. Now that you have the macro recorder started, use it to create a macro. The macro recorder will record your keystrokes in steps 5 through 7.

5. Choose Insert⇨Object. Word displays the Object dialog box.

6. Click the Create from File tab. Select the Windows 95 directory and the LEAVES.BMP file, as shown in Figure 7-3. (If LEAVES.BMP is not present, you can use any other small .BMP file located in your Windows directory.)

7. Click OK to complete the object insertion. You should see a display similar to the one in Figure 7-4. Notice the macro recorder dialog box on the upper-left side of the window. This dialog box allows you to stop or pause the macro recording process, as necessary.

8. Click the Stop button to stop the macro recording process.

9. To see the field code entry for this object, choose View⇨Field Codes or press Alt+F9. (Word for Windows uses field codes to show nontext entries — for example, OLE objects, special characters such as em dashes, or data fields such as the current date.) You should see **{ EMBED Paint.Picture }** in place of the picture. We now have an OLE-specific macro we can examine. Let's see what it actually contains.

10. Choose Tools⇨Macro. Word displays the Macro dialog box shown in Figure 7-1. Select the OLEConnect entry, and then click the Edit pushbutton. You should see a screen similar to the one in Figure 7-5. As you can see, our macro consists of three steps. The first entry, Sub MAIN, starts the macro. The second entry is the one that does the actual work. It tells the word processor to insert a Microsoft Paint object that uses the LEAVES.BMP file. The final entry ends the macro.

11. Double-click the control menu box to close the macro editor. Choose Tools⇨Macro to display the Macro dialog box. Select the OLEConnect entry, and then click the Delete pushbutton to remove the macro from your stylesheet. Close the document without saving it.

Figure 7-1:
Your starting point for performing any macro-related activity in Word.

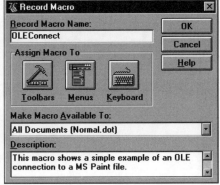

Figure 7-2:
Here's where you define and start the macro recording process.

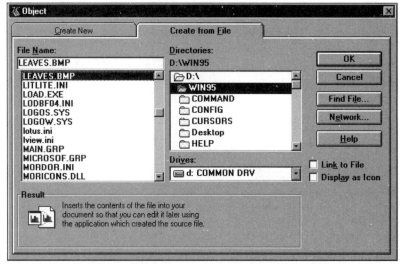

Figure 7-3:
Selecting an object to insert in the document.

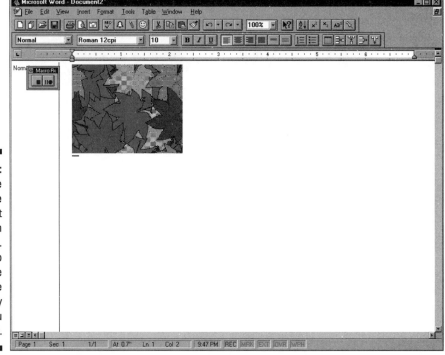

Figure 7-4:
Here's the result of the object insertion process. Your macro will produce the same result every time you run it.

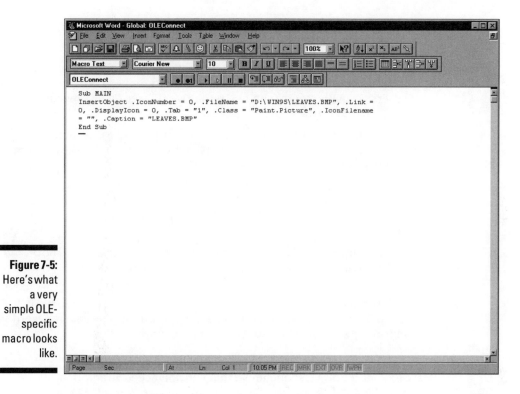

```
Sub MAIN
InsertObject .IconNumber = 0, .FileName = "D:\WIN95\LEAVES.BMP", .Link =
0, .DisplayIcon = 0, .Tab = "1", .Class = "Paint.Picture", .IconFilename
= "", .Caption = "LEAVES.BMP"
End Sub
```

Figure 7-5:
Here's what
a very
simple OLE-
specific
macro looks
like.

There are a few problems with the macro we just created. For one thing, it won't simplify your job much unless you want to insert the same picture all over the place. Another problem is that it depends on a specific machine configuration. We'll look at some realistic examples in the following chapters.

Planning Your Macro

One step is common to the creation of all macros: planning. No matter which application you use, you'll want to plan the macro recording process before you actually start it.

Unlike some macros you create, you'll almost never be able to use an OLE macro as is. You'll usually need to edit an OLE macro before you can use it. Editing a macro to make it truly useful is much easier if you start with a clean macro recording. A clean macro recording is one without typos or other errors. It also doesn't contain any unnecessary steps that you might have mistakenly added during the recording process.

The following steps will simplify your macro planning process. Make sure you carefully follow each step:

1. Determine what you'll start with and what you want to accomplish. You may simply want to place a company logo in the upper-right corner of your letters. A simple macro (such as the one we showed in the preceding section) may do the trick in this case.

2. Once you decide on your starting and ending points, figure out what you need to do to get the job done. If you don't know how to get the job done, how can you tell the computer how to do it?

3. Practice your procedure a few times until you can complete it without error. This is essential. The macro recorder will copy your every step. Missteps always result in extra entries in the macro that you'll have to clean up later.

4. Record the macro. Make sure you see the result you expected. If not, rerecord the macro. If you don't get the desired result, the macro is no good.

5. Test the macro. See if it produces the same result each time you run it. If it doesn't, the application must have tricked you. Repeat the macro recording process, keeping a close eye on that tricky application.

Never assume the macro you record will work correctly on the first try. Always test a new macro on a test document that you don't need. In addition, always save your files and close any other open applications. You never know when a macro will freeze the system and cause you to lose data.

By following this five-step process, you can ensure that you always start with the best possible macro base. A firm foundation always reduces the work you need to do manually. Following this process usually also results in a faster, more error-free macro.

The OLE Cast of Characters

Before you can begin the macro coding process, it helps to understand what is going on in the background. It would be impossible to provide you with a blow-by-blow description of the entire process, but we can look at some of the players in the OLE arena.

If you look in your \WINDOWS\SYSTEM directory, you'll find some files with OLE somewhere in their names (for example, OLESRV.DLL and OLECLI.DLL).

The number of files you see usually depends on the number of applications you have installed and which version of Windows you are using.

These files usually fall into one of three groups: client, server, or base. The client files control how a single application or Windows as a whole reacts when it is a client. The server files perform the same function for server applications. The base files are the glue that holds everything else together. They perform some of the basic tasks of interpretation, and other things that you really don't need to worry about.

The following list describes some of the most common OLE-specific files. Understanding the purpose of these files is helpful when you are creating macros. You'll definitely need to know about these files if you decide to write an OLE application using a general-purpose programming language such as Visual BASIC:

- OLE2.DLL — If you see this file, you know that some part of the Windows installation on your machine supports the OLE 2 standard. Windows 95 always installs this file. This dynamic link library (DLL) provides some base functions. (A DLL is a special Windows program.)

- OLECLI.DLL — This file contains all the basic client code your application needs. Your application uses this file as a base for building its own client features.

- OLESRV.DLL — This file contains all the basic server code your application needs. Like the client code, this DLL won't provide everything. Your application uses it as a basis for building its own set of features.

- OLE2CONV.DLL — Remember our discussion in Chapter 2 about the basic features that most programmers provide in OLE applications? This file provides the generic routines that a program uses to convert an object to the client program's native format.

- OLE2DISP.DLL — Every OLE client application uses this program to help it display the objects it contains.

- OLE2NLS.DLL — Most versions of Windows provide National Language Support (NLS). This program helps OLE keep pace with the rest of Windows in providing support for other languages.

- OLE2.REG — This is a registry file. The registry is a special database used by Windows for storing system settings and other types of information (see Chapter 21 for more details). You can import this file into your registry to install OLE 2 support. In most cases, your application will do this automatically, so you don't need to worry about it. You only need to use this file if you can't get OLE 2 to work and you discover that the registry doesn't contain the correct entries.

✔ MCIOLE.DLL — Under Windows, sounds require special handling. Unlike most objects, you don't display a sound. This special DLL provides the support an application needs for handling a sound object.

✔ OLE32.DLL — A group of OLE files in the SYSTEM directory have *32* somewhere in their name. These files provide the same services to 32-bit applications as their 16-bit counterparts do for 16-bit applications.

✔ MFCOLEUI.DLL — C programmers need every bit of help they can get. To make their workload a little lighter, they use something called Microsoft Foundation Classes. This file (and any others with similar names) provides the C interface to OLE. If you see a file with MFC in its name, you know that one of your applications uses the Microsoft Foundation Classes.

Windows 3.1 does not come with all these different OLE files. In fact, you will probably see only the OLECLI.DLL and OLESRV.DLL files in your SYSTEM directory (the directory may include other files specific to OLE 1). Only when you install an OLE 2-compliant application will you see the OLE2 files. Other files, such as MFCOLEUI.DLL, are installed by programs written in C. You might see the OLE32 files if you install a WIN32S program, a special 32-bit Windows application that can run under Windows 3.1. Windows 95 comes with a lot more OLE support than does Windows 3.1; an important fact to keep in mind if your programs need to run under both operating systems.

Test your newfound knowledge

1. Macros are:

   a. A strange food eaten by pygmy warriors from another planet.

   b. A new video game available at your local entertainment store.

   c. Various forms of programs that require a lot of user intervention.

   d. A method for automating repetitive tasks by storing the keystrokes you would normally make to perform those tasks.

2. Planning your macro before you record it ensures that it will:

   a. Blow up in your face, resulting in certain data loss.

   b. Create a new world order in a matter of moments. Up with computers; down with the human population!

   c. Forever change the way you look at computing.

   d. Allow you to edit the macro with the least amount of effort. A planned macro also runs faster and contains fewer errors than one that wasn't carefully planned.

Chapter 8

OLE for Graphics

....

In This Chapter

▶ All about using OLE within graphics applications

▶ Identifying the OLE capabilities of your graphics applications

▶ Putting OLE to work with your graphics applications

....

*T*he term *graphics* covers a wide range of Windows programs. When you mention graphics programs, some people immediately think of MS Paint or Paintbrush. Other people think about full-fledged drawing programs such as CorelDRAW!. Still others think of presentation graphics programs such as Corel Chart or Microsoft PowerPoint. It would seem that there is a lot of confusion over exactly what a graphics program is.

The quick definition of a graphics program is any application that produces a nontext result. This includes

- ✔ Icon drawing
- ✔ Painting
- ✔ Drawing
- ✔ Presentation graphics
- ✔ Animation
- ✔ CAD (computer-aided design)

This chapter provides an overview of OLE and graphics programs in general. It also looks at two of the more common types of graphics programs: paint and draw applications. The next chapter starts by looking at specialized server techniques. Then, we'll take a look at two of the more specialized types of graphics programs: CAD and charting applications.

Graphics Applications and OLE

The various types of programs mentioned in the preceding section all provide some graphics capabilities, but for different purposes. It makes sense, then, that each type of application will also provide different OLE capabilities.

The simplest type of graphics program we can discuss is the icon drawing program. This type of program has only one purpose: producing those neat-looking icons on your desktop. Icon drawing programs don't usually require OLE capabilities, so we won't discuss them further.

Among graphics programs that do support OLE, you can expect to find some fairly obvious differences in OLE capabilities. For example, Paintbrush doesn't provide a macro language because it is unlikely that anyone will use this program as an OLE client. In most cases, you use a paint program to produce a quick picture that you'll embed somewhere else.

Sophisticated drawing programs such as CorelDRAW! provide a subtle macro language. Like simple paint programs, however, these drawing programs are designed more for creating a picture or other graphic image than for acting as an OLE client. With this in mind, Corel designed CorelDRAW! to use an external macro language substitute and provide support for VBA (Visual BASIC for Applications). Still, you might use CorelDRAW! as a client for putting together a poster or other graphic design.

Corel Chart (or any other presentation graphics program, such as PowerPoint) is definitely intended to be used as a client. This type of application provides the finished output that you can use at a sales meeting or some other type of demonstration. It's unlikely that you would use a presentation graphics program to draw everything you need for a presentation. In addition to using a drawing program for graphics, you would probably rely on spreadsheets for calculations and word processors for text.

CAD programs round out the overall graphics picture. Some people use CAD programs as clients, others as servers. For example, someone who normally creates architectural drawings would probably use a CAD program as a client by adding the results from spreadsheet calculations or bitmapped graphics to a drawing. On the other hand, someone who uses CAD as a means for drawing images to include in a presentation would use it as a server.

A CAD program is typically used for architectural applications or other disciplines that require drafting capabilities. However, there's nothing stopping you from using a CAD program to create flowcharts or other abstract data presentations. A CAD program typically provides a robust macro language designed to make full use of OLE.

Using paint programs with OLE

Paint programs are versatile applications that allow you to create quick graphics. For example, you could use a paint program to create a logo for your letterhead and other office correspondence. Paint programs also come in handy for sketches and other simple pictures.

Paint programs work with raster graphics such as those contained in .PCX (Zsoft Paintbrush), .BMP (Windows bitmap), and .TIF (tagged image format file) files. A raster graphic stores the image you see on screen as a series of pixels. They're called paint programs because you paint an image on the file's canvas, just like a painter working with the real thing.

Some paint programs do not provide OLE services. For example, the Microsoft Paint program provided with Windows 95 doesn't provide full OLE services. Paintbrush, provided with Windows 3.x, does provide full OLE services as a server, but not as a client.

Can your paint program handle the job?

It always pays to check whether your application fully supports OLE. If your application does provide OLE support, you need to find out how well. In Chapter 5, we covered some general procedures for determining the level of OLE support you'll receive from an application. The following procedure is specific to graphics programs.

This procedure assumes you are working with either Windows 95 or Windows 3.1, and have copies of WordPad (or Write, if you are using Windows 3.1), Microsoft Paintbrush, and Microsoft Paint installed on your machine. Even if you don't have these applications, you can still follow the procedure and learn how to detect a paint program's capabilities.

1. Open Microsoft Paint.

2. Choose File⇨Open. The File Open dialog box is displayed. The upper portion of this dialog box contains a list of the folders and files on your machine. Find the Windows 95 directory.

3. Select LEAVES.BMP (or any other small .BMP file) from the list of files in this folder, and click OK.

4. Open the Edit menu. You should see the list of options shown in Figure 8-1. Notice that this list of options includes Paste, but not Paste Special. This tells you that Microsoft Paint does not support OLE as a client.

5. Use the Select tool to select the entire graphic.

6. Choose Edit⇨Copy. The selected object is copied onto the clipboard.

7. Open either WordPad or Write, and open the Edit menu. You should see a list of options similar to the menu shown in Figure 8-2. Notice that WordPad (Write) supports OLE as a client. The menu contains both a Paste and a Paste Special entry.

8. To open the Paste Special dialog box shown in Figure 8-3, choose Edit⇨ Paste Special. Notice that the Source field contains Unknown Source, the Paste Link radio button is deselected, and the As field does not contain a Microsoft Paint entry. This tells you that Microsoft Paint does not support OLE as a server. (At least, it doesn't support it in the normal way. For additional details about Windows 95 and OLE, see the accompanying sidebar.)

9. Click Cancel to close the Paste Special dialog box.

10. Close Microsoft Paint, and open Microsoft Paintbrush. Repeat steps 1 through 9. You should notice that Microsoft Paintbrush does support OLE as a server. The big difference is the Paste Special dialog box, which is shown in Figure 8-4. You can create a link to it or embed the graphic as an object.

11. Close WordPad (or Write) and Microsoft Paintbrush. There is no need to save the files.

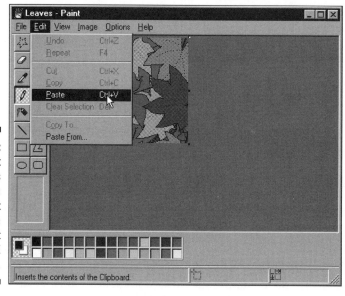

Figure 8-1:
The Paint program's Edit menu shows that this program does not support OLE as a client.

Figure 8-2:
The Edit
menu in
either
WordPad or
Write,
showing
that these
programs
support OLE
as a client.

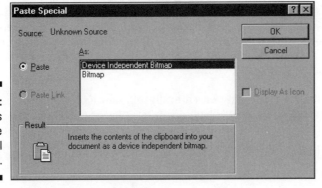

Figure 8-3:
WordPad's
Paste
Special
dialog box.

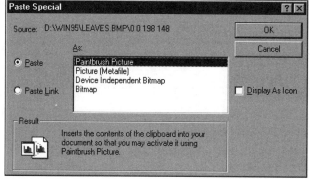

Figure 8-4:
The Paste
Special
dialog box
now shows
that
Paintbrush
supports
OLE as a
server.

Putting your paint program to work

Once you determine the level of support provided by your paint program, you can start to use it for some real work. (It's too bad that fun and games last only a short time but work seems to last forever.) Because most paint programs act as OLE servers, let's look at the types of things you can do with them.

First, you need to decide whether to create a link or embed your graphic. The answer is fairly simple. If you plan to use the graphic in many places (for example, as a logo), you'll probably want to create a link. On the other hand, if this is a one-time specialty graphic (such as a sketch), you'll probably want to embed it.

When you're using a paint program to create a graphic, linking has lots of advantages over embedding. Logos change. So do other small graphics that companies commonly use to dress up letters and other correspondence. Linking allows you to change all the graphics at once by changing a single file. You perform less work, and you can really impress the boss with your speed and accuracy in making the change.

Think about a large company with literally millions of pieces of correspondence. Wouldn't it be nice if you could update all that correspondence to a new look by simply changing one file? That's what linking allows you to do. The first person who opens a letter after you update the logo will also update it to the new look.

Windows 95 and OLE

Windows 95 (as well as a few Windows 3.1 applications) provides an additional method for linking or embedding an object into your application. The following procedure shows how you can use this new technique.

1. Open WordPad.

2. Choose Insert⇨New Object. WordPad displays the Insert Object dialog box.

3. Click the Create from File radio button.

4. Click the Browse button, and find the LEAVES.BMP file in your Windows 95 directory. (You can substitute any desired file here.)

5. Click OK. If Windows 95 displays an error message, there is no application associated with this file extension. If you see an error message, click Cancel to return to the WordPad menus. You will need to add an association using Explorer's View Options dialog box.

To check whether an application supports OLE, double-click the new object that you just inserted. If Windows 95 changes the menu and the toolbar on the client display or brings up the server application to allow you to edit the image, the program associated with that file supports OLE as a server. In this case, we find that even though Microsoft Paint doesn't support the cut-and-paste-special OLE technique, it does support the insert-object technique.

What does this mean to you as a user? The insert-object technique has several limitations. First, you can only insert whole objects. Second, you need to get used to a different method of inserting objects. Finally, the client application has to provide the means for using the insert-object technique, and most applications don't do this.

Let's look at the process for linking a paint graphic, because this is what you will probably do most often. In the following procedure, we assume you are using some version of Windows. We also assume that you have Microsoft Paintbrush (or another paint program that fully supports OLE as a server) and either WordPad or Write.

1. Open Paintbrush (or another paint program).

2. Use the various drawing tools to create a logo that looks similar to the one in Figure 8-5.

3. Use the Select tool to select the entire logo.

4. Place the logo on the clipboard by choosing Edit⇨Copy.

5. Open WordPad (or Write if you are using Windows 3.x).

6. Choose Edit⇨Paste Special to display the Paste Special dialog box.

7. Click the Paste Link radio button. Notice that you get only one choice for format when creating a link. As shown in Figure 8-6, you must create a Paintbrush Picture object.

8. To insert the logo in your word-processing document, click OK. You should see the logo on the page.

9. Using the File⇨Page Setup command under WordPad or the Document⇨Page Layout command under Write, change the left and right margins for your document to .75".

10. Click to the right of the logo. Change the font type to Arial and the size to 72. Center the logo using the Format⇨Paragraph command in WordPad or the Paragraph⇨Centered command in Write. Type **New Town Publishing**.

11. Press Enter. Change the font size to 22. Type **1919 Mockingbird Lane**. Press Enter. Type **Lavern, North Carolina 11223-4567**.

12. Click on the logo. Using the sizing handles, change the logo's size to match the header. Your letter heading should resemble the example in Figure 8-7.

13. Double-click the logo to open Paintbrush. Because we created a link instead of embedding the logo, Paintbrush is opened as a separate application.

14. Modify your logo as shown in Figure 8-8. All you need to do is use the roller tool to fill in the appropriate colors.

15. Close Paintbrush. Choose Yes when the program asks if you want to save the logo. As shown in Figure 8-9, the WordPad file contains the new version of the logo.

16. Close WordPad. Choose Yes when the program asks if you want to save the example file.

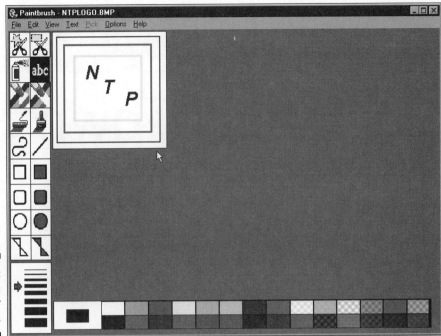

Figure 8-5:
A sample logo for your test file.

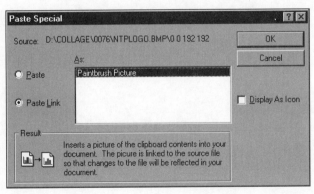

Figure 8-6:
Because the original application retains control over the file, you usually get a single formatting choice when linking a file to a compound document.

Figure 8-9:
The linking
process
automatically
updates the
logo in the
sample
letter file.

Using drawing programs with OLE

With sophisticated drawing programs such as CorelDRAW!, you have many more choices than you do with simple paint programs. In addition to supporting all the server capabilities found in paint programs, drawing programs usually provide client services.

A drawing program works with vector graphics such as those contained in .CGM (computer graphics metafile), .AI (Adobe Illustrator), and .CDR (CorelDRAW!) files. A vector graphic stores the image you see on screen as a series of equations. These equations describe every feature of the drawing in great detail. Because the graphic is stored as equations, a drawing program allows you to resize the image without losing any resolution. Most drawing programs also support the raster formats produced by paint programs.

Windows 95 and Windows 3.1 do not come with a drawing program; you need to buy one separately. CorelDRAW! is only one of many drawing programs on the market. Its many features make CorelDRAW! the most popular PC drawing program.

Sophisticated drawing programs usually provide some type of limited macro or scripting capability that allows you to automate many OLE processes. This isn't the same type of capability you'll find in a word processor or a CAD program. Artists seldom need advanced macros to perform repetitive tasks because art is seldom repetitive.

In the case of CorelDRAW!, this macro capability actually resides outside the application as a separate program, Corel Show. Other full-fledged graphics programs may include this capability as part of the product.

Drawing programs are typically used for producing artistic, nonrepetitive drawings. CAD programs are used for creating architectural or other drawings with precise measurements and repetitive elements. You can use either type of program to create abstract drawings that fall between these two extremes — for example, flowcharts or organization charts.

CorelShow: The other macro

If they don't provide an internal scripting language, high-end graphics programs such as CorelDRAW! usually include some type of presentation program. (Older versions of CorelDRAW! provided a scripting language, but the newer versions use CorelShow.) Although applications such as CorelShow are sometimes referred to as slideshow programs, the current version includes a lot more than that. CorelShow doesn't produce charts or pictures, it creates a presentation from existing materials.

CorelShow and other presentation programs are really a lot more than a macro, but less than a graphics application. As client programs, they use OLE to assemble all the elements of a presentation in one place. This includes pictures, charts, text, spreadsheets, database information, and sounds.

Once you get all the material together, a presentation program will help you add special effects. Some of these special effects are sounds; others include eye candy such as fades and wipes. All the eye- and ear-catching gizmos that computer science can provide come together in one program.

Of course, once you get the show together, the presentation program animates it, making it fun to watch. Presentation programs are useful for convincing other people to support your point of view. The more powerful the presentation, the better your chances of obtaining your goal.

Now, imagine the problems of updating this show with the latest information if you couldn't use OLE. Instead of making a quick fix to a graph or a chart, you'd get mired in a muck of presentation graphics every time you needed to make a change. See how useful OLE is?

Using CorelDRAW! with VBA

Microsoft envisions VBA (Visual BASIC for Applications) as the common language that most programs will eventually use to talk with each other. This capability depends on each program providing some type of documented means for communicating with other programs. Most books refer to this communication process as OLE automation. What this really means is that one program can activate another program's OLE capabilities and use them for its own purposes.

Low-end programs such as Microsoft Paint and WordPad don't usually document their interface. CorelDRAW! and other high-end programs do provide this documentation (although it's frequently buried in the most out-of-the-way place possible). With CorelDRAW!, you can use the following OLE automation commands:

- ✔ Open *filename*
- ✔ Print *filename*
- ✔ Export *filename*
- ✔ Import *filename*
- ✔ Save As *filename*
- ✔ Quit

You can use VBA to create the complex macros that CorelDRAW! does not support. For example, you might want to use a drawing within your Word for Windows document. You can use VBA to open a drawing in CorelDRAW!, export it in a format that Word supports, and then import it into Word. All you need to do is add one of the automation commands to a VBA program like this:

```
Dim DrawObject as Object
Set DrawObject = CreateObject("CorelDRAW.CorelDRAWApp")
DrawObject.Open "Somefile.CDR".
```

The first statement creates a variable to hold an object you plan to manipulate. The second statement tells VBA to create the object. In this case, you create a CorelDRAW! object of some type. The third statement tells the object to open a specific CorelDRAW! file. Once you open a specific file, you could create a link to it or embed it in your current document.

Special OLE capabilities in drawing programs

When it comes to OLE, most programs refuse to do more than the absolute minimum. They provide the common open, edit, and convert options, but not much more. However, graphics programs tend to be among the exceptions to this rule.

Graphics application programmers typically provide a few additional bells and whistles with their applications. The following procedure shows you just one of the special OLE features provided by a drawing program.

In this procedure, we assume you are using CorelDRAW! version 4.0 or later, and we show you CorelDRAW!-specific features. However, most other full-fledged drawing programs provide similar capabilities. It always pays to read your drawing program's documentation to find out which capabilities are supported.

1. Open CorelDRAW!.

2. Choose Edit⇨Insert Object. CorelDRAW! displays the Insert Object dialog box. Click the Create from File radio button. Find LEAVES.BMP (or a similar file) using the Browse button. Click OK. You should see a new graphic object on the screen.

3. With your right mouse button, click the object to display the Object Menu shown in Figure 8-10. Most applications provide a context menu for OLE. This one contains several entries you haven't seen before. The most important entry is the Object Data Roll-Up. The Object Data Roll-Up provides the means for using some OLE features that you might not have seen before.

4. Select the Object Data Roll-Up entry. CorelDRAW! displays the dialog box shown in Figure 8-11. This dialog box lets you associate descriptive information with the object.

5. Click the Object Data Menu button. You should see the menu shown in Figure 8-12.

6. Select the Field Editor entry. You should see a dialog box similar to the one shown in Figure 8-13. This dialog box allows you to change the kinds of descriptive information that CorelDRAW! stores about each object.

7. Click the Create New Field button. In the name field, type **Link Type**. Click the Add Selected Field(s) button. You should see a new field in the Object Data dialog box, as shown in Figure 8-14.

8. Select this field, and type **Embedded**. Now, whenever you select the object roll-up for that field, you'll know that this object is embedded and not linked.

9. Click the Object Data Manager button. You should see the dialog box shown in Figure 8-15. This dialog box will contain one entry for each group or object selected. You can use it as a database for all the OLE objects within a drawing or to simply manipulate the objects in a particular group.

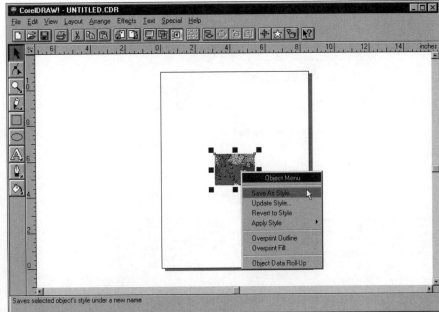

Figure 8-10:
Most
applications
provide
some type of
context
menu for
modifying or
otherwise
managing
OLE objects.

Figure 8-11:
The Object
Data dialog
box provides
the means
for
efficiently
managing
your
CorelDRAW!
OLE objects.

Figure 8-12:
The Object Data menu contains entries that help you maintain descriptive information.

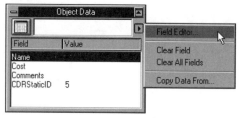

Figure 8-13:
The Field Editor allows you to determine what type of descriptive information each object contains.

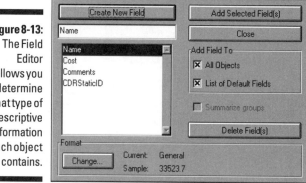

Figure 8-14:
To ensure that you can easily find what you need, always customize the information associated with an object.

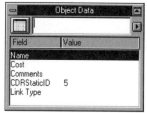

Figure 8-15:
CorelDRAW!
allows you
to select a
group of
objects and
then modify
them using
the Object
Data
Manager.

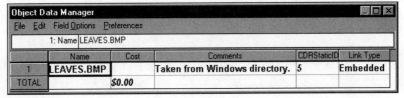

	Name	Cost	Comments	CDRStaticID	Link Type
1	LEAVES.BMP		Taken from Windows directory.	5	Embedded
TOTAL		$0.00			

Three areas in this dialog box are of special interest. The first is the Object Data Manager button in the upper-left corner. Clicking this button displays information about all the selected objects and groups within the current drawing. The second item of interest is the right-pointing arrow on the right side of the dialog box. Clicking this arrow opens the Object Data dialog box, which allows you to specify the types of descriptive information associated with this object. Finally, several fields of object information are displayed in rows at the bottom of the dialog box. These fields contain the descriptive information associated with the object.

Many applications do not allow you to attach descriptive data to an object. Fortunately, however, this capability for defining your objects isn't limited to CorelDRAW!. This capability is provided in other applications — especially drawing applications. You'll also find this capability in many CAD programs. In fact, this capability is likely to be provided in any application that must support complex interactions among numerous objects. If your application doesn't allow you to attach descriptive data to an object, you might want to find out whether the vendor provides some type of alternative.

The vendor determines which types of OLE capabilities a product supports. However, it's up to you to use them effectively. Features such as the Object Data Manager can greatly reduce the effort needed for using OLE on any project.

Test your newfound knowledge

1. Paint programs usually provide the following OLE capabilities:

   a. What capabilities? Paint programs don't need no stinkin' OLE capabilities.

   b. Paint programs typically provide server capabilities to varying degrees, but don't usually provide any type of client capability.

   c. A big sheet that's used to keep the bull residing in your computer at bay.

   d. Paint programs only provide the capability to draw stuff.

2. CorelDRAW! provides a VBA interface. What is this, and what does it do?

   a. VBA stands for Very Big Arsenal. The interface allows you to keep track of any guns or other munitions stored near the computer.

   b. The virtual buffer access interface allows you to maintain an OLE connection via modem.

   c. VBA stands for Visual BASIC for Applications. The interface allows another application to use CorelDRAW! as an OLE server.

   d. There's no such thing as VBA. It's a nice idea from Microsoft whose time hasn't come.

The 5th Wave   By Rich Tennant

"THIS IS YOUR GROUPWARE?! THIS IS WHAT YOU'RE RUNNING?! WELL HECK — I THINK THIS COULD BE YOUR PROBLEM!"

Chapter 9

Advanced OLE for Graphics

In This Chapter

▶ Using OLE with CAD applications

▶ Specialized graphics server applications

▶ All about OLE macros for graphics applications

▶ Charting with OLE

*O*nce you understand the basics of using OLE with graphics applications, it's time to look at some of the more advanced ways you can use OLE. Graphics applications provide several ways to automate OLE tasks. For example, you can use the macro capability provided with some CAD programs to create new OLE objects. As we'll discuss later in this book, many spreadsheet and word processor applications also have this capability. However, some graphics applications go even further. They allow you to embed OLE objects as part of your drawing. In other words, OLE becomes more than a way to share data; it becomes a form of artistic expression. In addition, just about every graphics program provides unique ways to manage objects.

You create macros by recording your keystrokes. The macro is stored as part of your document or on disk in a separate file. By recording your keystrokes, you can play them back later, much like you play a videocassette or audio recording. Application programs provide a macro capability so you can reduce the work required to perform repetitive tasks. Some applications allow you to enhance your macros so you can actually do more with the macro than you could originally do by manually entering keystrokes.

Specialized Server Methods

Graphics applications have one problem that no other application has under Windows. They must provide a way for the client to display the information they create. This isn't a problem for most applications. However, some graphics applications need special tools to display their information on a client screen.

CAD (computer-aided design) programs fall into this category. Other graphics applications — for example, painting, drawing, and presentation graphics programs — provide artistic or other nonprecise output. People expect CAD applications to provide precise output.

So, the problem for a CAD program is how to display this precise picture on a client screen that may not be designed to handle such a precise image. For example, a word processor isn't set up to display an image that's accurate to 0.0001 of an inch, but CAD programs normally work with this level of accuracy.

TurboCAD, a Windows-based CAD program, provides a special OLE server technique. It converts its vector graphics into a raster graphic (or bitmap) that can be displayed by the client program. Many applications can display a raster graphic with greater precision than a vector graphic. Here's how TurboCAD accomplishes this task.

If you have TurboCAD or another CAD application that supports this specialized server technique, you can use the following procedure directly. If not, follow along anyway so that you can at least see how this technique works:

1. Open TurboCAD (or any other midrange to high-end CAD application).

2. Draw a triangle or other simple object. Select it, and then place a copy of the selected object on the clipboard by choosing Edit⇨Copy.

3. Open Write or WordPad (depending on whether you are using Windows 3.x or Windows 95).

4. Open the Edit menu. As shown in Figure 9-1, you can't select Paste, Paste Special, or Paste Link. Even though you copied the object to the clipboard, it isn't in a format that the word processor can use. TurboCAD needs to convert the image into a usable format.

5. Press Alt+Tab to reselect TurboCAD. As shown in Figure 9-2, place a copy of the drawing on the clipboard by choosing Edit⇨Copy Special.

6. Press Alt+Tab to reselect Write or WordPad. To display the Paste Special dialog box shown in Figure 9-3, choose Edit⇨Paste Special. Notice that this dialog box doesn't allow you to select the Paste Link radio button. The reason is simple: You can't link to a file that the word processor can't display. You must embed the converted version of the file into the word-processing document. WordPad (or Write) will still start TurboCAD whenever you need to modify the drawing; this is still a true OLE object. All that's changed is your ability to link several documents to the same graphic.

7. In the Paste Special dialog box, select TurboCAD 2 Win Object, and click OK. You should see the triangle displayed in the WordPad (Write) document area.

8. Double-click the object. Notice that WordPad starts TurboCAD and places the image in a new drawing area. This tells you two things. First, TurboCAD doesn't provide the means for WordPad to display its controls and allow you to edit the file in the WordPad document area. Second, you embedded the object into the WordPad document.

9. Make some change to the object and close TurboCAD. It will ask if you want to save the original drawing. Choose No. Notice that TurboCAD didn't ask if you wanted to save the changes to the embedded object. What's more, the WordPad document doesn't contain the changes.

10. Double-click the object in the word-processing document. TurboCAD will start and display the object in the drawing area. Make some change to the object.

11. To update the object you embedded in the word-processing document, choose File⇨Update. Close TurboCAD. Now, the object embedded in the WordPad document contains the change. Some applications require you to update the object before you exit; others perform this task automatically. You should also note that you don't save the drawing. Saving it would create a file on disk that contained the vector graphic. Remember that WordPad can't use the vector representation of the drawing.

12. Close both WordPad (Write) and TurboCAD. There is no need to save the drawing.

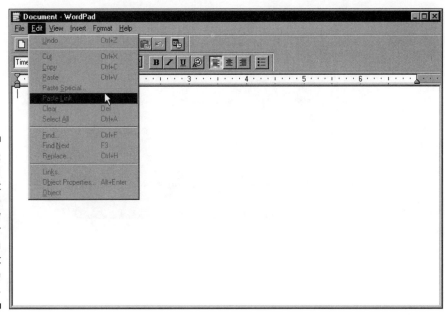

Figure 9-1:
TurboCAD doesn't support the normal copy method for placing an OLE object on the clipboard.

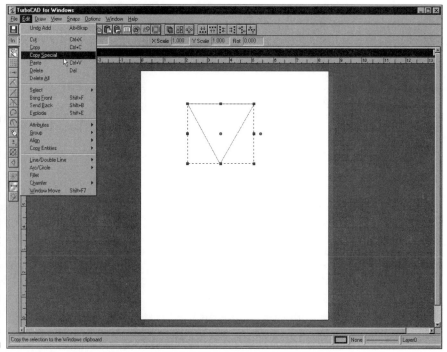

Figure 9-2:
TurboCAD
does
provide a
Copy
Special
command
that
converts the
raster
graphic
drawing into
a bitmap
representation.

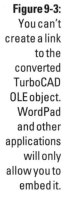
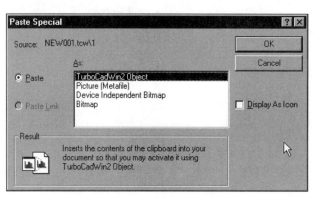

Figure 9-3:
You can't
create a link
to the
converted
TurboCAD
OLE object.
WordPad
and other
applications
will only
allow you to
embed it.

Always check the capabilities of your application. Otherwise, you might spend hours trying to figure out why OLE isn't working properly. You would think that the various vendors could get together and determine one way of handling these exceptions, but they don't want to cheat you of the pleasure of learning so many new things.

You may notice that TurboCAD (as well as most other CAD applications) doesn't support OLE as a client. High-end CAD programs such as AutoCAD do support OLE as a client. CAD programs never display anything as text. (Some CAD programs do store text, but they usually display it in a graphics mode.) They usually display everything as a vector graphic. This means the application won't be able to handle other types of data without first converting the data. The one exception to this rule is vector graphics from other applications such as CorelDRAW!. You'll find that many CAD applications allow you to paste information from one vector graphics program to another.

CAD Programs and OLE Scripts

CAD programs use scripts to automate just about every imaginable task. The reason is fairly simple: CAD drawings usually contain repetitive elements, and using a script reduces the time it takes for a draftsperson to create a drawing. For the same reason, CAD programs usually come with one or more libraries of predrawn objects.

From a conceptual point of view, scripts and macros are usually the same thing. Both contain sets of keystrokes that allow the computer to perform repetitive tasks. Word-processing and spreadsheet applications call a list of stored commands a *macro*. Just to be different, graphics programs call these lists *scripts*.

Depending on which CAD program you use, you may or may not have the ability to automate OLE commands. It depends on what type of access the program provides to the application menu. Some CAD programs — for example, TurboCAD — only provide script commands for drawing objects and importing or exporting files. Other, high-end CAD programs such as AutoCAD provide access to the application menu.

Most CAD programs use a somewhat cryptic scripting language similar to the languages used by programmers. For example, the following script opens a file, selects the entire drawing, and copies it to the clipboard:

```
OpenDrawing(SAMPLE.TCW)
SelectAll
CopySpecial
```

An application such as a word processor could use a DDE call to start the CAD program using this script, and then place the contents of the clipboard into the current document. Of course, this is only one approach.

Depending on the capabilities of your applications, there may be other, equally good solutions to your OLE automation needs. As mentioned in the preceding chapter, CorelDRAW! supports a VBA (Visual BASIC for Applications) interface. Many CAD programs also offer this type of interface. In the future, you won't need to write scripts to obtain the input you need. One application will directly manipulate another application using its VBA interface. For now, however, scripts at least provide a way to get your work done.

You can never be certain what kind of reaction you'll get from an application if you try to control it remotely — that is, from within another application. Some applications work just fine; others quickly send you to an early grave trying to figure out what went wrong. To avoid getting prematurely gray, always test a script within an application first, before you try to invoke it remotely using a client application.

OLE and Chart Programs

Most people think of a chart program as just another graphics application. As shown in Figure 9-4, a chart program (in this example CorelCHART) is actually a different kind of spreadsheet. In many ways, it's much simpler to use because it provides only a small number of the features you would expect to find in a spreadsheet. In other ways, a chart program is actually more complex because it provides graphics-related features that a spreadsheet doesn't need. You won't find a chart program that doesn't include at least a rudimentary spreadsheet as part of its package. However, you'd never want to replace your spreadsheet with a chart program; they're designed for two completely different uses.

If a chart program provided only a basic spreadsheet and a few minor graphics capabilities, you could probably replace it with a good spreadsheet. However, chart programs typically go beyond these simple features. Most of them also include

- Presentation graphics
- The capability for downloading your charts to a slideshow service or a printer
- An animation capability
- Some type of clip-art package

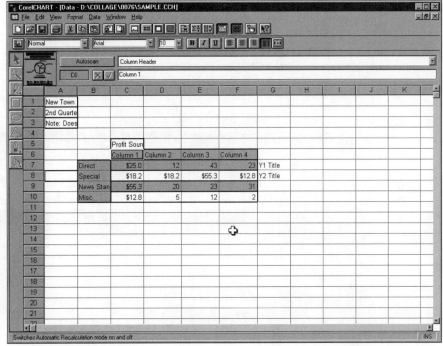

Figure 9-4:
The front
end of a
chart
application
may look
like a
standard
graphics
program,
but the back
end is a
spreadsheet.

Chart programs normally provide both client and server capabilities. Most of them also provide spreadsheet-style macro capabilities similar to the ones we'll discuss in Chapter 10. The big difference between the two application types is that chart programs normally provide more graphics-handling macro commands and fewer calculation-related features than typical spreadsheet programs.

Unlike some graphics applications, chart programs develop their own graphics and use the output of other applications simultaneously. In addition, chart programs usually handle both types of graphic images: vector (CAD and drawing program output) and raster (bitmapped). They also allow you to use a variety of clip-art images to dress up the various types of charts and graphics they produce.

You can use the output of a word processor to add information to a chart or graph; however, the text capabilities of most chart applications usually get the job done. As a server, a chart program allows you to place the compound documents into your favorite word processor, desktop publishing program, or presentation graphics package.

Chart programs also usually display their dual nature in the way they handle OLE. Figure 9-5 shows the Edit menu for the spreadsheet portion of CorelCHART. Notice that this menu has two OLE-specific entries. The familiar Paste Special command works just like the same command provided with other applications. The Paste Link Data command creates a link with the data from another source. CorelCHART highlights only this entry when the clipboard contains text.

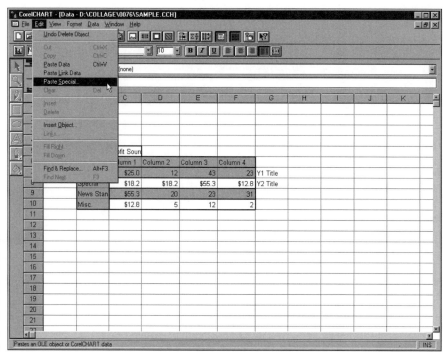

Figure 9-5:
CorelCHART
spreadsheet
supports
OLE as a
client.

If you switch to the presentation part of the package and look at its Edit menu, you may get a surprise. As shown in Figure 9-6, the presentation portion of CorelCHART doesn't support OLE as a client. The developers expect that you'll want to link or embed data from other applications into your chart program, but they expect you'll use the program as a server when it comes to graphics.

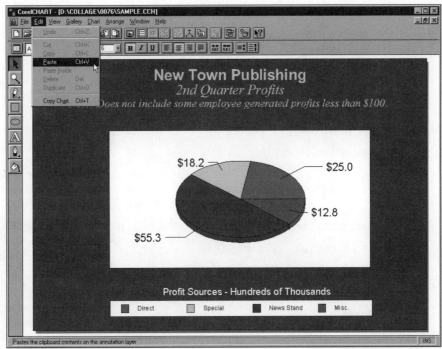

Figure 9-6:
The
presentation
part of
CorelCHART
doesn't
support OLE
as a client.

Always check the capabilities of your chart program. The capabilities in one portion of the program may not match those provided by other parts. This holds true for any application you use, but becomes a factor most often in chart programs.

When you look at the last entry in the Edit menu, it becomes clear that Corel expects the output of CorelCHART to be used as a server. This application provides a single-step method for copying an entire chart to the clipboard. This feature makes it easy to create a chart using data from another source — for example, a database — and then move the chart to an application that needs this graphical representation of the data — such as a word processor.

Test your newfound knowledge

1. You should always test your OLE scripts within the server application first, and then within the client application:

   a. To make certain the scripts work before you try to use them remotely from the client.

   b. Because they'll never work from a remote location.

   c. So you can say that you followed the rules.

   d. To avoid work by making it appear that the script needs more editing.

2. Which parts of a chart program support OLE? How do they support it?

   a. Chart programs never support OLE. They're an end in themselves and are completely self-sufficient.

   b. You should never use OLE with a chart program. Doing so could have seriously damaged the appearance of your output.

   c. The spreadsheet portion of a chart program normally supports OLE as a client so you can input data from another source, such as a database. The graphics portion of a chart program supports OLE as a server so you can link or embed the resulting graphics in another application.

   d. A chart program uses OLE only to display graphics on the screen. Unfortunately, even this is limited by an inability to edit the graphics image later.

Chapter 10

OLE for Spreadsheets

In This Chapter

▶ All about using OLE within spreadsheet applications

▶ OLE capabilities of spreadsheet applications

▶ Specialized spreadsheet server applications

▶ OLE macros for spreadsheet applications

Spreadsheets have come a long way since the days of VisiCalc. In fact, the original spreadsheet programs have as much in common with today's spreadsheets as a four-function calculator has with a Pentium-equipped computer. Modern spreadsheets such as Lotus 1-2-3, Quattro Pro, and Excel come equipped to handle a wealth of calculations that you once had to perform manually.

However, modern spreadsheets are distinguished by more than just their capability for handling complex equations. The new breed of spreadsheet programs provides other features such as presentation-quality graphics and the capability to integrate graphics with the final output. In fact, some folks even use their spreadsheet program as a primitive word processor.

Although this might lead you to believe that a spreadsheet could replace just about every application on your machine, that simply isn't so. You can use a hammer to pound a screw into a piece of wood, but that doesn't make a hammer the right tool for the job. Likewise, a spreadsheet doesn't make a particularly good word processor.

Always use the appropriate tool for the job. A spreadsheet isn't a word processor and it's only a barely adequate charting tool. Using OLE to combine the features of all the tools on your machine makes sense. Use each tool for the work it does best, and then combine the results using the tool that lets you create the most effective presentation. Spreadsheets are great analysis tools; in most cases, however, you won't want to use one for final output.

Spreadsheets and OLE

You can accomplish quite a bit using a spreadsheet for calculations or as a charting tool. Normally, you use a spreadsheet as an OLE server; its output appears as part of a report in a compound document created with a word processor or a desktop publishing application. However, you might sometimes want to use a spreadsheet as an OLE client.

For example, what would happen if you needed to create a presentation that reflects daily changes in sales for your workgroup or company? The presentation needs to include real-world statistics such as profits by sales area, and you need to perform what-if analyses while presenting the report. A charting program is designed for static, not dynamic presentations. The most appropriate tool on your computer in this case is a spreadsheet, because it's designed to work with dynamic — that is, changing — data.

As you might expect, the boss is breathing down your neck, and you really need to make this presentation look polished or you'll suffer the consequences. You will present the sales statistics to not only your boss, but your boss's boss as well. Using other applications to handle the tasks for which your spreadsheet isn't particularly well suited really makes sense. For example, you might want to add a bit of text created with your word processor and perhaps some bit-mapped graphics created with Microsoft Paint or Paintbrush.

Both Microsoft Excel and Lotus 1-2-3 provide superior OLE capabilities. You can create links using the standard Copy and Paste Special technique we've described in previous chapters (such as Chapters 4 and 8). Both products also support the Insert Object feature we've discussed. Figure 10-1 shows the Edit menu from Lotus 1-2-3. Figure 10-2 shows the same information for Excel.

The first thing you'll probably notice is that even though both products provide the same features, those features are arranged differently. Excel's Insert⇨Object command performs the same task as the Edit⇨Insert Object command does in Lotus 1-2-3. Both commands provide access to an Insert Object dialog box similar to the examples we've showed you in previous chapters. (You can also look at Figure 10-7 for an example of an Insert Object dialog.)

Even though the location of these commands differs, their names do not. To make their products easier for you to learn, software vendors typically use the same name for a command from one product to another. In addition, different programming specifications attempt to force software vendors to use similar menu configurations for all their products. The goal of these specifications — or programming guidelines — is to ensure that Windows users aren't faced with the hodgepodge of command names and menu structures that plagued users of DOS programs.

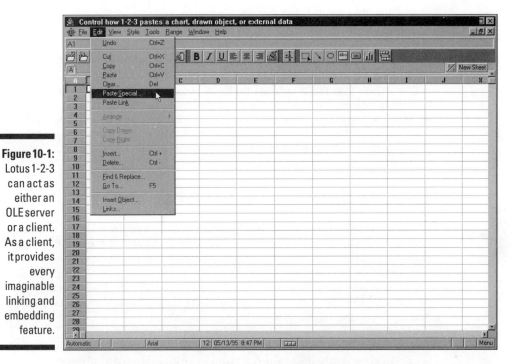

Figure 10-1:
Lotus 1-2-3
can act as
either an
OLE server
or a client.
As a client,
it provides
every
imaginable
linking and
embedding
feature.

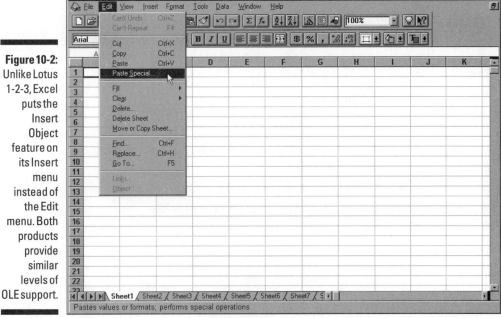

Figure 10-2:
Unlike Lotus
1-2-3, Excel
puts the
Insert
Object
feature on
its Insert
menu
instead of
the Edit
menu. Both
products
provide
similar
levels of
OLE support.

Objects Within a Spreadsheet

The one area in which spreadsheets provide a different interface from other applications is in the management of objects. Spreadsheets use a special macro language that relies as much on functions as on menu commands. As a result, most (if not all) of the functionality a spreadsheet provides for OLE purposes must also appear in some way on a menu or within a dialog. This reflects the origins of spreadsheets. Early spreadsheet programs provided a simple macro language that mimicked the commands you entered at the keyboard.

Linking data in spreadsheets

One of the first features you should examine in a spreadsheet is how it manages data links. Trying to manage one huge worksheet is much more difficult than managing lots of little ones. However, if you use many small spreadsheets, you need to create a central worksheet (a form of master document) from which you can see an overview of your data. For example, although you could put all the sales figures for every region on one worksheet, the data would be easier to manage if you put each region on its own worksheet.

That's where linking comes in. You need a good linking mechanism in spreadsheets because embedding the data won't work. Linking can automatically update multiple files, but embedding can't. To stay current, your master document must update itself from all those little worksheets, and that requires OLE links.

The following example shows how spreadsheets help you manage objects through linking. We'll list commands for both Microsoft Excel and Lotus 1-2-3. Because other spreadsheets will likely follow the example set by these two, you can probably use this procedure with a few minor modifications, no matter which spreadsheet you use.

1. Open either 1-2-3 or Excel.

2. Open Microsoft Word (or another high-end word processor to which you can link your spreadsheet).

3. Select Arial from the Font list and 22 from the Size list.

4. Click the Center Text pushbutton on the toolbar.

5. Type **This is a Title**.

6. Select the paragraph. Choose Edit⇨Copy to place the paragraph on the clipboard.

7. Press Alt+Tab to display the spreadsheet.

8. To create a link in 1-2-3, choose Edit⇨Paste Link. In Excel, choose Edit⇨Paste Special to display the Paste Special dialog box. Then, to create the link in Excel, click Paste Link, and then OK. You should see a display similar to Figure 10-3. Notice that the text is left justified, not centered.

9. Delete the object you just pasted.

10. Press Alt+Tab to display Word again.

11. Press End to place the cursor at the end of the line. Press Enter to create a new paragraph.

12. Repeat steps 6 through 8. You should see a display similar to the one in Figure 10-4. Notice that the text is now centered. Word processors usually require that you place an end-of-paragraph mark in the object before text can be displayed correctly in another application.

13. Choose Edit⇨Links to display the Links dialog box, which contains a list of OLE objects in the current worksheet. (Surprisingly, this command is precisely the same in both spreadsheet applications.) Figure 10-5 shows the result for 1-2-3. Figure 10-6 shows the same thing for Excel. Notice that both dialog boxes provide the same functionality.

14. Close all applications. Do not save anything unless you want to try this exercise again later.

Spreadsheets usually allow you to embed any kind of information. However, they are very picky about the types of applications to which you can create a link. In most cases, you can create links to word processors and other spreadsheets. Spreadsheets embed data from every other application, including note-taking applications such as Write and WordPad.

The preceding example showed you something important about the way spreadsheets manage OLE links. They use the same techniques for managing these links as they do for managing links to their own files. The same dialog that shows you the files linked into the totals worksheet will also tell you about any OLE links.

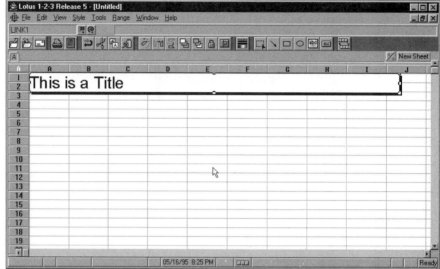

Figure 10-3:
You won't
always get
the
expected
results the
first time
you try to
create a link
to an object.

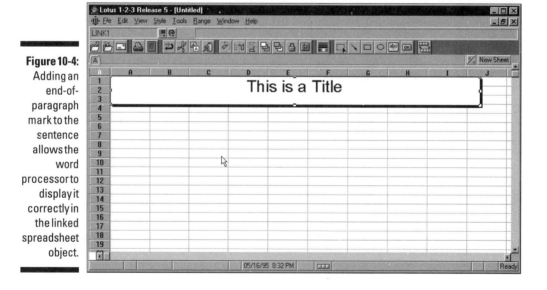

Figure 10-4:
Adding an
end-of-
paragraph
mark to the
sentence
allows the
word
processor to
display it
correctly in
the linked
spreadsheet
object.

Figure 10-5:
Lotus 1-2-3
provides an
easy-to-
read Links
dialog box
that allows
you to
create new
links.

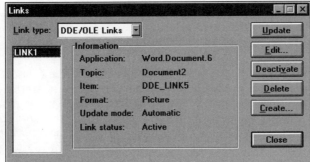

Figure 10-6:
Excel's
Links dialog
box allows
you to
choose
between
manual and
automatic
updates. It
also allows
you to
change the
source file
used for
a link.

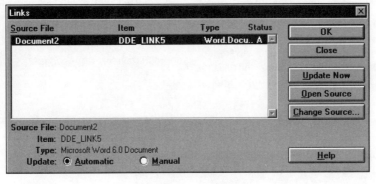

Embedding data in spreadsheets

In some cases, embedding an OLE object in a spreadsheet makes sense. For example, you might want to dress up your spreadsheet by adding a graphic stored in a BMP file. Embedding that file is a good idea, because the data is static; it won't change any time in the near future. Text you created in your word processor to make graphs and charts look more professional is also a good candidate for embedding.

Various spreadsheets react differently to embedded data. Figure 10-7 shows you the Insert Object dialog box for Lotus 1-2-3. Figure 10-8 shows Excel's version of the same dialog box. Notice that you can embed only a new object in 1-2-3. On the other hand, Excel allows you to embed either an existing file or a new one. This difference in functionality could prove essential if you normally use your spreadsheet to prepare in-house presentations. Using the existing file option allows you to embed clip art or other existing documents.

Word processors and spreadsheet links

There's a special relationship between word processors and spreadsheets that you probably won't find in many other OLE-capable programs. When you select text within a word processor, and then create a link to it by choosing a spreadsheet's Paste Link command, something also happens in the word processor document.

As part of the linking process, most word processors will automatically create a bookmark (or that word processor's equivalent of a bookmark). For example, if you create a link in a Word for Windows document, you will find an OLE_LINK*X* bookmark (where *X* is the number of the OLE link).

You can use this relationship to your advantage. Move the bookmark and you change the text that the spreadsheet displays when you update the link.

This feature comes in handy if you use the same spreadsheet to produce several different versions of the same graph. You could easily change graph titles by changing the bookmark location within your word processor document. In fact, you could even use this feature to support different languages by having them all in one word processor document.

Later in this chapter we'll look at how you can use DDE macros to automate your OLE connections. Using these DDE macros could allow you to change languages automatically with a simple control key combination. All you'd need to do is create a DDE macro that looks for a key word in the word processor document, and make the appropriate bookmark changes.

Figure 10-7:
Lotus 1-2-3's
Insert
Object
dialog box.

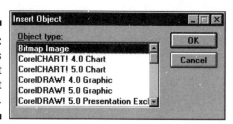

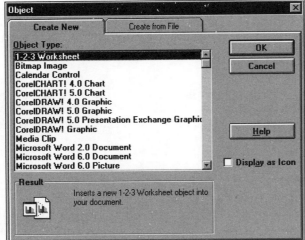

Figure 10-8:
Excel's
Insert
Object
dialog box
offers a
wealth
of tools.

Excel and 1-2-3 also differ in the way they react to embedded objects. If you try to embed a Microsoft Paint bitmap in Lotus 1-2-3, the spreadsheet always opens a new window when you want to edit that bitmap. As shown in Figure 10-9, Excel allows the server application to take over its menus and toolbar. Again, the difference between the two applications comes down to ease of use. (In this case, the difference is in the way 1-2-3 adds entries to the registry, a topic we discuss in Chapter 21.)

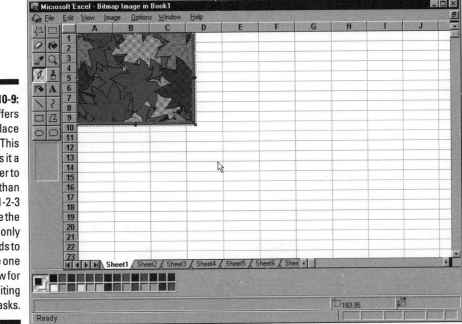

Figure 10-9:
Excel offers
in-place
editing. This
makes it a
lot easier to
use than
1-2-3
because the
user only
needs to
use one
window for
all editing
tasks.

One other point of interest in this figure is the hatching (diagonal lines) around the graphic. When you see hatching around an object, it tells you that you're no longer using the client application's controls. The server application tells you that it's in control by displaying the hatch marks. Click outside the object and the hatch marks will disappear.

Always pick an OLE application that includes all the features you need for getting the job done. Some products may provide excellent server capabilities, but fall short when it comes to acting as a client. Likewise, a good client does not always make a good server.

Spreadsheets and OLE Macros

In most cases, programming a spreadsheet to perform a repetitive OLE task is as easy as starting the macro recorder. Of course, you won't get the final result that way, but using the macro recorder is a good starting place. Lotus 1-2-3 uses the older macro method of recording keystrokes when creating a spreadsheet "application" that makes using OLE a little more automatic.

If you have Lotus 1-2-3, you can try the following example. If not, you can at least read along to see how a spreadsheet handles OLE in a macro.

1. Open 1-2-3.

2. Turn on the macro recorder by choosing Tools⇨Macro⇨Record. A Rec indicator will appear in the status bar at the bottom of the window.

3. Choose Edit⇨Insert Object. 1-2-3 displays the Insert Object dialog box shown in Figure 10-10.

4. Select Bitmap Image from the list, and click OK. 1-2-3 will display either Paintbrush or Microsoft Paint (depending on your version of Windows).

5. Update the spreadsheet by choosing File⇨Update (Update Untitled). We really don't need to add a functional image yet, so there's no need to draw anything. Choose File⇨Exit to return to the spreadsheet.

6. To complete the macro, choose Tools⇨Macro⇨Stop Recording.

7. Display the macro by choosing Tools⇨Macro⇨Show Transcript. You should see a dialog box similar to the one in Figure 10-11.

8. Simply cut and paste the macro from the transcript window to the worksheet. Save the worksheet as OLE.WK4 (or whatever extension your version of 1-2-3 uses). Now, you can move the macro from worksheet to worksheet as needed.

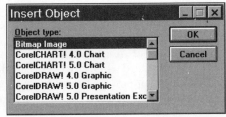

Figure 10-10:
By creating
OLE-specific
macros in
1-2-3, you
can make it
easier to
insert new
objects.

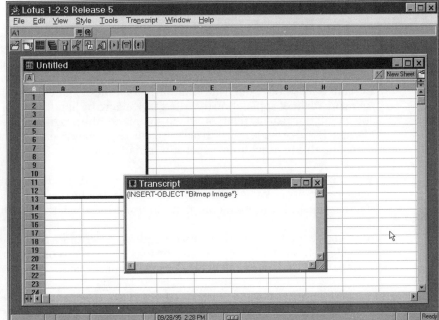

Figure 10-11:
Our
completed
one-line
macro
doesn't do
much, but it'll
help you
insert
objects
quickly.

This is a starting point for an OLE macro. You could save this tiny macro for later use, just like any other Lotus 1-2-3 macro.

Of course, this sample macro leaves a lot to be desired when it comes to OLE automation. Wouldn't it be nice if you could have the spreadsheet automatically insert a specific icon whenever you ran the macro? That's the topic we cover in the next section.

Spreadsheets and OLE Automation

Several different forms of OLE automation will soon be available. One type is VBA (Visual BASIC for Applications). We look at this particular topic a little later in the book. Lotus and Novell also seem intent on introducing their own versions of VBA. (Why adhere to one standard when two or three will confuse the issue?) The Lotus version provides a superset of the VBA instruction set. The bottom line is that these application interfaces are still a few years away.

The type of automation you're most likely to find today is not VBA. It's a lot more likely that you will find something called a DDE macro. In previous chapters, we described DDE as a predecessor to OLE. However, even OLE 2 still relies on DDE to accomplish one important job: automation of OLE-related tasks.

There's no way to write a DDE macro using the macro recorder provided with your spreadsheet. The reason is simple. The macro recorder can't read the keystrokes you make in the server application, so it can't record them for you.

You can usually find enough information in the vendor manual supplied with your spreadsheet application to write a DDE macro by hand. The vendor documentation usually tells you which commands the program supports. Both 1-2-3 and Excel provide a wealth of DDE macro commands, enough that you should be able to provide any level of automation you like.

A novice user won't want to tackle programming a DDE macro. Writing this type of macro requires a knowledge of both the client and the server applications' macro languages as well as some inside information about the way DDE works.

You can do a few things to speed up the process of writing a DDE macro. For example, you can break down the job into easily managed components. Writing a macro to automate your OLE tasks requires four steps:

1. Writing a macro to handle the task you need to perform in the server application.

2. Embedding this macro in your client application using DDE instructions.

3. Writing any steps the client requires for opening the server application and performing its own internal processing.

4. Testing your macro using a real-world situation.

DDE macros usually look pretty strange. They normally contain long lines of seemingly incoherent instructions. That's why you want to write the bulk of your DDE macro using the server application's macro recorder.

You need to remember another important rule when writing a DDE macro. Never try to place a single instruction on two macro lines. DDE macros don't have continuation characters like the ones you'll find when using formal programming languages.

Now that you have a basic idea of what you need to do to prepare a DDE macro, let's look at an example. The following code is a typical, eight-line DDE macro:

```
{LAUNCH "D:\WIN\WINWORD\WINWORD"}
{DDE-OPEN "WINWORD","SYSTEM"}
{DDE-EXECUTE "[InsertObject .IconNumber = 0, .FileName =↲
            ""D:\WIN95\LEAVES.BMP"",
.Link = 1, .DisplayIcon = 0, .Tab = ""1"", .Class =↲
            ""Paint.Picture"", .IconFilename = """", .Caption
            = ""LEAVES.BMP""]"}
{DDE-EXECUTE "[CharLeft 1, 1]"}
{DDE-EXECUTE "[EditBookmark .Name = ""DDE_LINK1"", .SortBy =↲
            0, .Add]"}
{SELECT A1}
{LINK-CREATE
            "LINK1";"Word.Document.6";"Document1";"DDE_LINK1"↲
            ;"Picture";"Automatic"}
{LINK-ASSIGN "LINK1";"A:A1"}
```

The macro may look confusing, but it's actually pretty easy to figure out. The following paragraphs break down the macro line by line.

1. The first line opens Word for Windows. The LAUNCH command always opens an OLE server.

2. Once you start the server, you have to open it for use with DDE macro commands. In this case, we tell Windows to open a DDE conversation with WINWORD. We tell Windows that we plan to use Word for Windows system commands. You can use the registry information we discuss in Chapter 21 as a basis for opening a DDE conversation. The file associations a program creates usually contain the required information. (In Windows 95, you can also find this information on the File Types page of the Explorer Options dialog box.)

3. Now that we've told both Word and Windows that we want to talk, it's time to start a conversation. This first DDE-EXECUTE command uses Word's Insert⇨Object command to insert an OLE object in a Word document. In this example, the object is LEAVES.BMP, but you could also insert any other object. The important thing to remember is that all three DDE-EXECUTE commands were created using Word's macro recorder. You don't have to worry too much about how to format these commands.

4. The second DDE-EXECUTE command highlights the OLE object, just as you would with the mouse.

5. The third DDE-EXECUTE command creates a bookmark called DDE_LINK1. We talked about bookmarks at the beginning of this chapter. A spreadsheet creates an OLE link to a word processor document using a bookmark.

6. Now that we've inserted an object in our Word document and created a bookmark for it, we can access that bookmark from 1-2-3. This command selects cell A1 in the current worksheet. That's where we'll place the OLE object.

7. The LINK-CREATE macro command creates a link to the word processor document. Let's take this command apart, because you will have to create it manually. LINK1 is the name of the link within 1-2-3. Word.Document.6 is the Registry form of the OLE 2 entry for Word for Windows. (Chapter 21 tells you how to find this information.) The next part of the command references the DDE_LINK1 bookmark we created in the Word document. The next entry tells 1-2-3 that this is a picture OLE object. Finally, we tell 1-2-3 that we want this link updated automatically.

8. The final command, LINK-ASSIGN, places the object LINK1 in cell A1 of our worksheet.

Once you break down the task into logical steps, it's not too difficult to understand what's going on. You can use DDE macros to accomplish any task in the server that you could normally perform with a macro. In fact, you can even use DDE to execute macros that you created in the server.

Test your newfound knowledge

1. When you consider the availability of OLE features that make it easier to share information between applications, spreadsheets are the best tools to use when you need to:

   a. Create a long document such as a book.

   b. Hammer a screw into a piece of wood or perform other chores around the house.

   c. Create charts or worksheets.

   d. Sleep during lunch, because most spreadsheets also include an alarm clock.

2. Linking is more important than embedding in a spreadsheet because:

   a. It's not more important. Embedding is always more important than linking. Up with embedding, down with linking!

   b. This book says so.

   c. Very few people know how to use embedding within a spreadsheet. It's much too complex for the average human mind to comprehend.

   d. A worksheet usually contains more dynamic data than static data. Using links will allow you to automatically update all the files on which a master worksheet depends.

Chapter 11

OLE for Database Managers

In This Chapter

▶ All about using OLE within database management applications

▶ OLE capabilities of database management applications

▶ Using OLE in forms and reports

▶ Enhancing macros using OLE

*P*C database managers have come a long way since the days of dBASE II. They're faster, more reliable, and able to serve the needs of users in many more ways than earlier products. In fact, database managers have come so far that many PC-based versions are replacing their mainframe counterparts. Early database managers served the needs of a single person or perhaps a workgroup. Newer versions can meet the needs of an entire company.

Database management systems (DBMSs) differ in various ways from every other application we've discussed in the previous chapters. For one thing, all the other applications are designed for use by one person at a time. It's unlikely that you'd find more than one person updating a worksheet, a graph, a drawing, or a word processing document at one time. DBMSs are truly useful only when more than one person is using them.

There's another important difference between DBMSs and other applications you use. A user rarely uses the DBMS engine or edits the data directly. (A DBMS engine controls access to the data, processes all the commands the user or your application makes, and takes care of database management tasks such as adding and deleting records.) You normally access the power of the engine and the contents of the database through a *front end*.

A DBMS front end is a combination of forms, queries, reports, and other components created by an advanced user or a programmer. A DBMS normally manages the data using a combination of program code and macros. The program code displays a form and retrieves the data the user places in the form. Once retrieved, the data is entered into the appropriate tables of the database.

The final major difference between a DBMS and other applications (at least from an OLE point of view) is that the database is normally kept on a file server or a host (mainframe) computer. The OLE capabilities of your DBMS are affected as much by the capabilities of the product as by the capabilities of both the workstation and the network operating system. This important difference makes the DBMS one of the most complex OLE environments from a user perspective.

DBMSs and OLE

A DBMS normally acts as both a client and a server, with heavy emphasis on the server role. Its role as a server is fairly easy to understand. A DBMS contains a huge amount of data entered by more than one person. One person can't possibly keep track of which data has changed. By using the built-in OLE server capabilities of a DBMS, you don't have to manually update a document, a graph, or a worksheet.

There are at least two ways to create DBMS OLE objects. You can link a range of data from a database table into a graph, a document, or a worksheet. Depending on the format of the forms you use, you could also create a link to the form. Some DBMSs also provide a means for creating links using macros, VBA (Visual BASIC for Applications), or other methods.

The DBMS's role as a client is a little more difficult to understand, especially when you consider how some people perceive DBMSs. Many people view a DBMS as a central repository of information, offering only crude output capabilities. Although this was once quite true, it is no longer the case. A DBMS's capability for generating beautiful reports, such as those used for presentations or a company's annual report, is limited only by the imagination of the programmer and the tools the DBMS engine provides.

Using products such Access, FoxPro for Windows, dBASE for Windows, or CA-Visual Objects, you can easily add some word processor text or a bitmap to your form or report. All you need to do is insert the object into the form or report, just as you would any other document. The object will appear as part of the form or report when the user activates it as part of a database edit.

You could use a DBMS as an OLE client in several ways that aren't even related to reports. For example, you could create a multimedia database containing graphics, sounds, or even video clips. Of course, your DBMS engine has to support a special form of data called a binary large object (BLOB) before you can use the DBMS in this way.

Windows DBMSs have another capability that's important to consider. Many Windows DBMSs now support open database connectivity (ODBC). This new specification allows a DBMS to look at the data stored in other DBMS's format. For example, you could create a database in FoxPro, but view it using Access. The technical details of how this actually works are a little too complex for our current discussion, but it's important to know that the capability exists.

You can determine whether your DBMS supports ODBC by looking at the Control Panel entries. Any DBMS that supports ODBC will add some entries to an ODBC icon you'll find there. You can look at the same icon to see which other applications on your machine support ODBC. Figure 11-1 shows a typical ODBC Data Sources dialog box.

Figure 11-1:
Applications
that support
ODBC can
act as data
sources for
other
applications.

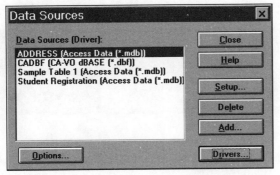

Every application implements ODBC in slightly different ways. Check the DBMS manual to learn how to configure it for using ODBC. In most cases, you'll need to create a data source entry in the Data Sources dialog and a special entry in the database itself.

Using ODBC requires a knowledge of SQL (structured query language) in addition to the DBMS native language. SQL provides a common language that allows your application to communicate with other applications.

Objects within a DBMS

Adding OLE objects to a database is a little different from anything else we've explored so far in this book. A user normally adds an OLE object by selecting it in the source document, copying it to the clipboard, and then choosing the Paste Special command in the destination file. As an alternative, many newer programs provide an Insert Object command.

You use the same technique to insert data into a database, but you have to do a few other things first. A DBMS requires you to design a database before you can use it. The data part of a database contains tables. They're just like the tables you use on paper or in a word processing document. The rows are called records, and the columns are called fields.

Each field in a table must contain some type of data. You can't put different types of data in the same field. For example, if you create a number field, it won't accept text such as "Hello World." Figure 11-2 shows the table view of a typical Access table.

Figure 11-2:
Tables
contain
rows
(records)
and columns
(fields) of
information.

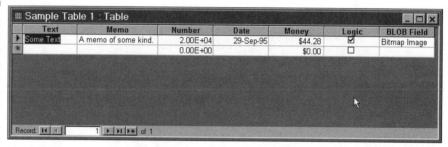

Earlier in this chapter, we mentioned a special field type called a BLOB (binary large object). When using Microsoft Access, you will find BLOBs referred to as the OLE Object field type. On the other hand, Borland Paradox for Windows actually has a BLOB field type. Other vendors will use other names. If you look at Figure 11-2, you'll see that the last field contains a BLOB.

Most BLOB fields can contain WAV (sound), PCX (ZSoft paintbrush), and BMP (Windows or OS/2 bitmap) links. They may not support Word for Windows or 1-2-3 links. You'll need to check your vendor documentation to see which types of BLOBs your database supports. It's also important to see which OLE objects you can place on a form and in a table. Some vendors provide additional object types for forms.

You can't see what your OLE object looks like by checking the table view. As you can see in Figure 11-2, the table view simply shows the words *Bitmap Image*. To see OLE objects in a DBMS, you must use a form.

Table view does allow you to add or remove object links. All you need to do is right-click the field to see its context menu, which is shown in Figure 11-3. Choosing Insert Object from this context menu brings up the same Insert Object dialog we have seen so many times in the past. You can choose to link or embed the object. The Insert Object dialog also allows you to create the object from either a new file or an existing one.

Figure 11-3:
Once you get past the context menu, the process for adding an object to a database is much the same as in any other application.

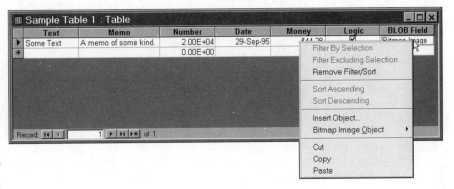

In most cases, Windows 3.x doesn't provide a context menu; however, you may find one when using your DBMS. The products that don't provide a context menu usually allow you to create a new OLE object by double-clicking the field. When the program sees that the field is empty, it automatically asks if you want to create a new object.

As shown in Figure 11-4, once you create a form for your data, the OLE object will appear. To create this view, we simply used the Columnar Form Wizard. You don't have to do anything fancy, just create a form in which the data can appear.

Figure 11-4:
In most DBMSs, OLE objects appear in Form View, not Table View.

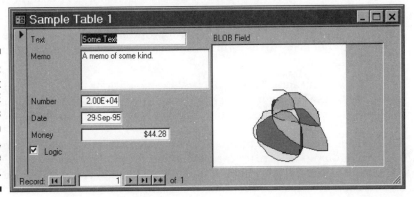

Using OLE in DBMS Forms and Reports

Adding BLOBs to your database tables isn't the only way you can use OLE with a DBMS. You can also add OLE objects to your forms and reports. You usually add the object to the form or the report when you're working in *design mode*, and then display it when the user runs the program you've created (during what's known as *run-time*).

The following example shows how to add an OLE object to a database form. You can use the same process to add an OLE object to any form or report. In this example, we'll add a leaf bitmap (the LEAVES.BMP file provided with Windows 3.x) to an Access database form. You'll probably recognize the form; it's a modified version of the one we showed previously:

1. Open a bitmap file using Paintbrush or MS Paint.

2. Select the entire bitmap using the selection tool.

3. Copy the bitmap to the clipboard by choosing Edit⇨Copy.

4. Open Access (or any other database that supports OLE in forms and reports).

5. Open a database by choosing File⇨Open (unless your DBMS uses a different command to open a database).

6. Open the form or report that you want to modify. In this case, we opened Sample Form 1 - Sample Table 1.

7. Create a link to the bitmap by choosing Edit⇨Paste Special, as shown in Figure 11-5.

8. Position the bitmap and add an appropriate label. We added the name of the company to the form's header to produce the display shown in Figure 11-6.

9. You can't actually see what the graphic will look like until you view the form. In Microsoft Access, you can produce the display shown in Figure 11-7 by clicking the Form View button on the toolbar.

You don't have to limit the objects you use on a form to something the user can see. Adding a sound to the form could serve a number of purposes. For example, you could add a special error sound for a special event such as the user trying to stick text in your numeric field. You would sound the alarm by adding it to a macro.

Access doesn't limit you to using the Edit⇨Paste Special technique for adding OLE objects to forms and reports. You can also use the Insert⇨Object technique we discussed earlier in the book.

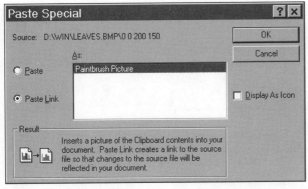

Figure 11-5:
The
Edit⇨Paste
Special
technique
lets you add
OLE objects
to DBMS
forms and
reports.

Figure 11-6:
Unlike
BLOBs, OLE
objects
appear in
Access's
design view
as well as
its form
view.

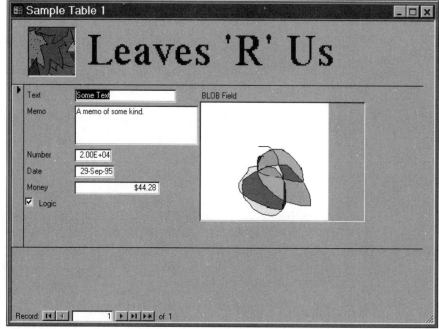

Figure 11-7:
Use form
view to see
the results
of your
object
addition
when using
bitmaps.

There's also a third method for creating OLE objects. You might not immediately notice the Toolbox shown in Figure 11-8, but it contains controls. Three of those controls — Image, Bound Object Frame, and Unbound Object Frame — allow you to add graphics to your forms and reports. You can use the two object frames for OLE-specific tasks.

Figure 11-8:
Look at the
Toolbox
provided
with your
DBMS
frame
design tool
to see if an
OLE tool is
hiding there.

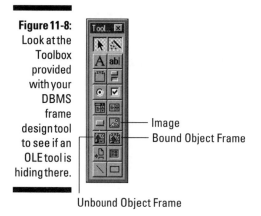

Image

Bound Object Frame

Unbound Object Frame

Using the object frame is easy. You simply draw a square the desired size on your form or report, and then add the name of the file you want to use to the Source Doc property of the object.

A Bound Object Frame stores the OLE object in the table — in other words, the object is embedded in the form or report. An Unbound Object Frame creates a link to the OLE object — in other words, the object is stored outside the table. To either link or embed an object, you must use the correct object frame in your form or report. Unlike object frames, BLOBs can either link or embed an OLE object. There is only one type of BLOB.

Using OLE in DBMS Macros

One of the unique features of Access is that it includes both a macro language and a programming language. Other DBMSs — for example, FoxPro and dBASE — typically include only a programming language. We'll tell you all about the programming language in Chapter 15. This chapter discusses the macro language.

Object properties

To create macros, the first thing you need to know is that many DBMSs assign properties to OLE objects. Figure 11-9 shows the properties Access assigns to OLE objects.

These properties are broken into four categories:

- ✔ Format
- ✔ Data
- ✔ Event
- ✔ Other

The Format properties control an object's on-screen appearance. For example, you can choose whether Access clips a bitmap to fit the screen or squeezes it to fit the space provided. You'll also find the Visible property here; this is an important property when you're writing programs or macros. In some cases, you can't access hidden controls. In other cases, using a hidden control allows you to perform tasks in the background in a way that the user can't see.

The Data properties specify how Access interacts with the data. You can control whether the object is linked or embedded using these properties. The all-important Source Item property is part of this category. This property allows you to control which part of the file appears in the Access window, making it possible to move from section to section in the file, as needed.

Unbound Object Frame: OLEUnbo... ✕

| Format | Data | Event | Other | All |

Name	OLEUnbound17
Size Mode	Clip
OLE Class	Paintbrush Picture
Auto Activate	Double-Click
Display Type	Content
Update Options . . .	Automatic
Verb	0
OLE Type	Linked
OLE Type Allowed .	Either
Class	PBrush
Source Doc	D:\WIN\LEAVES.BMP
Source Item	0 0 200 150
Visible	Yes
Display When	Always
Enabled	No
Locked	Yes
Tab Stop	Yes
Tab Index	0
Left	0.0833"
Top	0.125"
Width	0.7465"
Height	0.7465"
Back Style	Normal
Back Color	16777215
Special Effect	Sunken
Border Style	Solid
Border Color	0
Border Width	Hairline
Shortcut Menu Bar .	
ControlTip Text . . .	
Help Context Id . . .	0
Tag	
On Updated	
On Enter	
On Exit	
On Got Focus	
On Lost Focus	
On Click	
On Dbl Click	
On Mouse Down . .	
On Mouse Move . .	
On Mouse Up	

Figure 11-9:
DBMSs
allow you to
control OLE
objects by
changing
their
properties.

Events are the method Access uses for calling your programs or macros. For example, you can tell Access to call a specific macro every time the user clicks on the object, making it act just like a pushbutton. An Updated event allows you to do something whenever the object is updated.

Forms also have events that could affect OLE objects. For example, you could add a macro to the Got Focus property to change the picture in the OLE object every time the user moves to a different record. This would come in handy when you're using objects to group items — for example, the type of movie in a movie database.

The other properties include a variety of entries, such as the control name and its Auto Activate event. This is the event that allows a user to access the OLE object. For example, you might add a sound object to your form and allow the user to play the sound whenever they double-click this object.

By changing an object's properties using a macro or a program, you can change the bitmap object displayed on a form or a report to match the situation. For example, you might want to change the icon displayed at the top of a form to match the type of movie in a movie database. This feature makes your DBMS considerably more flexible than some other applications you use.

Creating a simple form macro

The form is the central component that holds the rest of a database system together. This isn't some new Windows idea; from the very first product that appeared on a PC, database managers have used forms. Even dBASE II used forms as a central area for gathering data contained in diverse tables.

Forms have three purposes. First, they control access to the data. You can hide data or make it visible. Second, they force the user to input the data in a certain way. For example, the controls on a form can prevent a user from entering a nonexistent state in a state field. Third, forms organize the data, making it more understandable for the user.

The idea of using macros to control the appearance of a form is relatively new, but it has its origins in those original DOS programs. dBASE II used an FRM file to hold the macro-like commands used to draw a form on screen. Macros and object properties work hand-in-hand to automate many parts of a form or a report. The events associated with the form and the controls on the form activate macros. In turn, the macros control the appearance of objects by changing their properties.

A form macro usually modifies the appearance of the form. For example, when you move from one record to the next, Access must update all the edit controls on the form. Likewise, if you need to change a control when the user moves from record to record, you can do so by adding a macro to the form.

The following example shows how you could change the bitmap file displayed by a database as it moves from record to record. We use Access in this example, but you could use the same techniques with just about any database product that supports either macros or a programming language. In fact, by substituting macro commands with functions, you could even use this technique with a DBMS that only supports a programming language.

The following example assumes you're familiar with using Microsoft Access. We'll provide the parameters for accomplishing some tasks, but not the actual steps. The example also assumes you're using Microsoft Access for Windows 95. (For the most part, however, the example should also work with Microsoft Access 2.0.)

Creating some tables

The first step in designing any DBMS is identifying which types of data you want to store and the most efficient way to store them. Data is stored in tables.

Part of the table design process is to create queries, which provide a sort of window into the database. Using queries makes life a lot simpler when you're working with Access, because you get only the data you need and it's arranged in the way you need it. For example, you might need just the names and addresses of presidents of companies, not everything a database contains. The following procedure shows how to create the tables and queries needed for this example and several others in the book:

1. Open Access.

2. Select the Blank Database radio button. Call your database anything you like; we named ours "My Database."

3. To create a new table, click New.

4. Select Design View.

5. Define a table that contains the fields shown in Figure 11-10. This table contains the inventory of foods we have on hand. The four fields are: Food Name, how many we have (Quantity), the cost per item (Cost), and the food group to which the food belongs (Category). Notice that there are two primary index fields: Food Name and Category. The Category field also has a default value of Meat.

6. Save the table as Food Itemizer by clicking the Save tool and entering a table name.

7. We need another table to store the food groups. Repeat steps 3 and 4 to begin the process.

8. Define a table that contains the fields shown in Figure 11-11. Notice that there are only two fields: Category and Food Picture. We'll use the Category field immediately. The other field will appear in the example in the next section.

9. Save this table as Food Types by clicking the Save tool and entering a table name.

10. Open MS Paint and create five drawings. Save them as: MEAT.BMP, DAIRY.BMP, VEGETABLE.BMP, FRUIT.BMP, and BREAD.BMP. The actual content of the drawings doesn't matter, but it would help if they actually looked like the food group they are supposed to represent.

11. Close MS Paint.

12. Select Access again. Switch from design view to table view by clicking the Table View pushbutton on the toolbar.

13. Enter five records into the Food Types table. Use the following categories: Bread, Dairy, Fruit, Meat, and Vegetable. In the Food Picture field, create OLE links to each of the five drawings you created.

14. Close all open tables.

15. Select the Queries tab of the Database dialog. We need to create a query to access the data in our Food Itemizer table. Using a query is the most efficient way to combine data found in multiple tables and to specify an order for displaying it.

16. Click the New pushbutton.

17. Select New Query, and click OK.

18. Select the Food Itemizer table, and click Add. Click Close. Adding a table to the query allows us to access its fields. You also have to add tables to define relationships between them. For example, there is a relationship between the Food Itemizer and the Food Types table, which we'll discuss in Chapter 15.

19. Define the query. Figure 11-12 shows the query we'll use for this example. Notice that we selected the Food Name field to sort the table in ascending order.

20. Save the query as Food Select 1 by clicking the Save tool and entering a query name.

21. Close any open queries.

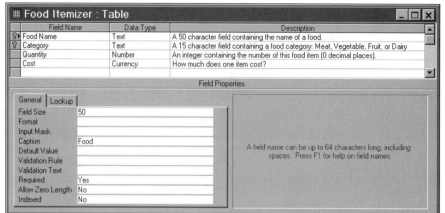

Figure 11-10:
The Food
Itemizer
table
contains an
inventory of
our stock.

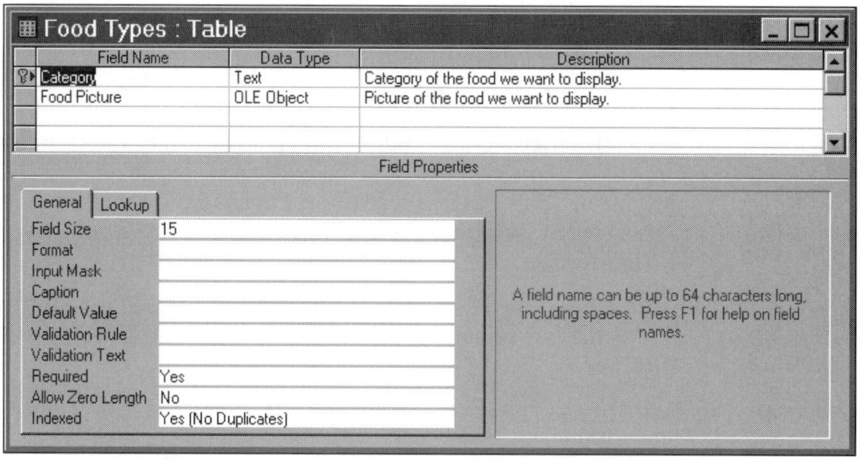

Figure 11-11:
The Food
Types table
contains a
complete list
of the food
groups in our
inventory.

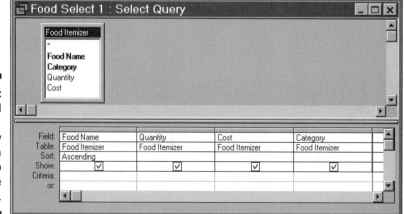

Figure 11-12:
The Food
Select 1
Query
creates a
window into
the
database.

Designing a form

Forms let you add information to a database, and reports let you display your stored data. We need only one form for this example. Before you create the form, make sure you've create the required tables and queries by following the procedure in the preceding section.

1. Select the Forms tab in the Database dialog. We need to create a form for displaying our data.

2. Click New.

3. Select Autoform: Columnar.

4. Select the Food Select 1 query as the source of information. Remember that we defined this query to make it easier to access the data that the table contains.

5. Click OK. Access will automatically display all four fields of the Food Itemizer table on a form for you. Notice that the form appears in Form View.

6. Switch to design view by clicking the Design View pushbutton on the toolbar. Your display should look similar to the example in Figure 11-13. Now that we have a default form, let's customize it a bit.

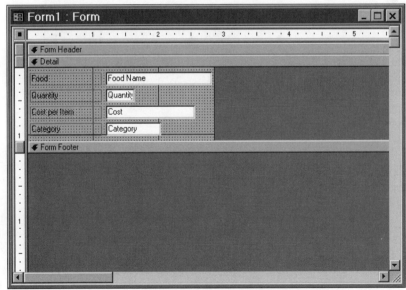

Figure 11-13:
The Form Wizard can give you a head start when you're designing a basic form.

7. Delete the Category field and its associated label. This will allow us to add a combo box which will provide the user with a list of responses from the Food Type table.

8. Select the Combo Box tool, and place a new combo box in the same position as the Category field. Using a combo box makes it easier for the user to select the correct food group. The Combo Box Wizard will ask which source you want to use.

9. Select table or query (the first radio button). Click Next.

10. Select the Food Types table, and then click Next.

11. Select the Category field (move it from the left list box to the right one), and then click Next. The Combo Box Wizard should show you a dialog similar to the example in Figure 11-14.

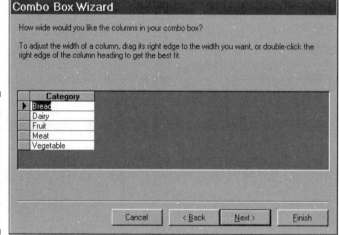

Figure 11-14:
The Combo
Box Wizard
provides an
easy method
for adding
combo boxes
to your form.

12. Click Next. It's important to make this as automatic as possible, so we'll store the value the user selects from the Food Types table in the current record of the Food Itemizer table.

13. Select the radio button. Store the value in this field, and then select the Category field. Click Finish. Now that we have an easy method for selecting a food type, let's display a picture of the food type for the user. This will make it easy for the user to see at a glance which type of food is currently selected rather than actually reading the category field.

14. Using the Picture tool, add a picture to the right side of the form. Once you insert a picture, you have to set it up so that it displays the picture correctly.

15. Select any of the five drawings you created for the Food Types table.

16. Make the picture 2" square by changing the Width and Height properties.

17. Change the Size Mode property to stretch, so we can see the entire picture.

18. Change the Picture Type property to linked, so any changes to the external pictures will also be reflected in our form.

19. Change the Name property to Food Picture.

20. Select the Category combo box that we created previously.

21. Change the Name property to Food Group.

22. Save the form as Food Inventory Control 1 by clicking the Save tool and entering a form name.

23. Close the Properties dialog. Your form should look like the example in Figure 11-15.

24. Keep the form open if you plan to go immediately to the next section. Otherwise, close all forms before you exit Access.

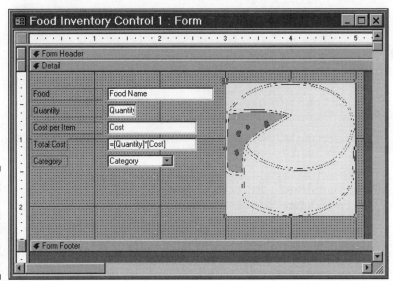

Figure 11-15:
Our final
form for this
example
shown in
Design.

Programming a macro

Automating OLE connections isn't always a matter of convenience. If you've added any records to your database, you already know that the picture on the form we created in the previous section never changes. A macro can solve this problem; it can automatically update the form picture.

In some respects, using macros can be troublesome. For one thing, when compared with the features of a full-fledged programming language, macros are quite limited. They have no looping or other control structures, and you can call only a limited number of functions.

Another problem with macros occurs with the DBMS itself. A form or a report in Access monitors many events, and there is some duplication. For example, the On Current event for the form won't affect the controls it contains. To get a better idea of what this means, look at our form. The On Current event for the forum will automatically update all the data fields as we move from record to record, but it won't update the picture. We have to add a macro to do that. In essence, we're duplicating the effort of the On Current event. We'll see in the following example how that replication comes into play when it comes to keeping your OLE links up to date.

1. Open the Food Inventory Control 1 form in design view (if necessary). We need to add some macros to the form to allow it to handle such tasks as automatically updating the picture for the user.

2. Select the entire form, and open its Properties dialog to the Event page.

3. Click the On Current event, and then click the ellipsis that's displayed next to the blank. This will display the Choose Builder dialog.

4. Select the Macro Builder entry in the Choose Builder dialog. You should see a blank Macro dialog box.

5. Select the SetValue action in the first row. This will allow us to assign the value of the Food Group (category) control to the Picture property of the Food Picture control.

6. Click the ellipsis next to the Item field in the lower half of the dialog. You will see the Expression Builder dialog. This dialog allows you to create expressions using a point-and-click technique rather than trying to write them by hand.

7. Select the Picture property of the Food Picture control on the Food Inventory Control 1 form, as shown in Figure 11-16. The Picture property determines which picture is displayed on the form in form view. We want to assign a new picture to it every time the user moves to a new record.

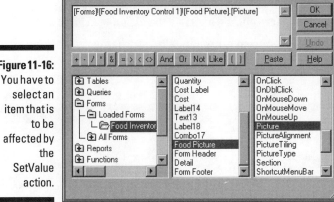

Figure 11-16:
You have to
select an
item that is
to be
affected by
the
SetValue
action.

8. Click OK.

9. Click the ellipsis next to the Expression field in the lower half of the dialog. You will see the Expression Builder dialog. We need to create a complex expression this time, so you will have to type part of the expression by hand.

10. In the Expression field, type the path in which you stored the five database pictures, followed by a plus sign (+).

11. Select the Value property of the Food Group control on the Food Inventory Control 1 form. Type a plus sign and **".BMP"**. Your expression should look like the example in Figure 11-17. You're telling the Food Picture control to display a picture of the food group that the user selected from the Food Type table using the Food Group combo box.

Figure 11-17:
Once you
select an
item to act
upon, you
need to
assign it a
value using
an
expression.

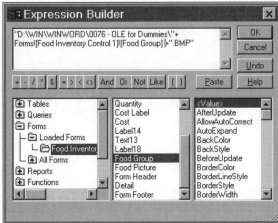

12. Click OK.

13. Save the macro as Change Category by clicking the Save tool and entering a macro name. Your macro should look like the example in Figure 11-18.

14. Close the Macro dialog. Access automatically returns you to the Food Inventory Control 1 form.

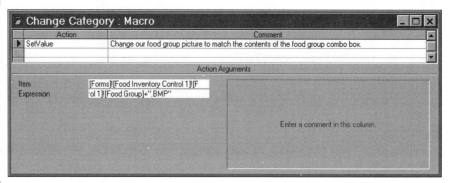

Figure 11-18:
The completed macro contains only one step, but the program won't work correctly without it.

Creating a simple object macro

In the preceding section, we showed you how to create a macro that reacted whenever you updated a form. At this point, you could switch to form view and see the picture change as you move from record to record, as shown in Figure 11-19. Before long, however, you would notice that the picture doesn't change when you change the contents of the Category combo box. This is one of the programming considerations you'll need to think about when writing OLE-specific macros.

Every Access form has a set of events. Those events do not necessarily affect the controls or other objects on the form. You need to work with the control and object events as a separate issue from the form events. This procedure will fix our problem with the Category combo box:

1. Change views to design view by clicking the Design View pushbutton on the toolbar (if necessary).

2. Select the Category combo box.

3. Display the Properties dialog for the combo box.

4. Select the On Change event.

5. Select the Change Category macro from the drop-down list.

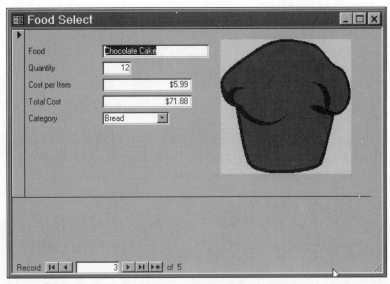

If you change to form view, you'll see that the picture now changes whether you move from record to record or simply change the contents of the Category field. The need for using the same macro in two places wasn't obvious until we actually tried to change the contents of the form.

Objects present other problems, too. For example, you can't easily pass information from Access to another application using a macro. DDE commands won't work from within an Access macro, but they do work well from within a program module. (Chapter 15 talks about using Access BASIC.)

When using objects, don't make the programming environment more difficult than it needs to be. For example, there are times when you should use a picture like the one in our example program. We don't want to edit the pictures, we simply want to create an OLE link to them for viewing purposes.

What if you wanted the ability to edit the picture? Although it's very tempting to say that you would need to resort to Access BASIC to do so, don't forget that you can also display a picture using either bound or unbound object controls. Either control allows users to edit the picture whenever they double-click it.

Test your newfound knowledge

1. One way to use a DBMS as an OLE client is as a:

   a. Bull in the ring.

   b. Central repository for nonessential gibberish spoken by a politician during a campaign speech in the rain.

   c. Ding/bat manipulation scenario document.

   d. Multimedia database.

2. Objects and controls often require OLE linkage handling separate from forms because:

   a. Objects and controls are very antisocial and demand their own macros.

   b. The form events don't necessarily interact with those monitored by controls and objects.

   c. Access was poorly designed and now we have to make up for it.

   d. There's no way to get there from here; we have to go somewhere else first.

Chapter 12

OLE for Word Processors

In This Chapter

▶ All about using OLE within word processors

▶ OLE capabilities of word processors

▶ Using OLE in documents

▶ Enhancing word processing macros using OLE

*T*he most common, and probably the oldest, type of application on the market today is the word processor. Few of us can get by without using at least some form of word processor to somehow record our thoughts.

Word processors aren't limited to the large applications used by those of us who produce copious quantities of nearly indecipherable text. A word processor could also be a simple note taker such as NotePad, Write, or WordPad.

Almost everyone uses these handy applications for any number of purposes. Consider the programmer who used a form of word processor (a text editor) to write portions of the Windows software. It doesn't take too much thought to figure out that the word processor is the most generic, widely used category of software tools.

The short definition for a *word processor* is any application that stores and manipulates text. A much tighter definition — the one used in this chapter at least — is an application that stores documents such as letters and books in human-readable form.

Word Processors and OLE

More often than not, you'll use a word processor as an OLE client, even though you could also use it as a server. For the vast majority of people who use word processors, these applications are used to produce the final output of a document. In other words, a word processor acts as the central storage area for all the information a document will contain.

Although word processors are well-suited for formatting text, they aren't quite as effective for performing some other types of data manipulation. Consider a table of numbers. If you need to perform calculations with those numbers, a spreadsheet is the best tool for the job. The spreadsheet is the OLE server, and the word processor is the OLE client.

Mailing lists are common elements in letters and other mass media applications. A word processor is the best tool for printing those letters, but a database management system (DBMS) is the best tool for maintaining the mailing list. The DBMS is the OLE server, and the word processor is the OLE client.

Take a look at this book. There's hardly a page on which we haven't included some kind of picture. Word processors are good tools for integrating text and graphics, but they won't work at all for producing those graphics.

As you can see, word processors are commonly used as formatting and output applications for a variety tasks. They are seldom used for creating anything other than the original text in a document. Word processors are commonly used for combining all the elements of a compound document — for example, tables and graphics created in other applications — and printing them in their final form.

So, when will you ever use a word processor as a server if it's so good at producing output such as books, brochures, and pamphlets? For specialized applications such as presentations, a word processor probably won't provide the best output. Charts and graphs are best produced in a charting program. However, producing the text used to enhance the graph or chart is best done within a word processor.

A word processor is the best tool available for formatting documents that are at least half text. This feature makes a word processor the perfect OLE client. However, you can still use the superior formatting capabilities of a word processor in a server capacity within other applications.

Objects Within a Document

You'll quickly discover that word processors are almost as generic in their handling of OLE objects as they are in their capability for formatting data. There's nothing really new or interesting in the actual implementation of objects within a word processor that we haven't covered in the preceding chapters. Word processing programs can usually use both the Copy⇨Paste Special and the Insert⇨Object methods of linking or embedding objects. They also act as both OLE servers and clients. In addition, you can use a wide variety of macro programming techniques in word processors — including the DDE macro technique we discuss in Chapter 10.

However, when it comes to manipulating objects, word processors do provide some capabilities that you won't find in other types of applications. As detailed in Chapter 8, some graphics applications provide an actual OLE database. Chapter 10 describes a special link management dialog that spreadsheets provide. For their part, word processors provide a context menu.

Accessing an object's context menu is easy. You simply right-click (instead of left-click) the object. Windows 95 users will be familiar with this action because they use the right-hand mouse button to display the context menu for various objects in Windows 95. However, this is a new concept for Windows 3.x users.

What you find on this context menu depends on the type of object you select and whether it is linked or embedded. Figure 12-1 shows the context menu for a linked MS Paint object. Figure 12-2 shows the context menu for an embedded version of the same object.

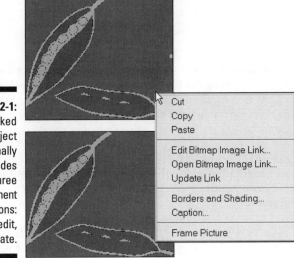

Figure 12-1:
A linked object normally provides three management options: open, edit, and update.

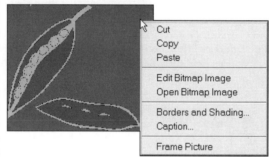

Figure 12-2:
An
embedded
object
normally
provides
two
management
options:
open and
edit.

The linked version of the object provides three different management options. However, within a word processor, both the edit and the open options act like the standard open action. Both actions open the originating application allowing you to edit the object. The update option reads a new copy of the object into the document from the disk.

The embedded version of the object provides two management options. The open option opens the originating application allowing you to edit the object. The edit option provides in-place editing of the object if both the client and the server are OLE 2 compliant.

As shown in Figure 12-3, the options listed in a context menu may differ depending on the type of object you select. In this case, we created a link to a wave audio file. The open option from the previous context menu is replaced by a play option.

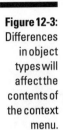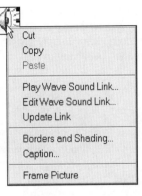

Figure 12-3:
Differences
in object
types will
affect the
contents of
the context
menu.

A context menu always reflects the characteristics of the object. This process is almost the same as defining a word by reading the words around it. You learn the word's meaning from the context in which it is used. An OLE object's context menu always defines the object in a way that reflects its use.

Some context menus contain an unexpected set of options. For example, although it seems unlikely that you'd be allowed to edit a video clip from within your word processor, a look at the context menu options in Figure 12-4 shows that you can. The context menu for an object often reveals options that you may not find elsewhere.

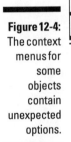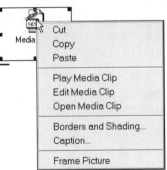

Figure 12-4:
The context
menus for
some
objects
contain
unexpected
options.

Unlike other applications, a word processor's context menu is directly controlled by the Windows registry. Editing the registry may give you access to undocumented OLE features in a DLL or a VxD (virtual anything driver). In Chapter 21, we tell you more about the registry and how to edit it.

OLE as Part of Documents

High-end word processors such as Word for Windows typically provide more than one way to insert an object. Middle-of-the-road word processors such as Write or WordPad usually provide one method for inserting an object. Low-end word processors may be limited to acting as an OLE server, not a client.

To let you see the diverse options available, we'll focus on the high-end word processors in this section of the chapter. The options your word processor supports may vary from what we show here; check the vendor documentation to see which OLE features the product supports.

In other chapters, we show you the Insert⇨Object and Edit⇨Paste Special commands many word processors provide. Because we aren't politicians, we won't bore you with yet another demonstration of those features here.

Word processors do provide some unique methods for inserting objects. The following example assumes you have Word for Windows, but other word processors support similar features. Just follow along even if you don't have Word for Windows on your computer.

Inserting pictures

Graphics represent one of the most common objects found in a document. It makes sense, then, that Microsoft and other vendors try to provide some special options for handling graphics:

1. Open Word for Windows (or any other word processor that supports pictures as a special OLE object).

2. Choose Insert⇨Picture. Word opens the Insert Picture dialog box.

3. Click the Link check box. You should see a dialog box similar to the one in Figure 12-5.

4. Select a graphic. Word for Windows supports the WMF (Windows metafile), .PCX (Zsoft Paintbrush), and .BMP (Windows bitmap) formats.

5. Click OK. Word inserts the selected picture at the current cursor position in your word processing document.

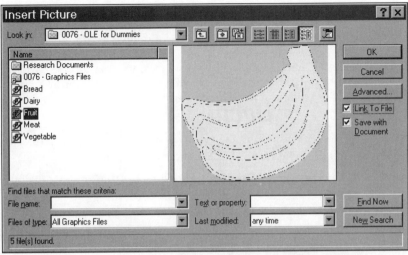

We should note one special feature of the dialog shown in Figure 12-5. Remember that we told you linked files are always stored on disk. Moving a compound document with linked OLE objects requires moving the linked files as well.

Word for Windows provides a means for getting around this problem. You can create an OLE link and still store the object with your compound document. Moving the document also moves the linked object. When you open Word, it updates the linked object from the file on disk. If the object isn't available, Word tells you so, but still displays the object it has stored with your document.

If you look at the context menu for this OLE object, you'll see something strange. The context menu looks like a combination of the menus for linked and embedded objects shown earlier in this chapter. The two OLE-specific options are: Update Links and Edit Picture. As you can see, it's never safe to assume anything about the objects stored in a document. Always check to see which editing options are available.

Inserting databases

Mail merge and other data-intensive uses of word processors often also involve using a DBMS. A company is unlikely to store its client list in a word processor. It will use a DBMS for that task.

When it's time for writing letters to those clients, someone usually has to transfer the data from the database to a word processing document. Word and other high-end word processors offer a way around this problem. They use OLE to create a link between a database and a document.

However, the problem doesn't quite stop there. The person preparing the letters may be very experienced with the word processor, but may not fully understand the inner working of the company's DBMS.

The following example shows one way around this knowledge barrier. It uses a special database OLE feature provided by Word for Windows. Follow along even if you use a different word processor, because the same principles apply to a variety of products:

1. Open Word for Windows (or any other word processor that supports databases as special OLE objects).

2. Choose Insert⇨Database. Word displays the Database dialog box shown in Figure 12-6.

Figure 12-6: The Database dialog box provides a systematic method for importing data into your document.

> **Database** `? X`
>
> Data Source:
>
> [Get Data...]
>
> Data Options:
>
> [Query Options...] [Table AutoFormat...]
>
> Insert the Data into the Document:
>
> [Insert Data...]
>
> Cancel

3. The first thing we need to do is get some data. Click the Get Data button.

4. Select your database type from the File Types list box. (The default setting is a Word for Windows document.)

5. For this example, we're using an existing mailing list database. Select your mailing list database from the list provided.

6. Click the Select Method check box. Doing so allows you to select the method Word for Windows uses to talk with your DBMS. Your dialog box should look similar to the example shown in Figure 12-7.

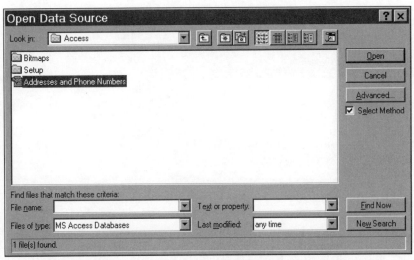

Figure 12-7:
The Open
Data Source
dialog box
lets you
select the
location, the
type of
database,
and the
method for
importing
your data.

7. Click Open to finalize your database choice. Word displays the dialog box shown in Figure 12-8.

Figure 12-8:
This dialog
box allows
you to
choose the
method
Word
uses for
interacting
with your
database.

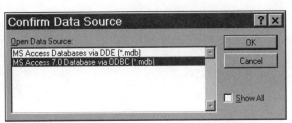

8. Select the ODBC method for importing data.

9. Click OK. You should see a dialog box similar to the one in Figure 12-9. Notice that Word lists only the tables in the database. You can also view queries by clicking the Options button and checking the Views option.

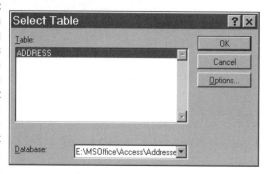

Figure 12-9:
Even though
this dialog
box appears
to indicate
that you can
only select
tables, you
can also
select
queries as a
data source.

10. Select the ADDRESS table, and click OK. Word returns you to the Database dialog box. Notice that the dialog box shows the name of the table you selected. It also highlights the Query Options, Table AutoFormat, and Insert Data buttons.

11. Click Query Options. You will see a three-tab dialog box like the one in Figure 12-10. The first tab in the Query Options dialog allows you to select the filter criteria. A filter allows you to select specific records from a table.

12. Use the combination of list boxes and data entry fields to create a filter similar to the one shown in Figure 12-10.

Figure 12-10:
You can
use a
combination
of data entry
fields and
values to
control
which
records the
database
provides.

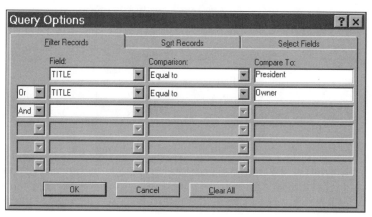

13. Click the Sort Records tab. A page in the Query Options dialog box appears, similar to the one shown in Figure 12-11. This tab allows you to modify the way Word orders the data. For mass mailings, post offices usually require zip-code order.

14. Use the list boxes in this dialog box to create a sort order similar to the example in Figure 12-11.

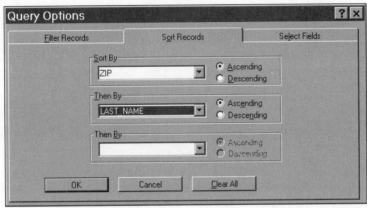

Figure 12-11: By sorting your data as you import it into Word, you can reduce the amount of work you need to do later.

15. Click the Select Fields tab. A page in the Query Options dialog box appears, similar to the one shown in Figure 12-12. The Select Fields tab allows you to choose which data appears in the table. In this case, we only need the information required for filling out and mailing a letter.

16. Choose the appropriate fields from your table. Our suggested list appears in Figure 12-12.

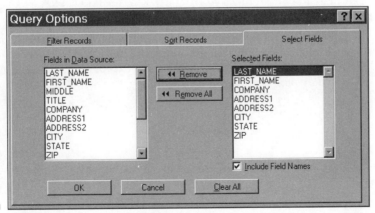

Figure 12-12: By carefully choosing the data fields you want in a table, you reduce the time required for creating the table.

17. Click OK to accept all the query parameters. Word takes a few moments to create an SQL (structured query language) query for you. (We'll take a look at the query later in this example.) After it creates a query, Word displays the Database dialog box. Notice that the dialog box tells you the query parameters are complete.

18. Click the Table AutoFormat button. A dialog box similar to the one shown in Figure 12-13 appears.

Figure 12-13: Word provides a wealth of automatic formats you can use to reduce the time required to put your table in its final format.

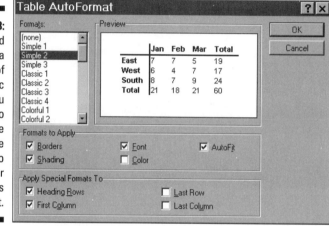

19. Select one of the formats from the list. We chose Simple 2, but you can use any of the formats listed, depending on how you plan to use the table. These formats simply change the appearance of the data in your document; the picture in the Preview field shows you how Word will format your table.

20. Click OK. Word returns you to the Database dialog box.

21. Click the Insert Data button. The Insert Data dialog, shown in Figure 12-14, appears. Notice the Insert Data as Field check box at the bottom of the dialog box. Check this field to insert the data as an OLE object. If you leave the field blank, Word converts the database information into a standard table.

Figure 12-14:
The Insert
Data dialog
box is the
last step
required for
inserting a
database
object into
your
document.

22. Click OK. Word grinds away for a few moments, then a few more, and a few more. When you finally start to wonder whether your hard disk is worn out, you'll see a display similar to the one in Figure 12-15. Notice that the database output looks like a standard table.

Figure 12-15:
You could
use a
database
object like
this one for
a variety of
purposes,
including
mail merge
and
presentations.

LAST_NAME	FIRST_NAME	COMPANY	ADDRESS1	ADDRESS2	CITY	STATE	ZIP
Casey	Helen	Wildwood Cafe	320 S. Main Street		Adams	WI	
Klodner	Jan	SofDesign					
Koffman	Eli	Hero Enterprises			San Diego	CA	
Mann	Gary	Mann Media			San Diego	CA	
Miller	Jeffrey	Forward	13010 Rancho Penasquitos Blvd	Suite 2	San Diego	CA	

23. Right-click the table to see the context menu.

24. Select the Toggle Field Codes option. An SQL statement similar to the one shown in Figure 12-16 appears. This is the query required for creating the table you saw in Figure 12-15. Every time you select the Update Field option, Word sends this query to the DBMS.

25. Close Word for Windows. (You don't need to save the document unless you want it for future reference.)

Figure 12-16:
Word uses
this SQL
statement to
get the data
you
requested
from the
DBMS.

```
{ DATABASE  \d "E:\\MSOffice\\Access\\Addresses and Phone Numbers.mdb" \c "DSN=MS
Access 7.0 Database;DBQ=E:\\MSOffice\\Access\\Addresses and Phone
Numbers.mdb;DriverId=25;FIL=MS Access;UID=admin;" \s "SELECT `LAST_NAME`,
`FIRST_NAME`, `COMPANY`, `ADDRESS1`, `ADDRESS2`, `CITY`, `STATE`, `ZIP` FROM
`ADDRESS` WHERE ((`TITLE` = 'President')) OR ((`TITLE` = 'Owner')) ORDER BY `ZIP`,
`LAST_NAME`" \l "2" \b "183" \h }
```

The DDE method of importing data is slower than ODBC, but allows you to access tables created by non-ODBC-compliant versions of a DBMS. The ODBC method also allows greater flexibility in choosing how to format and order the data once you select it.

By now, you're probably wondering why there was no edit or open option in the database object's context menu. Many complex reasons exist for this fact, but we'll take a quick look at two of the more important reasons.

First, a DBMS must preserve the integrity of its tables. The programmer who creates the forms, reports, queries, and other components of a DBMS does so by adding rules to the data entry program. If your word processor were allowed to edit the database, you could inadvertently corrupt the contents of one or more tables.

Second, opening a table or a query might involve a lot more than just a simple exchange of data. Some programs rely on forms containing calculated fields or other constructs for entering data. Opening a database without using the required forms may cause data entry problems.

Using OLE in Word Processing Macros

When it comes to macro capabilities, word processors are more flexible and powerful than DBMSs. You can even build spreadsheet-like applications in a word processor using tables and its macro capability. Tables also provide a method for managing data like a single-table database would. A programmer normally uses a programming language to create applications in a DBMS, but you can create simple tables in a word processor without any programming at all. However, once you get past simple tables, the DBMS quickly overtakes the capabilities of your word processor. For example, creating a multi-table database using your word processor would be difficult. Don't mistake flexibility for capability; a word processor can't replace your DBMS.

Word processors also lack some features of spreadsheets. For example, you can build complex applications in spreadsheets using macros. There are even compilers on the market for making these macro programs into full-fledged executable files (.EXEs). The macro capabilities of word processors are more in tune with the needs of a single user who needs to automate some repetitive task.

Word processors do provide a programming language. Word for Windows uses a form of BASIC similar to that used by Access. (See Chapter 15 for an example of Access BASIC.) In fact, once VBA (Visual BASIC for Applications) gets fully integrated into both products, the differences between the two programming languages will be minimal.

Word for Windows doesn't create an artificial difference between its macros and its programming language. The macro recorder actually uses the same language you would use for manually writing a program. As a result, you can start creating a program using the macro recorder and then add any special elements by hand. We show you how to do this later in this chapter.

The preceding sections of this chapter showed how you can easily insert picture and database objects using options from Word's Insert menu. What would happen if you needed to insert sound files on a regular basis? You'd have to go through the somewhat time-consuming procedure of using the Insert⇨Object command.

Word does allow you to modify its menus. You can even create macros and add them to the menu system. With this feature, we can create an Insert⇨Sound File (or any other OLE object) macro and add it to Word's menu.

The following procedure uses Word for Windows to create a specific macro. You should follow along even if you don't have Word for Windows because the principles illustrated work equally well with other products.

Creating the initial macro

The fact that Word's macro language and its programming language are really the same thing can work to your benefit. We'll start this example by creating a shell with the macro recorder:

1. Open Word for Windows.

2. Choose Tools⇨Macro. Word displays the Macro dialog box. The first thing we need to do is set up Word for recording the macro.

3. Click Record. You'll see the Record dialog box. This is the dialog box in which you enter the macro name and specify where it appears in the Word menu structure.

4. Type **InsertSoundObject** in the Record Macro Name field.

5. Click the Menus button. The Menus page of the Customize dialog box appears.

6. Select the &Insert entry in the Change What Menu field.

7. Select the &Picture entry in the field labeled Position in Menu. Click the Add Below button.

8. Type **Sound...** in the Name on Menu field. Click Rename. Your dialog box should look like the example in Figure 12-17.

9. Click Close. You'll see the macro recording dialog box shown in Figure 12-18. Word is now ready for us to create the macro shell.

10. Choose Insert➪Object. Word displays the Insert Object dialog.

11. Select the Create from File tab.

12. Click Browse, and select any existing file — for example, the Windows sound file.

13. Check the Link to File check box.

14. Click OK to accept the selection.

15. Click the Stop button in the macro recording dialog.

You have created a macro shell — a simple form of the more complex program we'll soon create. Creating macro shells can greatly reduce your workload and the number of mistakes you make. You can even break down a complex program into simple steps and create each step using a separate macro. Then, to create the program, you simply paste all the pieces together. We look deeper into the programming process in the next section.

Figure 12-17: The Customize dialog box lets you add your macro to the Word for Windows menu structure.

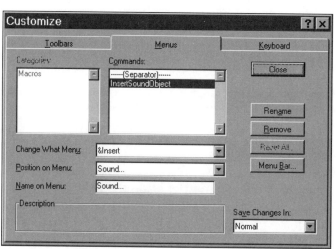

Figure 12-18:
The macro
recording
dialog box
allows you
to stop or
pause the
macro
recording
process.

Adding a dialog box

If you ran the macro we created in the preceding section, Word for Windows would faithfully create a link to the wave audio file you selected. However, that's not what we had in mind when we started this exercise. Our goal is to provide a generic Insert⇨Sound command for Word.

To meet this goal, we need a method for obtaining a filename from the user. Dialog boxes are one means Windows provides for getting input from a user. This example won't go to the extreme of providing a complex dialog box for getting the name of a wave audio file, but it will show the basics of how this is done.

For this part of the example, you need a copy of the Word for Windows Dialog Editor. Microsoft provides this tool as part of the Word for Windows product, so all you need to do is install it (if you haven't already done so):

1. Open the Word for Windows Dialog Editor. The first thing we'll do is insert the controls we need in a blank dialog box.

2. Choose Item⇨Button. As shown in Figure 12-19, the Dialog Editor displays the New Button dialog.

3. Select the OK button, and then click OK.

4. Choose Item⇨Button. Again, the Dialog Editor displays the New Button dialog box. Select the Cancel button, and then click OK.

5. To insert a text block for holding user instructions, choose Item⇨Text.

6. Choose Item⇨Text Box to insert a box in which the user can enter a filename.

7. Arrange the dialog box as shown in Figure 12-20. Placing the controls in some kind of order will make the dialog box easier to use. Now that we have the controls arranged, we can add the code required for making them do something.

8. Double-click the text control. The dialog box shown in Figure 12-21 appears.

9. In the Text$ field, type **Type a Filename**. Then click OK.

10. Double-click the text box control.

11. In the .Field field, type **.Filename**. Then click OK.

12. Choose File⇨Exit. The Dialog Editor asks if you want to save the changes to the clipboard. Click Yes. Now that we have a complete dialog box, we can add it to the macro shell we created previously.

13. Open Word for Windows (if you haven't already done so).

14. Choose Tools⇨Macro. Word displays the Macro dialog.

15. Select the InsertSoundObject macro, and click Edit. You should see the initial macro shown in Figure 12-22.

16. Use the Paste button on the toolbar to insert the code required for creating the dialog box just below the Sub MAIN line of the macro. Now that we've inserted the dialog box where we need it in the program, we can do a little customization.

17. In the Begin Dialog line, change Microsoft Word to Sound Select. Adding a dialog description to the macro won't activate it. We need to add some code to make the dialog visible.

18. Add the following text just below the End Dialog line. The first line allocates a variable called GetSound that will contain our user dialog. The second line detects whether the user pressed OK or Cancel in the dialog box.

```
Dim GetSound As UserDialog
If Dialog(GetSound) Then
```

19. Remove the specific filename (but not the path) from the InsertObject line. Add the following text immediately after the path:

```
+ GetSound.FileName.
```

20. Every If statement must have a corresponding EndIf statement. Add the following statement on a separate line just above EndSub:

```
EndIf
```

21. Your macro should look like the example in Figure 12-23. Save the macro, and then close the editing window.

If you try the Insert⇨Sound command, the first thing you'll see is the dialog box you created using the Dialog Editor. Once you enter a filename, Word will insert a new sound object on the screen.

Of course, you could add a huge array of enhancements to this simple example. For example, you could add a File Open dialog box. This example only shows you the basics of creating an OLE-specific Word for Windows macro.

Figure 12-19:
The Dialog
Editor
allows you
to create
several
predefined
buttons.

Figure 12-20:
The
arrangement
of our
filename
entry dialog
box.

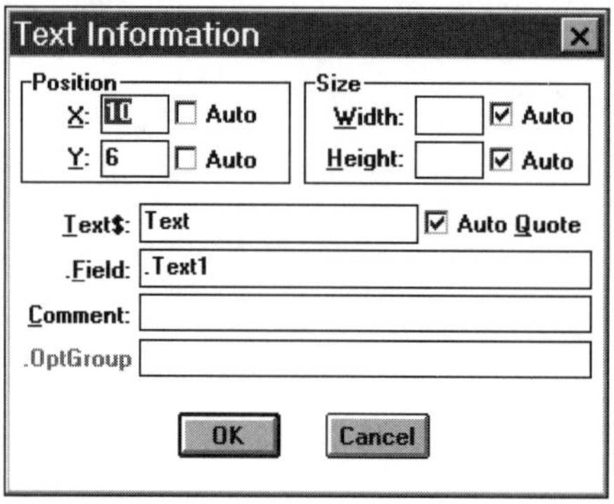

Figure 12-21:
Double-
clicking a
control
displays its
property
dialog box,
which lets
you control
its
appearance.

Text Information ✕

┌─ Position ─────────────┐ ┌─ Size ──────────────────┐
│ X: [10] ☐ Auto   │ │ Width: [   ] ☑ Auto   │
│ Y: [6]   ☐ Auto   │ │ Height: [   ] ☑ Auto │
└────────────────────────┘ └─────────────────────────┘

Text$: [Text   ]   ☑ Auto Quote
.Field: [.Text1   ]
Comment: [   ]
.OptGroup [   ]

[OK   ]   [Cancel]

Figure 12-22:
These are
the Word
BASIC
statements
the macro
recorder
created.

```
Sub MAIN
InsertObject .IconNumber = 0, .FileName = "D:\WIN\BELLS.WAV", .Link = 1,
.DisplayIcon = 0, .Tab = "1", .Class = "SoundRec", .IconFilename = "",
.Caption = "BELLS.WAV"
End Sub
```

Figure 12-23:
This macro
will allow us
to insert a
sound
object using
one
command.

```
Sub MAIN
Begin Dialog UserDialog 320, 144, "Sound Select"
    OKButton 22, 109, 88, 21
    CancelButton 206, 109, 88, 21
    Text 14, 16, 131, 13, "Type a Filename:", .Text2
    TextBox 15, 55, 160, 18, .FileName
End Dialog
Dim GetSound As UserDialog
If Dialog(GetSound) Then
    InsertObject .IconNumber = 0, .FileName = "D:\WIN\" +
GetSound.FileName, .Link = 1, .DisplayIcon = 0, .Tab = "1", .Class =
"SoundRec", .IconFilename = "", .Caption = "BELLS.WAV"
EndIf
End Sub
```

Test your newfound knowledge

1. Word processors provide this special OLE object manipulation feature.

   a. A context menu that shows which tasks the object will support (such as editing or playing).

   b. A manual on psychology so you can learn to out-think the object.

   c. Large hammers for crushing any object resistance.

   d. An object blaster, a new device for removing troublesome objects without any trace.

2. Word processors normally won't allow you to edit database records directly because

   a. They are stubborn and obstinate.

   b. Microsoft won't allow them to.

   c. Directly editing the database could damage it in some way.

   d. No one's smart enough to create a word processor that can perform such a feat.

Part IV
Programming OLE with Application Programs

Real Programmers strive to insult users with error messages.

In This Part...

More and more users are asking for OLE capability in their application programs. More important than that (at least to some vendors) is the requirement by Microsoft that Windows 95 compatible programs include OLE capability. To get the Microsoft Windows 95 Compatible logo, you must add OLE to your application.

Adding this capability to your programs doesn't have to come at the loss of any sanity you may still possess (contrary to common belief). This part of the book shows you just how easy it can be to cut through the megabytes of documentation found in most OLE programming books to add simple OLE capabilities to any application. We won't make you an OLE programming guru, but we will give you a push in the right direction.

Chapter 13
Why Program?

In This Chapter

▶ All about programming and OLE

▶ Types of OLE programming

▶ Macros versus programming languages

Most people think they can never learn to program. They believe that writing a program that can do anything worthwhile must be difficult, or at least mysterious. After all, programmers are strange people who live in dark rooms and drink copious quantities of coffee while muttering in unintelligible languages.

In reality, programming takes many forms, most of which are neither difficult nor mysterious. For example, you are actually programming — to a limited extent — when you enter a command at a DOS prompt. Such a simple program could consist of a single DIR command, telling the computer to list the contents of a floppy disk.

Of course, a single command isn't terribly useful. To complete more complicated tasks, you need to enter a whole string of commands. If you were to write a series of commands and put them together in an ASCII text file with a .BAT filename extension, you'd have a program.

Your computer's AUTOEXEC.BAT file is a program that DOS uses to configure the machine on startup. This simple program is called a *batch file*, and many people write this type of program without realizing they are programming.

OK, so you're not adept at entering commands at the DOS prompt, and the last time you created a batch file, the machine was out of control for a week. Well, Windows (and DOS, in special circumstances) provides another means for programming your computer.

When was the last time you recorded a macro? Macros are yet another form of programming, and, in most cases, you don't even have to write them. Many applications can write macros for you by recording the keystrokes and mouse clicks you make.

Of course, most applications allow you to modify these macros so you can enhance them in some way. Macros are particularly useful in spreadsheets. Most serious spreadsheet users have probably written macros for gathering information from other files or automating other complicated tasks. Macros are another form of programming that many people use without realizing they are programming.

There are also subtler forms of programming. For example, anyone who has created a letter with a mail-merge file has programmed his or her computer. Using a search-and-replace command to change a word or a phrase qualifies as a simple excursion into programming. Even setting up a stylesheet with pre-defined bits of text is a form of programming. None of these activities seem like programming, but they are.

OK, you get the idea; being a programmer doesn't necessarily involve sitting under mushrooms for hours at a time. (We don't mean to imply that program-mers never inhabit dark places; we're just saying you don't have to live that way to program.) Whether or not you consider yourself a programmer, there are more programmers in the world than most people realize.

Programming always provides some way to automate a task. If a task is repeti-tive, you can proboably write a program that tells your computer how to do it for you. In most cases, the program simply repeats the same steps you would normally do yourself.

All About Programming and OLE

You can perform a variety of tasks with OLE and never write a single program. In fact, you may think that OLE doesn't lend itself to programming. After all, cutting and pasting hardly qualifies as programming.

However, OLE doesn't stop with cutting and pasting; that's where it starts. To take full advantage of OLE, you have to learn how to program.

OLE programming is a vast topic for Windows programmers. The programming aspects of OLE can be quite complex. That's why bookstores sell those fat books about OLE that you can barely lift without using a dolly or throwing your back out.

If you really want to dig into the depths of OLE programing, you have to learn C and write vast amounts of code. Fortunately, you can learn enough OLE pro-gramming for most tasks by using the built-in OLE capabilities of your favorite programs, such as Microsoft Word or Lotus 1-2-3.

Types of OLE Programs

Although we only look at two kinds of OLE programming in this book, there are three ways to program OLE:

- ✔ Macros
- ✔ High-level languages
- ✔ Low-level languages

As we detail in the following sections, each type is useful in different situations.

The distinction between high-level languages and low-level languages isn't very clear-cut. One programmer may view C as a low-level language, while another may see assembler in that role. It would be nice if programmers could get together and define exactly what *high-level* and *low-level* mean, but that would take all the mystery out of programming for users — wouldn't it?

Macros

Macro programming comes in handy when you need to automate a fairly simple task — for example, searching a database for names and addresses in a certain part of the country. The disadvantage to this type of programming is that macros only use the OLE capabilities provided by the program you're using. In other words, macros aren't as flexible as a full-fledged programming language.

On the other hand, you can usually get the job done using your program's built-in macro recorder. As a result, building an OLE program with macros is fast and easy.

High-level languages

BASIC and Pascal are considered high-level programming languages. You can use a high-level programming language to create a program that combines features found in two or more applications or to perform a task that a single application can't handle using macros.

For example, you could use macros in Microsoft Word to build a mailing list manager; but using Access or Visual BASIC is probably a lot easier. Both of these products have built-in OLE support, so part of the work is already done for you.

Low-level languages

Unless you need to write something that is speed critical or directly interacts with the computer hardware, you probably want to stay away from low-level languages such as C or C++. Programmers with computer science degrees and lots of experience use low-level languages to write operating systems and other really complicated programs that never seem to work right.

We won't cover low-level programming languages in this book; that topic is better discussed by those huge programming tomes on your local bookstore's computer shelves.

Macros Versus Programming Languages

So, when should you use macros and when should you use a programming language? You should consider the following factors when making this decision:

- ✔ *Time* — Recording a macro is fast; using a programming language is not. Even if you have to modify a macro to make it do what you want, getting a macro to work usually takes less than a day. Writing a successful program often takes weeks or even months.

- ✔ *Reusability* — If you only need to perform a task once or twice, writing a program hardly pays if a macro can do the job. On the other hand, if you need to perform the same task over and over again, a program may be the way to go.

- ✔ *Audience* — How many people will use this application? If you're the only user, you need to decide whether writing a program is worth the time and effort. If lots of people will use the application, a macro — with all its inherent weaknesses — will probably give you more grief than help.

- ✔ *Application need* — You can only use a macro if your application supports the features you need. For example, if you are using a word processor and you need to add columns of numbers, a macro may not do the job.

- ✔ *Availability* — Sometimes, you have to make the decision based on what's available. If you're a full-time programmer, you probably have a whole shelf of programming tools at your disposal. Unfortunately, most of us have to rely on the handful of applications installed on our computers. If your boss won't spring for a new programming language, the choice is obvious; you have to write a macro (or ask someone else to write the program for you).

- ✔ *Flexibility* — Each application is designed to perform one general task, and the macros you can create with a particular application tend to be limited to that task as well. For example, you wouldn't want to build a spreadsheet using macros provided by a database. General-purpose languages such as Visual BASIC don't have these limitations; they're designed to do practically anything.

✔ *Extensibility*—This $50 word is really pretty simple once you figure out what it means. You'll usually find only a few third-party products that you can use to extend the the capabilities of an application. For example, Microsoft Word is supported by a few third-party products that allow you to print labels, and that's about it. Languages such as Visual BASIC provide hundreds of third-party products to do just about anything.

✔ *Learning curve*—Learning about macros always takes less time than learning a programming language. Visual BASIC is very flexible, but this flexibility comes at the price of being harder to learn. It may be months before you can really write something useful in Visual BASIC. Learning to accomplish the same task using a macro may only take minutes.

Always look ahead when programming. Chances are that someone will see what you've done and want to add a few bells and whistles (that's programmer talk for "extra work"). If you're not careful, your program can get progressively bigger, harder to understand, and harder to modify.

Test your newfound knowledge

1. Programming consists of:

   a. Sitting under a mushroom and reciting bad poetry.

   b. Typing commands and saving them for re-use. Examples of simple programs include batch files and macros.

   c. Performing herculean tasks such as lifting OLE manuals and actually reading them.

   d. Becoming a hermit and learning obscure languages that no one else understands.

2. One of the best reasons for programming instead of using macros is:

   a. Programmers make more money than most people.

   b. Telling people you are a programmer sounds a lot more impressive than saying you can write macros.

   c. Programming languages give you more flexibility than macros. They allow you to write applications with a great deal more capabilities than you could create using macros.

   d. You can waste a lot of time using big words that other people won't recognize.

Chapter 14

OLE Programming Principles

* *

In This Chapter

▶ Making the required programming decisions

▶ Including all the necessary stuff

▶ Implementing your strategy

* *

*P*rogramming in OLE can become complex. In fact, Microsoft's overview of the OLE specification fills 8MB of hard disk space.

Do you really need to know that much to add OLE 2 features to your program? Not really. OLE 2 can get complicated if you want to do something really weird, but we'll concentrate on the "normal" stuff.

You can also simplify your OLE programming workload by choosing the right tools for the job. C programmers need to look at every detail associated with OLE. We can get by with an overview because we're using Visual BASIC and Access. Both of these products do some of the work for you. (Makes those C programmers look a little stupid, doesn't it?)

Deciding What to Program

Before you can write an application that provides OLE services, you need to decide what that program will include. OLE is complicated enough when you do plan ahead. Trying to writing an application without prior planning will cause you to lose all your hair (or worse).

You need to decide whether your application will provide client, server, or both types of services. (Chapter 2 explains the differences between OLE client and server applications.) The following sections will guide you through this decision making process.

The people who invented computer terminology apparently decided confusing us would be fun. They used the same terms to talk about two different things. In the database world, a *client* is a workstation, and the *server* is a mainframe, minicomputer, or file server that sends information to the client. In the world of OLE, a *client* is the application which creates a file (called a compound document or a container) containing all your information, and the *server* is a program that sends information to the client.

Is it a client or a server?

As a client, your application needs to know how to use files created by other programs. For example, a user might want to stick a spreadsheet into a file created by your graphics program. Before you start to write code for your graphics program, you need to decide how to handle this situation.

Clients also need to call on the server to provide editing and other services. A client doesn't have to know how to work with your data; it just needs to know where to find the application that's designed to do the job. As a server, your program needs to update its files when asked to do so by other applications. Many of these capabilities are provided by high-level programming languages such as Visual BASIC. All you need to do is tell your program to use them.

When deciding whether your application should provide client, server, or both types of services, you need to base the decision partly on what type of application you are creating. The following list looks at some typical applications:

- ✔ Word processors (for example, Word for Windows) and desktop publishing applications (such as Ventura Publisher) typically provide both client and server services. For example, as clients, these applications offer features that make combining parts of a proposal easy (at least, easier than it would be in a spreadsheet). These applications provide formatting features that make documents look like they just came back from the printer. As a server, a word processor comes in handy for creating those bits of text that users add to charts or as explanatory text on a spreadsheet.

- ✔ Spreadsheets (for example, Lotus 1-2-3) and databases such as Microsoft Access typically act as servers. Users don't expect these applications to provide the fancy text and graphics formatting features of a word processor or a desktop publishing program. Instead, spreadsheets and databases typically provide information that a client application uses in assembling a compound document.

- ✔ A notepad application usually acts as a client. It doesn't offer much in the way of formatting features, and you really wouldn't want to use its output in a formal proposal. However, it does come in handy for quick printing of the text in your document. If memory is in short supply, using the notepad as a client can help the user become more efficient and productive.

> ✔ Graphics applications may provide either or both services. In most cases, a drawing program acts as a server. On the other hand, a charting program typically acts as a client. Some complex graphics programs (for example, CorelDRAW!) act as both clients and servers because you can use them to create an entire presentation.

Using the command line interface

OLE doesn't use magic to perform its work. It uses some of the same techniques you already use. How many times have you used the command line interface in one of your Windows applications? That's what we thought; we haven't done it much either.

In some situations, however, a Windows application needs a command line interface. For example, a Windows application needs a command line to start an OLE server. When you drop a text file on the Notepad and tell it to print, how do you think Windows tells the Notepad to perform that task? It uses a command line, just like you would if you had to type the filename. The command line looks something like this:

```
NOTEPAD %1 /p
```

Wow! This command almost looks like something you might see in a DOS batch file. Windows replaces the %1 with the name of your file. The /p tells Notepad to print.

DDE: The other command line

Some applications (for example, Word for Windows) are a lot more complex than Notepad. They use more than just a simple command line to get their work done. You use this command line to tell Word for Windows to print a document:

```
WINWORD /w
```

This command line looks incomplete. How does Word for Windows know that it needs to print a document? It uses a subset of OLE called DDE (dynamic data exchange) to print the file. The /w switch stops Word for Windows from displaying a tip of the day. A switch changes the way an application acts when it starts. But that still doesn't explain how Windows gets Word to print. Here's the DDE message that Windows sends to Word once it gets Word started:

```
[FileOpen(""%1"")][FilePrint()][DocClose(2)]
```

This DDE message looks a lot like a macro. It opens the file, prints it, and then closes Word for Windows. Note that Windows substitutes a filename for the %1 in the DDE message. In some cases, you will use messages like this in your Visual BASIC and Access applications to control the way other applications work.

There are also lots of other command line switches. Many of them aren't even documented, but Windows knows what they mean. The appropriate command line switches are usually recorded in the registry during application installation. In fact, you may want to browse through the registry some time just to check it out. You might be surprised by what you find.

At a minimum, you should always provide the capability to print using a command line switch. The standard switch for print is -P (some programs use /P). We take a closer look at the techniques required for adding this capability in Chapters 15 and 16.

Things Every OLE Program Needs

There are a few things every OLE program needs to do. We show you the specific programming requirements in Chapters 15 and 16, but now is a good time for an overview of those requirements.

The four OLE programming modes

As a client, an application needs to know how to display an object and what to do when the user tries to edit that object. As a server, an application needs to know how to respond to a client's requests for specific services.

An object is anything you copy from a file created by another program. The file in which you place the object is called a *container* or a *compound document*. A compound document contains information created by the application that created the compound document, as well as one or more objects created by other applications.

To make it easier for programs to keep track of what each object is doing, the OLE specification defines four OLE programming modes. Whether your application is an OLE client, a server, or both, it needs to know about the following OLE modes:

- **Inactive** — Windows places an object in the inactive state when the object is not part of a selection and it isn't open for editing. This state is the one in which you see an object when you first open a compound document. As a client, your program displays the object in its presentation format — that is, the format in which Windows would print the object if you sent it to the printer. When you see an object in its inactive state, you can't tell where the object ends and the rest of the document starts.

- **Selected** — An object can be selected in two ways. You can either single-click it or use the group select tool (providing the application has one). The client highlights selected objects just like any native data the compound document contains. As shown in Figure 14-1, some objects also allow the client to display sizing handles. The user can move these handles to resize the selected object as needed.

✔ **Active** — An object enters the active state when the user selects it and then selects the Edit option of the object menu. In some applications, a user can accomplish the same thing by double-clicking the object. When an object is active, the server accepts editing requests from the client. The client allows the server to overlay its menu and toolbar on top of the native menu and toolbar. As shown in Figure 14-2, the client and the server share the application window. Notice that the client displays a hatched border around the object. The hatched border shows the limits of the area occupied by the object.

✔ **Open** — This mode provides compatibility with the OLE 1 specification. When an object enters this state, the client sends a DDE message to the server with the name of the file that contains the object. The server opens a new window and displays the object. This action allows the user to edit the object in a separate window. Any changes the user makes will appear simultaneously in both the server and the client windows. Figure 14-3 shows a typical client and server setup when the object enters the open state. Notice that the object is overlaid by hatching in the client window. This arrangement shows that the object is no longer available there; instead, the user needs to view it in the server window.

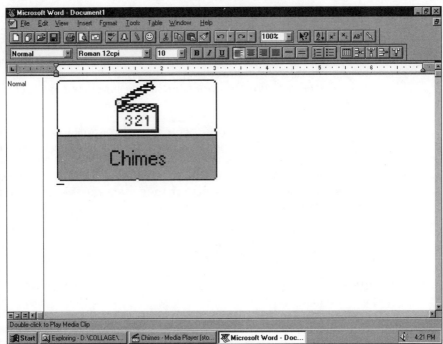

Figure 14-1: A client application always highlights a selected object. In some cases, it also displays sizing handles.

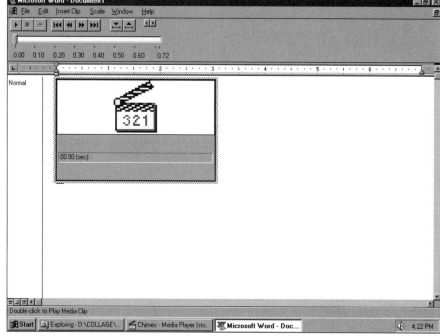

Figure 14-2:
When an
object
enters the
active state,
the client
and the
server share
the
application
window.

Selecting an object doesn't require any action from the server. The Selected mode allows the user to perform some action with the object, but it doesn't actually perform the action. For example, selecting an object usually enables the menu selections that allow you to open the object or edit it in place. Most object menus also provide a convert option that allows you to change the selected data from its native format to the one supported by the current application.

Most objects spend the majority of their time in the inactive mode. This means they just hang around waiting for someone to do something with them. After an update, the server always provides the client with a printable view of the object. This way, the client can show you what the object will look like when printed, and it doesn't need to disturb the server when you finally send the document to the printer.

Actions that OLE programs perform

In two modes, active and open, a server needs to work with the client to perform some OLE-related tasks. The exact nature of those tasks depends on what the user decides to do and the type of data the object contains.

The two standard actions are open and edit. In addition to these standard actions, an application usually provides a convert action.

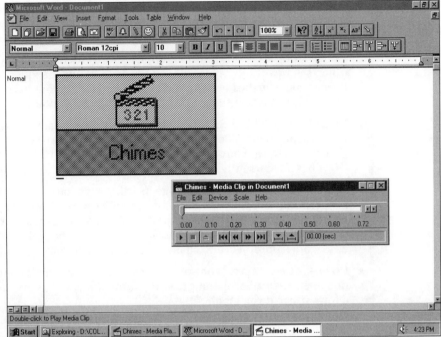

Figure 14-3:
When an
object
enters the
open state,
the client
and the
server use
separate
windows.

Applications that use special file types provide additional default actions. For example, a sound file object will probably provide a play action so that you can hear the contents of the file.

The following list describes some of the standard actions OLE programs perform. In most cases, these actions appear as menu items on the object menu that appears when you right-click an object. The actions you provide in your application depend on which types of actions the object needs to perform and the type of file:

- **Convert**—Changes the object's format. In most cases, this action changes the object into the client application's native format. However, the convert action could simply update the format to match the format of a new version of the same product. For example, if you upgrade from version 1.0 to 2.0 of your favorite word processor, the convert option allows a user to update the word processor objects embedded in another application's file to the new 2.0 file format. Most OLE applications automatically tell you that you need to update a file to the new format when you use a feature that the new version provides.

- **Edit**—The edit action changes the menu and the toolbar of the client application to match the configuration of the application used to create the object. By providing some of the functionality of the client application, the server allows the user to edit the embedded object.

✔ **Open** — This action opens another window. The server opens the original version of the object and allows the user to edit it in a separate window. Each change the user makes is also recorded in the client window.

✔ **Play** — The play action normally appears with video, voice, or wave objects. A wave object contains sounds or short music sequences. They are contained in the files with the .WAV extension on your hard disk. The play action allows the user to hear what the object contains.

✔ **Undo/Redo** — The Undo action allows users to reverse any changes the user made to the object. The Redo action undoes your undo. Make sense? Unfortunately, you can only provide an undo or redo feature for open objects. OLE does not currently support a compound document undo or redo.

✔ **Text Properties** — Embedded objects will not let you adjust their text properties directly. This menu entry simplifies the task of having the server change the text as needed. Of course, if the changes get too complex or you need to use more than one font, your only choice is to either edit or open the object and change everything manually.

✔ **Copy** — There is no reason you can't copy an object from a compound document instead of opening the original document. This menu command allows you to do just that.

✔ **Cut** — This menu entry doesn't really serve a useful purpose. Using the Cut command from the application menu accomplishes the same task.

✔ **Paste/Paste Special** — The standard paste selection is no real surprise when you consider that the menu also holds copy and cut entries. The surprise here is the paste special entry. Yes, you can actually link or embed another object into the current object. That's one of the new features that OLE 2 provides. OLE 1 allowed only one level of linked or embedded objects.

You can always determine whether an application supports OLE 1 or OLE 2 by checking which types of interaction it supports. If you try to edit or open the object and the client tells you it can't do so, the server only supports OLE 1. One of the upgrades Microsoft included in OLE 2 was to allow a two-way relationship between the server and the client. In other words, the server can talk to the client. One of the ways in which this new relationship shows up is when the server takes over the client's menu. For example, your word processor might suddenly have graphic commands added to its menu when you click on a graphic object.

Inside-out or outside-in?

The folks at Microsoft had to come up with some terms for describing the way a client allows the user to edit data contained in an object. These methods are known as *activation techniques*. An activation technique is the method a client uses for calling the server. Only the server can provide the editing tools a user needs for changing the contents of an object.

There are two major types of client activation techniques, and two derivatives for displaying information. Each type has advantages and disadvantages.

The first type of client application uses the outside-in activation technique. Most applications currently use this technique. It gets its name from the fact that you start outside the object and work your way in, activating the server application by either clicking or double-clicking the object.

The second type of client application uses the inside-out activation technique. Only a few applications currently use this new OLE 2 technique because it's unfamiliar to most users (as well most programmers). The inside-out activation technique works much as its name implies. From the user's viewpoint, the object is always active. Moving the mouse cursor near the object always provides some type of instant feedback. In such cases, the server is activated with the client application and remains active during the entire editing session. Whenever your mouse cursor is on an object, the server for that object takes over from the client application. (The actual process is a lot more complex than this, but we could end up writing an entire book on just this subject.)

The outside-in activation technique gives the user an additional layer of control and protection. The user must take the extra step of telling the application that it is time to edit the object. The drawback is that the object (for example, a piece of text, some sound, or a graphic) always seems like something added to a document, almost as an afterthought. The outside-in activation technique is best suited to workgroup projects in which you want to make certain that each edit is there because someone really wanted it there.

The inside-out activation technique creates the impression that a compound document was created without the aid of any other applications. You can move from object to object without realizing you have done so. The inside-out technique is particularly useful for presentations. For such applications, your primary consideration is ensuring that everything goes smoothly, not preventing someone from accidentally changing the contents of an object. Of course, you better make a backup copy of that file because someone will invariably change it (or even delete it).

These two activation techniques have two subsets. Applications that regularly handle very large and very small data elements may use the activation technique known as *outside-in plus inside-out preferred*. These applications use the outside-in activation technique for large objects that the user is unlikely to edit. Small data elements use the inside-out activation technique, which makes them seem like part of the original compound document.

The second subset is *switch between inside-out throughout and outside-in throughout.* (Yes, that's really the name for this technique, as listed in the Microsoft documentation.)

Programs such as Microsoft Access and Visual BASIC use this activation technique to make their design and runtime environments easier to use. (A design environment is where you draw the forms and define the way controls such as pushbuttons will react. A runtime environment is where the user actually gets to use what you created.) They use the outside-in activation technique when in design mode so the programmer doesn't accidentally change an important piece of information. The inside-out activation technique comes in handy in run mode because it provides the application user with a seamless user interface.

So, how does Windows know the difference between an outside-in and an inside-out OLE application? Every application that supports OLE has to register itself with Windows; otherwise, Windows won't know where to find the application. In fact, Windows won't even know the application exists.

These registry entries also contain something called *flags.* Think about the registry flags just as you would any other flag. For example, if you see someone waving a white flag, you know he's ready to surrender. If Windows doesn't see a flag in the application's registry entry, it assumes the application supports the outside-in activation method. An application that supports the inside-out activation method can use two flags.

The first flag is OLEMISC_INSIDEOUT. This flag tells Windows that the application can use the inside-out activation technique. Every application must support the outside-in activation technique; the inside-out technique is a special feature an application can add to its repertoire.

The second flag is OLEMISC_ACTIVATEWHENVISIBLE. This flag tells Windows that the application prefers to use the inside-out activation technique. When Windows sees this flag, it makes every effort to activate the application using the inside-out activation technique.

Applications that use the outside-in activation technique provide a menu that allows the user to select when and how to change the object's data. The inside-out activation technique allows the user to modify the object's data at any time; it's like the object was always a part of the document and not embedded.

Registering your application

One of the final pieces of the OLE programming puzzle is registering your application with Windows. The Windows registry tells Windows which programs support OLE. Windows needs this information so it can call your application when someone tries to use its OLE capabilities.

The registry also tells Windows how to interact with your application. Because each OLE-capable program can use different command line switches and provide different types of services, Windows can't assume anything. You need to tell Windows what to do with your application.

Program registration usually happens during installation. The setup program tells Windows all about the application and how to talk with it. As you are writing your application, you may need to spend a little time figuring out exactly what you want to tell Windows. (The Setup Wizard included with Microsoft Access and Visual BASIC usually does some of the registry setup for you; adding OLE support is fairly straightforward.)

We'll take a look at the registry to find out what these OLE entries are all about. Somewhere on your hard disk is a program called REGEDIT.EXE, a Windows utility that hides in either the SYSTEM or the WINDOWS directory. (Microsoft hides REGEDIT because it's a powerful editor that can cause significant damage to your system if you don't use it carefully.)

Never change any of the entries in the registry database unless you are certain about that entry's purpose. Any change to the registry database could prevent Windows from opening the next time you start your machine. The registry holds all your system's configuration information; without it, Windows doesn't have a clue as to what your system contains or how to use it.

Windows 3.x does include the REGEDIT (registry editor) utility. However, its interface is quite different from the one used by Windows NT and Windows 95. The following procedure talks about the Windows NT and Windows 95 version of REGEDIT. Please refer to your Windows 3.x documentation when using the registry editor utility.

1. Load and run the REGEDIT file. If you are using Windows NT or Windows 95, the display will resemble Figure 14-4. The Windows 3.1 display looks a bit different, but it performs essentially the same task.

2. Find the HKEY_CLASSES_ROOT entry, and click the plus sign (+) next to the entry.

3. Use the scroll bar to look at some of the entries. You should run across one for Notepad.

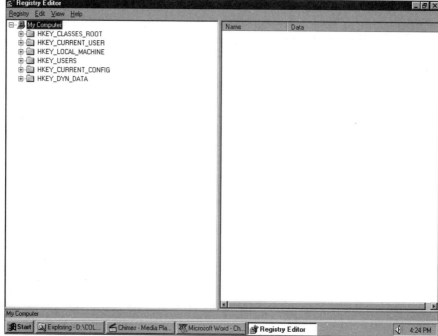

Figure 14-4:
The registry
is the
central
storage area
for all your
Windows
configuration
information.

Although some people think the registry database is an incomprehensible mess, it is actually a well-organized method for configuring Windows. A look at the registry can tell you a lot about how Windows and OLE interact. The registry can also tell you a great deal about your system in general.

Look for the registry entries made by other applications. You can use these entries as a template for creating your application's entries. Figure 14-5 shows some typical registry entries that include OLE-specific information.

The entries on the left side of the screen are called *keys*. Think of the keys as the headings in a book. The registry is like a book that contains six chapters, and each chapter has many subheadings (subkeys). The entries on the right side of the screen are called *values*. Think of values as the paragraphs in a book. They help fill out the registry and define the keys.

For this example, we're looking at a key called `CorelDRAW.CorelDRAWApp.5`. The value for this key indicates that it defines the CorelDRAW! 5.0 OLE Automation Application. The important word is OLE; this subkey is the one in which we're really interested.

Notice that this is the *Clsid subkey*, which stands for class identifier. Every object in Windows has a class identifier. Windows uses this number to identify the object in all the places it appears in the registry. Find an OLE entry for one of the applications on your machine, and write down its 32-digit class identifier.

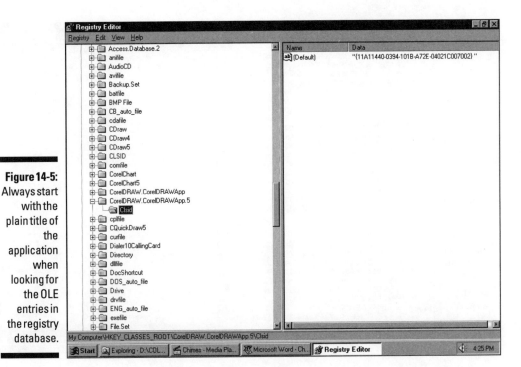

Figure 14-5:
Always start
with the
plain title of
the
application
when
looking for
the OLE
entries in
the registry
database.

Now, scroll up and find the CLSID entry under HKEY_CLASSES_ROOT. This is where the registry database stores all the information about each class (object) that Windows can identify. Click the plus sign (+) next to the entry and you should see a display similar to the one in Figure 14-6.

Look at the 32-digit number highlighted on the left side of the screen. This is the same class identifier we saw in the CorelDRAW.CorelDRAWApp.5 | Clsid key value. Notice the keys under this entry. From the listing, we can tell that CorelDRAW! 5.0 is an OLE server. Look for the 32-digit entry that you recorded earlier. Compare the entries you find for your application with those recorded for CorelDRAW!. You will definitely see some differences, but you may find a few similarities as well.

Writing the OLE Portion of Your Program

No matter which programming language you use (even if it uses macros), every OLE program requires some additional development steps. You could consider writing the work-related part of the program itself as phase one and writing the OLE interface as phase two. A third phase is testing all the interactions between your application and other OLE-capable applications. These are the twelve steps to good OLE programming:

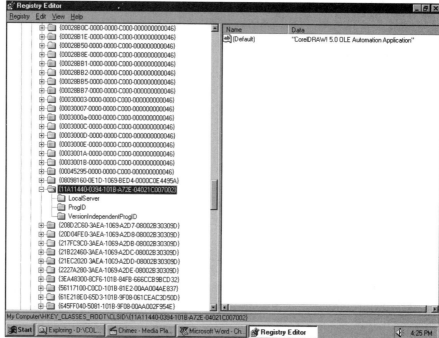

Figure 14-6:
The class
identifier
key contains
OLE and
other
application-
specific
information.

1. Write the application and test it for errors (bugs). Don't even attempt to check any of the OLE features until the rest of the application is bug free (or as close as you can get it).

2. If your application is a client, try to link some data from a spreadsheet into a sample file. Break a few pencils as you watch the hard disk eat every piece of data your machine ever contained.

3. Now do the same thing with word processing and database files. You should test all three application types because each type sends the data to your application in a different format.

4. Perform steps 1 through 4 over and over again until you get the application right. Doing so should take the rest of your lifetime because the OLE specification is so clear and easy to understand.

5. Now it's time to test the embedding part of your application. Embed data from each application type into a sample file. This time, you also need to add some graphics and sound samples because they use yet another communication method when talking to your program.

6. Repeat the previous steps over and over again until your brain is totally fried. Proceed to the next step after having a good long talk with your tennis shoes.

7. Try saving your file to disk. Close the application, and reopen the file. If all your linked and embedded data is still in place, you have a successful OLE client application!

8. If you wrote an OLE server application, create a small data file. Now copy the contents of the file onto the clipboard. Perform a paste link in three or four applications. Save the file and close your application.

9. Restart the application and open the file. If all the links remained intact, double-click the object. Edit the data, and then save and close everything again.

10. Restart the application and recheck data integrity.

11. Repeat steps 9 and 10 until the linking portion of your application works perfectly.

12. Perform steps 8 through 11 with embedded, instead of linked, data.

Test your newfound knowledge

1. OLE clients and servers consist of the following elements:

   a. Two applications running on one machine. One application sends its data to the other in the form of an object. The combined data structure is called a compound document.

   b. A lawyer taking care of business for a customer, and a deputy giving someone a summons to appear at the trial.

   c. Someone you take to lunch at a tennis club, and the man in white tossing a ball in the air.

   d. A book about the trial of a waiter accused of killing his boss.

2. The two standard OLE actions are:

   a. Making life difficult for the programmer and easy for the user.

   b. Causing the display to flash on and off in shades of purple and green and turn the sound up and down randomly.

   c. Causing massive destruction to the registry and your data.

   d. Open and edit.

3. You have to register your application with Windows:

   a. Because Microsoft is being really silly and forcing you to do more work than necessary.

   b. To enable OLE support and to help Windows understand how to communicate with your application.

   c. Every week or so to prevent Windows from forgetting that you installed it.

   d. Because your application should vote for who it likes best.

4. What is the major difference between the outside-in and the inside-out activation techniques?

   a. One refers to the standard condition of the socks in your drawer. The other refers to their condition after you take them off for the night.

   b. It's the difference between the person looking out from inside the candy store and the one on the outside looking in.

   c. The inside-out technique maintains a constantly active editing capability. The outside-in technique forces you to open a menu to enable editing.

   d. One refers to the desire of a fly once it checks out your house; the other refers to the fly before you open the screen.

Chapter 15

Writing OLE Programs with Access BASIC

In This Chapter

▶ Using the right tool

▶ Adding table objects

▶ Manipulating form objects

In this chapter, we explore the ins and outs of OLE programming with Access BASIC. Although we focus specifically on Microsoft Access 7.0, just about everything we describe also works fine with Access 2.x. You can even use some of the principles we describe with other DBMSs (database management systems) that provide direct support for BLOBs (binary large objects) and OLE 2. (FoxPro and other Xbase derivatives do not directly support BLOB fields, but you can usually gain BLOB support using an add-on product.)

DBMS programming is a complex undertaking. A DBMS programmer has to think about many issues that might not even affect another programmer. For example, you have to think about the problem of manipulating more than one table in a database that doesn't even reside on a workstation. A database is usually stored on a file server, which means you must deal with not one, but two, operating systems (maybe Windows 95 on your workstation, and NetWare on the file server).

Dealing with two operating systems may not seem like much of a problem until you have to add security to your program. You don't want everyone to gain access to your database, so your program needs security. The problem is so complicated that entire libraries are available to help programmers deal with the problem of implementing security under network operating systems such as NetWare.

Another two-operating-system problem involves the NetWare Transaction Tracking System (TTS). This is a method for tracking every database event on the file server. Tracking events allows your program to recover in the event of a power failure or other disaster. It also allows you to back out of failed transactions (when users turn off their machines without first exiting Windows for example). The only problem is that you have to make special operating system calls to use TTS, something Access doesn't provide as a built-in feature.

Problems are also associated with multiple users. What would happen if two users decided to change the same record? Which record would appear in the database when they tried to save their edits? A DBMS programmer has to incorporate locking mechanisms and other multiuser features in a database. A *locking mechanism* ensures that only one user can edit a record at a time, but many users can read the record (they can't edit it).

So, what does all this have to do with OLE? Using OLE with a word processing document is easy. You can make all kinds of assumptions about that object. For one thing, you can assume the object is always available.

A database programmer can't make any assumptions about the objects in a database. Think about the example we presented in Chapter 11. What would happen if your program needed access to the fruit picture, but that picture was unavailable because someone was editing it? Access would correctly point out that the file was in use by displaying an error message at the workstation requesting access to the file.

The only problem with error messages of this type is that they tend to be ambiguous. Users pull out their hair by the handfuls trying to figure out what they did wrong. Unless you want a lot of bald users in the office, solving this type of problem before it happens is wise.

You can solve the problem by making those picture files read-only. No one can edit the picture unless they have the right to change the status of the file from read-only to read-write. Of course, this solution limits your ability to use OLE to its full potential. It works for static data such as the pictures in our example, but not for dynamic data such as graphs or charts showing this week's sales figures.

Another solution — the one we examine in this chapter — is to store the pictures in a table. With this approach, you can write rules governing how people can access the files. This solution also allows you to provide friendly messages that tell users it really isn't their fault when they need to access a record that's already in use.

In this single chapter, we can't solve every programming problem you'll ever encounter when using Access. Entire books are devoted to the subject (such as *Access For Dummies*, from IDG). What we can do is provide you with tips that can help you use OLE in the best way possible in a multiuser situation.

Programming, Macros, Forms, or Queries

Not every problem requires programming. Just as every fastener isn't a screw requiring the services of a screwdriver, every problem in Access doesn't require programming. Some design problems are nails requiring the service of a hammer, or hex nuts requiring the services of a socket wrench. Using the right tool for the job is the first step in creating an efficient database design.

Always try to solve database design problems at the highest level possible. Every time you go down a level, the number of automatic controls that Access provides decreases. Using automatic controls means you have less work to do and less chance exists for any errors in the final program. In order from highest to lowest, here are the five solution levels that Access provides:

- ✔ Table
- ✔ Query
- ✔ Form
- ✔ Macro
- ✔ Programming

The reason for the name of this section should now be evident. Access provides validation rules and other table-related resources for every type of data field except OLE objects. The lack of validation rules for OLE objects is significant.

You could write a program that uses a validation rule to ensure the user inputs the correct information. (A *validation rule* makes sure the user provides the right type of input data.) More importantly, some programmers use validation rule code to perform other types of work as well. For example, you could use the validation rule program to update the contents of the form.

Queries are essential for defining who gets what level of access. Queries are one way to solve the data access problem we mention earlier in this chapter. You can use one type of query for users who are allowed to edit the database pictures and another query for those who aren't.

Chapter 11 demonstrates the usefulness of forms for controlling data access. Even if a table contains a specific data field, the user can't access that field unless the form contains it. This is only the first use of a form.

A form can also be used for manipulating the objects. Each control on a form has associated properties and events. You can attach macros or programs to the events to change the contents of the control. The properties allow you to change the way the user sees those contents.

As we describe in Chapter 11, you can use macros to provide some level of OLE services. The example in that chapter shows how to use a macro to control the picture the user sees, based on the food group (category) that's displayed. A macro can also perform other types of work. You can use a macro to change the way the user enters data or to perform some type of automatic service.

Macros have limits, but some people still try to use them for completing every task under Access. When you reach the limit of a macro's capabilities, you have to resort to writing a module in Access BASIC. (Chapter 13 describes the differences between a programming language and macros.) For example, because macros don't provide looping controls, you can't allow the user to switch between food categories with a mere click on the food group picture. That's what this chapter is all about: learning to use Access BASIC when a macro can't do the job.

Changing the Contents of a Table

OLE objects in a database aren't much good if you can't change them. That includes adding, deleting, and modifying the contents of the object fields. One of the problems with the example program in Chapter 11 is that you can't perform any of these tasks.

The examples in this chapter rely on the results of the example in Chapter 11. You should be familiar with the example programs in Chapter 11 before you start the examples in this chapter.

Modifying OLE objects

We can easily add the capability for modifying the food group pictures to our example database. We already have the required tables in place. The first step is defining a new query that makes use of the OLE objects in the Food Types table. Once we do that, we can create a new form that uses this query.

1. Open Access and the example table we created in Chapter 11. (We called our table My Database.)

2. Click the Queries tab of the Database dialog box.

3. Right-click the Food Select 1 query, and select Copy. Right-click within the list box, and select Paste from the context menu that's displayed. You'll see a Paste As dialog like the one shown in Figure 15-1.

4. In the text box, type Food Select 2, and then click OK.

Figure 15-1:
Access
allows you
to create
copies of
forms,
queries, and
other
database
objects
using the
standard
Copy and
Paste
commands.

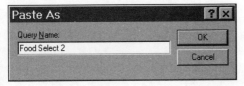

5. Open Food Select 2 in design mode. Right-click in the upper half of the Query Select dialog box. Select Show Table from the context menu. You'll see the Show Table dialog box shown in Figure 15-2.

6. Select the Food Types table, and click Add. Click Close. Access adds the new table to the query and automatically creates a relationship between the Category fields of both tables.

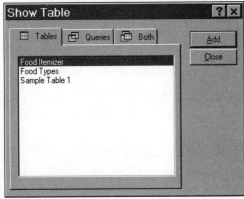

Figure 15-2:
Modifying
the first
program's
query
includes
adding a
new table.

7. Add the Food Picture field to the fifth column of the query. Your query should look like the example in Figure 15-3.

8. Click the Save button on the toolbar. Close the query.

9. Click the Forms tab of the Database dialog.

10. Using the same procedure you followed in steps 3 and 4, create a copy of the Food Inventory Control 1 form. Name the new form Food Inventory Control 2.

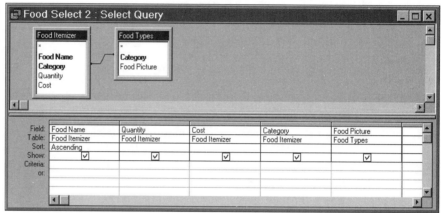

Figure 15-3:
Our new
query will
allow us to
grab the
pictures
directly from
the
database
rather than
rely on disk
copies.

11. Open Food Inventory Control 2 in design mode.

12. Open the Form Properties dialog. Change the Record Source property to Food Select 2. Doing so enables us to use the new query.

13. Delete the Change Category macro entry from the On Current event. Close the Form Properties dialog box.

14. Delete the Food Picture control from the form.

15. To display a list of fields associated with this form, choose View➪Field List.

16. Drag the Food Picture field from the list to the form.

17. Open the Food Picture Properties dialog. Change the Size Mode property to Stretch, and the Width property to 2".

18. Click the Category field. Delete the Change Category macro entry from the On Change event. Close the Properties dialog box. Your form should look like the one in Figure 15-4.

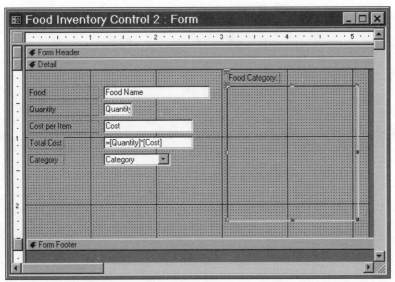

Figure 15-4:
The new form may look similar to the old one, but it includes important enhancements.

19. Click the Form View button. Try changing records. Notice that the picture changes automatically as the contents of the Category field change.

20. Double-click the picture. Access will open MS Paint, allowing you to change the contents of the picture.

21. Click the Save button on the toolbar.

As you can see, this new method for displaying a picture offers several advantages over the old method. For one thing, you don't need a macro to change the contents of the picture block. In addition, this method allows someone to edit the picture. (Of course, this ability could be a disadvantage if you didn't want to give users this capability.)

This new method also has several disadvantages. Did you notice the slower access time? Access has to go through more layers of code to display a picture than Windows does, which results in slower display times.

Another problem with this method is that the pictures are no longer stored on disk. Only people with access to the database can see and edit them. That can be a disadvantage in some cases because you may be forced to give database access to someone who only needs to change the pictures.

Notice something else about our new version of the form? It uses a Bound Object Frame control instead of a picture. Bound and Unbound Object Frame controls allow you to edit the OLE object they contain. Pictures merely display the object.

Adding OLE objects

Now that the user can modify a picture, what about adding a new one? It's quite possible that you won't anticipate every category users will ever need. Even if you don't allow users to remove old objects, adding new ones is essential.

You can approach this problem in several ways. Three events lend themselves to adding a new record: On Got Focus, On Click, and On Dbl Click. Of the three, On Got Focus is the least acceptable because the user constantly faces the decision of whether or not to add a new graphic.

What we really need to do is give users a choice. Do they want to add a new picture, delete an old one, or modify the current one? That's why this example modifies the action of the On Dbl Click event. It presents the user with a choice, and then allows Access to perform its task automatically:

1. Open Access and the My Database database (if necessary).

2. Click the Forms tab of the Database dialog. We need to create a new form for this exercise. Its only purpose is to allow us to add data to the Food Types table, so we don't need anything fancy.

3. Click New. Select Autoform: New, and the File Types table. Click OK. Access displays a simple form with two fields: Category and Food Picture.

4. Click the Save button on the toolbar. When asked, name the form **New Category**.

5. Close the New Category form.

6. Open the Food Inventory Control 2 form in design view.

7. Right-click the Food Picture control, and select Properties from the context menu that's displayed.

8. Click the On Dbl Click event. Choose [Event Procedure] from the drop-down list, and then click the ellipsis next to the event. An Access BASIC module appears.

9. Type the following program into the module. You do not need to add the Private Sub or EndSub lines.

```
Private Sub Food_Picture_DblClick(Cancel As Integer)

    'Declare some variables.

    Const MB_YESNOCANCEL = 3      'Type of message box.
    Const MB_ICONQUESTION = 32    'Icon displayed in message box.
    Const MB_DEFBUTTON2 = 256     'Default message box button.
    Const ID_CANCEL = 2           'Cancel button pressed?
    Const ID_YES = 6              'Yes button pressed?
```

```
Const ID_NO = 7           'No button pressed?
Const OLE_INS_OBJ = 14    'Display the Insert Object dialog.
Dim Title1 As String      'Message box title.
Dim Msg1 As String        'Message in message box.
Dim DlgDef1 As Integer    'Message box definition.
Dim Answer1 As Integer    'User response.
Dim Title2 As String      'New category title.
Dim Msg2 As String        'New category message.
Dim NewCategory As String 'New category name.

'The first thing we need to do is display a decision
'dialog so the user can choose an action.

Title1 = "Modify Picture"
Msg1 = "Do you want to create a new category?"
DlgDef1 = MB_YESNOCANCEL + MB_ICONQUESTION + MB_DEFBUTTON2
Answer1 = MsgBox(Msg1, DlgDef1, Title1)

'Now that we know what the user wants to do, let's act
'on it.  The Cancel and No options don't require much
'processing, but Yes requires us to add a new record to
'the File Types table and a new object to the record.

Select Case Answer1
    Case ID_CANCEL
        Cancel = True
    Case ID_NO
        Cancel = False
    Case ID_YES

        'The first step in creating the new category is
        'to determine its name.

        Msg2 = "Type the name of the new category."
        Title2 = "New Category"
        NewCategory = InputBox$(Msg2, Title2)

        'Once we've given it a name, we need to add a
        'new record to the Food Types table.  To
        'do this, we open a form in add mode and enter
        'the new category name.  (Notice that the
        'form remains hidden.)

        DoCmd.OpenForm "New Category", , , , A_ADD, A_HIDDEN
        Forms![New Category]![Category] = NewCategory

        'Now we have to give the user a chance to add
        'a graphic image.  We'll do that by displaying
        'the Insert Object dialog.
```

(continued)

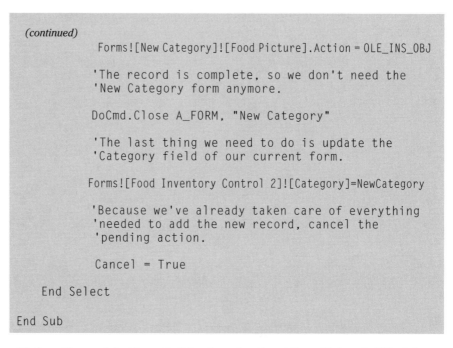

```
(continued)
                    Forms![New Category]![Food Picture].Action = OLE_INS_OBJ

                    'The record is complete, so we don't need the
                    'New Category form anymore.

                    DoCmd.Close A_FORM, "New Category"

                    'The last thing we need to do is update the
                    'Category field of our current form.

                    Forms![Food Inventory Control 2]![Category]=NewCategory

                    'Because we've already taken care of everything
                    'needed to add the new record, cancel the
                    'pending action.

                    Cancel = True

            End Select

End Sub
```

10. Save the module. Compile it by choosing Run⇨Compile Loaded Modules.
    Close the module.

11. Open MS Paint.

12. Create a new .BMP (Windows Bitmap) picture, and store it in the same
    directory as the other five pictures we created in Chapter 11. Call this one
    SWEETS.BMP.

13. Close MS Paint.

14. Click the Form View button for the Food Inventory Control 2 form.

15. Double-click the Food Picture control. The dialog box shown in Figure 15-5
    appears. This is the first dialog box we created in the program. Pressing No
    allows us to modify the picture, while pressing Cancel returns us to the form.

Figure 15-5:
Modifying
the On Dbl
Click event
allows us to
ask which
action the
user would
like to take.

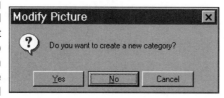

16. Click Yes. The New Category dialog shown in Figure 15-6 appears. This is the second dialog box we created. It appears in response to an answer of Yes from the user.

Figure 15-6:
The first
step in
adding a
new
category is
to ask the
user for the
category's
name.

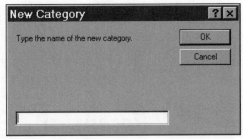

17. Type Sweets, and then click OK. Access grinds away while it creates a new record and inserts the name of our new category. The familiar Insert Object dialog box appears.

18. Click the Create from File radio button. Type the location and the name of your new SWEETS.BMP file in the File field. Check the Link check box. Click OK.

19. As shown in Figure 15-7, Access automatically inserts the new category and updates the picture in the current record.

Figure 15-7:
The On Dbl
Click event
automatically
updates the
form so that
the current
record uses
the new
category.

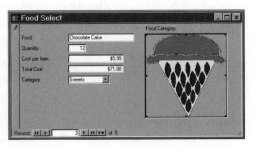

So, how would you use this form? The form in Chapter 11 would work well for most of the people doing data entry because they wouldn't need to add new categories to the database. Managers and administrators could use this form so they could define new categories or modify old categories as needed.

One capability is still missing from this database. It lacks a capability for deleting old categories. To provide this functionality, you actually need a separate maintenance program or a longer On Dbl Click event procedure. Before allowing an administrator to delete an old category, the delete procedure needs to assign a new category value to all the records that belonged in the old category.

Using Forms to Their Full Potential

We've described forms as the central processing area for most database applications. It's too difficult to manage tables without using a form. For you as the programmer, this fact means that you need to find better ways to use forms without adding a lot of code.

Access can perform a great deal of work without requiring you to add even a single line of code. Chapter 11 shows that even a one-line macro can do a lot of work, and our first example in this chapter certainly wasn't all that long.

However, these examples didn't take one thing into account. A piece of code can help you enhance a form's capabilities, but it can't save on-screen real estate. A form should never extend outside the screen area, which means you have to start adding subforms and other messy constructs if you waste space on a form.

Some forms need so much data that Advanced buttons leading to subforms really are necessary. Other forms, such as the example in this chapter, are simple enough that they barely fill the screen, much less use all of it.

We have space wasted on our form. Notice that we have a Category field and a category picture. That's wasted space you could use for something else (if it was really needed).

Pictures are helpful whenever you want the user to see something at a glance. The food group (Category field) is a good example of information you would want the user to see at a glance, so the text representation is wasted space.

We can't remove the Category field right now because there isn't any other way to change categories. However, we can take care of that by attaching some code to the On Click event of our Food Picture control. If the user single-clicks the picture, the category changes. A double-click allows the user to add a new category or modify an existing one. (We'll also add this single-click procedure to the other form to make it easier to use.)

Using a single-click technique on the Category field works fine because we're unlikely to have more than 10 selections. However, think twice about using a single-click technique when you get beyond that 10-selection limit. Users tend to get a little frustrated single-clicking a picture more than 10 times to find the right category. To make things more convenient for the user, use a drop-down list if you have more than 10 items.

1. Open Access and the My Database database (if necessary).
2. Click the Module tab of the Database dialog.
3. Click New. An Access BASIC module appears.
4. To create a new module, choose Insert⇨Procedure. Complete the Insert Procedure dialog box as shown in Figure 15-8.

In this case, we need to create a public Access BASIC module so we can use the same procedure from both the Food Inventory Control 1 and the Food Inventory Control 2 forms. Using the standard event procedure won't provide this flexibility; we'd have to duplicate the same code in two modules.

Figure 15-8:
The Insert Procedure dialog box defines the name and type of a new procedure.

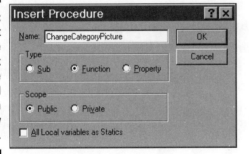

5. Click OK to create the module.
6. Type the following program into the module. You do not need to add the Public Function or End Function lines:

```
Public Function ChangeCategoryPicture()

    'Create some variables.

    Dim FoodGroups As Control    'A copy of our Food Group control

    'Initialize our control.

    Set FoodGroups = Forms![Food Inventory Control 2]![Food Group]

    'Set the focus to the Food Group control.

    FoodGroups.SetFocus
```

(continued)

(continued)

```
'Change the List Index property as needed to advance the picture
'to the next item.  If we're at the end of the list, go to the
'beginning of the list.  Otherwise, increment the list count.

If FoodGroups.ListCount = FoodGroups.ListIndex + 1 Then
    SendKeys "{F4}"           'Open the combo box.
    SendKeys "^{HOME}"        'Go to the beginning of the list.
    SendKeys "{ENTER}"        'Accept the new value.
Else
    SendKeys "{F4}"           'Open the combo box.
    SendKeys "{DOWN}"         'Select the next value.
    SendKeys "{ENTER}"        'Accept the new value.
End If

End Function
```

7. Save the module. When asked for a module name, type **Form Functions**.

8. Compile the module by choosing Run⇨Compile Loaded Modules. Close the module.

9. Select the Forms tab of the Database dialog box.

10. Open the Food Inventory Control 2 form in design view.

11. Right-click the Food Picture control, and select Properties from the context menu that's displayed.

12. Click the On Click event. Choose [Event Procedure] from the drop-down list, and then click the ellipsis next to the event. An Access BASIC module appears.

13. Type the following statement between the Private Sub and End Sub lines:

```
ChangeCategoryPicture
```

14. Save the module. Compile the module by choosing Run⇨Compile Loaded Modules. Close the module.

15. Delete the label associated with the Food Group combo box.

You'll sometimes need to keep a control visible even though you don't want the user to access it anymore. You can effectively hide a control while retaining access to it by setting the dimensions of the control to 0. Changing the background color of the control to match that of the form background and setting the Special Effect property to flat completes the task.

16. Change the Food Group combo box Width and Height properties to 0.

17. Change the number of List Rows to 1.

18. Change the Back Color property to match that of the form (just select gray from the Color dialog box accessed through the ellipsis next to the property field).

19. Change the Special Effect property to flat.

20. Click the Form View button for the Food Inventory Control 2 form.

21. Click the Food Picture control. The category changes to the next one in the list. (You may also see a momentary flash from the Food Group control, an unavoidable effect of this particular object control method.)

22. Save the form by clicking the Save button on the toolbox.

23. Close the Food Inventory Control 2 form.

As you can see in Figure 15-9, we now have one additional line available on our form. Another benefit of this design is that less chance exists of confusing the user with two fields that serve the same purpose. Using forms to their full potential can mean a variety of things, depending on the current application. However, using resources efficiently should be the goal of every application.

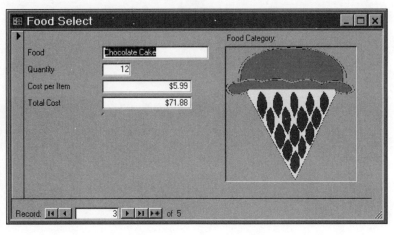

Figure 15-9: Our modified form shows one of the benefits of form space optimization: extra room for another data field.

Test your newfound knowledge

1. Access allows you to modify graphical OLE objects by using:.

   a. A Bound or an Unbound Object Frame control.

   b. A paintbrush and some paints.

   c. A secret password known only to Microsoft programmers and a few members of the press.

   d. Large quantities of memory and extreme patience.

2. You can never assume anything about database OLE objects because:.

   a. They're very unreliable and tend to run away at a moment's notice.

   b. Access deletes them at random just to make life difficult.

   c. Databases can hide the objects based on the phase of the moon and the position of the sun.

   d. They may be located on a network drive and become inaccessible when the user logs out or someone else is using them.

Chapter 16

Writing OLE Programs with Visual BASIC

In This Chapter

▶ Using the Insert Object dialog box

▶ Using the Paste Special dialog box

▶ Adding in-place activation

▶ Creating OLE servers

*V*isual BASIC is an easy-to-learn programming language which you can use to create programs that can be OLE servers or OLE clients. To write a Visual BASIC program, you just have to design your program's user interface and then write BASIC commands to make your program work.

This chapter focuses exclusively on Visual BASIC version 4.0, which can be used to write OLE servers or clients for both 16-bit (Windows 3.1) and 32-bit (Windows 95) operating systems. Older versions of Visual BASIC (3.0, 2.0, and 1.0) can create only OLE client programs.

Using the Insert Object Dialog Box

The Insert Object dialog box lets you embed or link whole files into an OLE client Visual BASIC program. The following steps show you how to create a simple Visual BASIC program that displays an Insert Object dialog box.

The following sample Visual BASIC programs don't support in-place activation, which we discuss later in this chapter:

1. Load Visual BASIC.

2. Click the OLE control on the Toolbox and draw the OLE container on the form, as shown in Figure 16-1. An Insert Object dialog box appears.

3. Click Cancel to remove the Insert Object dialog box. (This dialog box lets you, as the programmer, link or embed OLE objects into your program at design time.)

4. Click the CommandButton control on the Toolbox and draw two buttons on the form.

5. Use the Properties window to change the caption of Command1 to **Use OLE** and its name to **cmdOLE**.

6. Use the Properties window to change the caption of Command2 to **Exit** and its name to **cmdExit**.

7. Double-click the Exit button to open the Code window.

8. Type **End** in the Private Sub cmdExit_Click( ) procedure as follows:

```
Private Sub cmdExit_Click();
    End
End Sub
```

9. Click in the Object list box and choose cmdOLE.

10. Type **OLE1.InsertObjDlg** in the Private Sub cmdOLE_Click( ) procedure as follows:

```
Private Sub cmdOLE_Click()
    OLE1.InsertObjDlg
End Sub
```

Even though this Visual BASIC code looks deceptively simple, it actually tells your Visual BASIC program how to use the Insert Object dialog box to link or embed files.

OLE control   OLE container

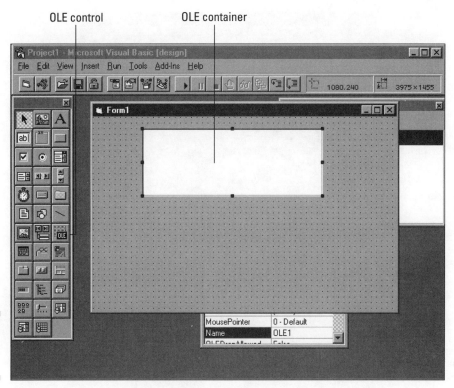

Figure 16-1:
The OLE
container.

Testing OLE embedding

Once you've created your Visual BASIC program, you can test its OLE embedding capabilities by following these steps:

1. Press F5 to run your program.

2. Click the Use OLE button. The Insert Object dialog box appears, as shown in Figure 16-2.

3. Click the Create New radio button.

4. Choose Bitmap Image or Paintbrush Picture from the Object Type list box, and click OK. As shown in Figure 16-3, a Microsoft Paintbrush (or Microsoft Paint) window appears.

5. Draw a picture. When you're done, choose File⇔Exit & Return to. As shown in Figure 16-4, your Visual BASIC program displays your drawing in the OLE container.

6. Click the Exit button to stop your Visual BASIC program.

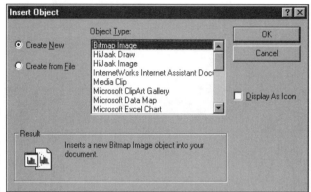

Figure 16-2:
The Insert
Object
dialog box.

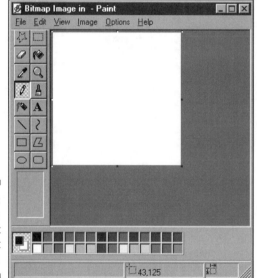

Figure 16-3:
The
Microsoft
Paint
window.

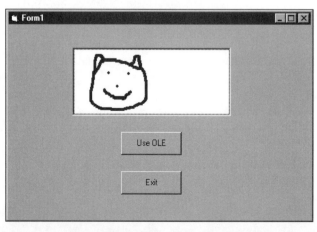

Figure 16-4:
A Paint
picture
embedded
in the
sample
Visual
BASIC
program.

Testing OLE linking

After you've created your Visual BASIC program, you can test its OLE linking capabilities by following these steps:

1. Load Microsoft Paintbrush (or Microsoft Paint) and draw a picture.

2. Choose File⇨Save (or press Ctrl+S). A Save As dialog box appears.

3. Type a filename for your drawing and click Save.

4. Switch to Visual BASIC and run your program by pressing F5.

5. Click the Use OLE button. The Insert Object dialog box appears (see Figure 16-2).

6. Click the Create from File radio button. The Insert Object dialog box changes its appearance, as shown in Figure 16-5.

7. Select the Link check box.

8. Click the Browse button. A Browse dialog box appears.

9. Choose the filename (such as a Paint file) that you want to link to your Visual BASIC program, and click Insert.

10. Click OK. Your Visual BASIC program displays the linked file.

11. Switch to the program that created the file you chose in step 9 (such as Microsoft Paint) and edit and save the file.

12. Switch back to your Visual BASIC program and double-click the linked OLE object. Notice that the OLE link displays the changed file in your Visual BASIC program.

13. Click the Exit button to stop your Visual BASIC program.

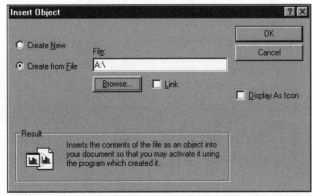

Figure 16-5:
The Insert Object dialog box, ready to create an OLE link.

Using the Paste Special Dialog Box

The Insert Object dialog box embeds or links whole files into an OLE client Visual BASIC program. If you just want to use part of a file as an OLE object, you can use the Paste Special dialog box instead. By using the Paste Special dialog box, you can copy an OLE object to the clipboard and then embed or link it to your Visual BASIC program.

This sample Visual BASIC program doesn't support in-place activation.

1. Load Visual BASIC.

2. Click the OLE control on the Toolbox and draw the OLE container on the form (see Figure 16-1). An Insert Object dialog box appears.

3. Click Cancel to remove the Insert Object dialog box. (You may use this dialog box later for linking or embedding OLE objects into your program at design time.)

4. Click the CommandButton control on the Toolbox and draw two buttons on the form.

5. Use the Properties window to change the caption of Command1 to **Use OLE** and its name to **cmdOLE**.

6. Use the Properties window to change the caption of Command22 to **Exit** and its name to **cmdExit**.

7. Double-click the Exit button to open the Code window.

8. Type **End** in the Private Sub cmdExit_Click( ) procedure as follows:

```
Private Sub cmdExit_Click();
  End
End Sub
```

9. Click in the Object list box and choose cmdOLE.

10. Type the following code in the Private Sub cmdOLE_Click( ) procedure. You don't have to type the first and last lines because Visual BASIC will do that for you automatically.

```
Private Sub cmdOLE_Click()
  If OLE1.PasteOK = True Then
    OLE1.PasteSpecialDlg
  End If
  ' Display a message if there is nothing on the clipboard
  If OLE1.OLEType = 3 Then
    MsgBox "Nothing has been copied or cut to the clip-
        board."
```

```
      End If
   End Sub
```

This simple Visual BASIC procedure tells your Visual BASIC program how to paste an OLE object stored on the clipboard. If nothing has been copied or cut to the clipboard, a message box appears and displays, "Nothing has been copied or cut to the clipboard."

Testing OLE embedding

Once you've created your Visual BASIC program that uses the Paste Special dialog box, you can test its OLE embedding capabilities by following these steps:

1. Load Microsoft Paintbrush (or Microsoft Paint) and draw a picture.

2. Use the Selection tool to select part or all of your drawing.

3. Choose Edit⇨Copy (or press Ctrl+C).

4. Switch to Visual BASIC and press F5 to run your program.

5. Click the Use OLE button. The Paste Special dialog box appears, as shown in Figure 16-6.

6. In the Object Type list box, choose Bitmap Image. Click OK. Your Visual BASIC program displays the embedded OLE data.

7. Click the Exit button to stop your Visual BASIC program.

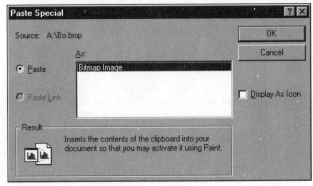

Figure 16-6:
The Paste Special dialog box.

Testing OLE linking

Now that you've created your Visual BASIC program you can test its OLE linking capabilities by following these steps:

1. Load a program such as Microsoft Word or Microsoft Excel, and type some text or numbers.

2. Choose File⇨Save (or press Ctrl+S). A Save As dialog box appears.

3. Type a filename for your drawing and click Save.

4. Highlight your text or numbers.

5. Choose Edit⇨Copy (or press Ctrl+C).

6. Switch to Visual BASIC and run your program by pressing F5.

7. Click the Use OLE button. The Paste Special dialog box appears (see Figure 16-6).

8. Click the Paste Link radio button.

9. Click OK. Your Visual BASIC program displays the linked OLE data.

10. Switch to the program that created the file you saved in step 3 (such as Microsoft Word) and edit the file.

11. Switch back to your Visual BASIC program to verify that the OLE link displays the changed file in your Visual BASIC program.

12. Click the Exit button to stop your Visual BASIC program.

A program can use both the Insert Object and the Paste Special dialog boxes. The previous examples simply isolate the minimum amount of code necessary for using either type of dialog box.

Adding In-Place Activation

An OLE 2 client program must support in-place activation, which lets you edit an embedded OLE object by replacing the client's menus with the OLE server's menus.

To allow for in-place activation within a Visual BASIC program, your Visual BASIC program must display pull-down menus. When you click an embedded OLE object, the pull-down menus of the OLE server (such as Microsoft Excel) appear.

The OLE server can display its pull-down menus within a Visual BASIC program in two ways:

✔ By replacing one or more titles on the Visual BASIC program menu bar

✔ By adding its own menu titles to the Visual BASIC program menu bar

Figure 16-7 shows a typical menu bar in a Visual BASIC program. If an OLE server (such as Microsoft Excel) replaces the menu titles in the menu bar, the Visual BASIC program menu title changes as shown in Figure 16-8.

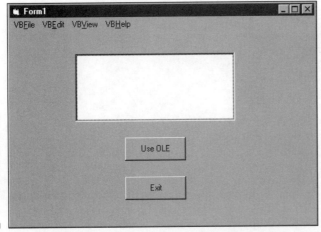

Figure 16-7:
A typical
menu bar in
a Visual
BASIC
program.

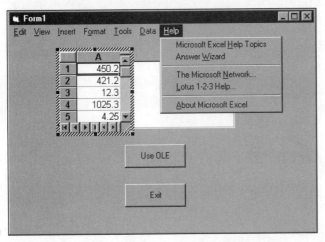

Figure 16-8:
Microsoft
Excel's
menu bar
wiping out
the entire
Visual
BASIC menu
bar.

In many cases, you may want to keep portions of your Visual BASIC menu bar intact and just include the menu bar of the OLE server, as shown in Figure 16-9. For example, you won't want an OLE server (such as Microsoft Excel) to wipe out your Visual BASIC program's File menu title or else your Visual BASIC program won't be able to save, print, or exit until the OLE server's menu bar goes away.

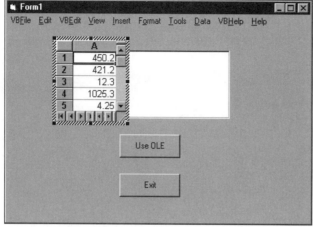

Figure 16-9:
Microsoft
Excel's
menu bar
keeping part
of the Visual
BASIC menu
bar intact.

To keep your Visual BASIC program's menu titles intact when the OLE server's menus appear, you have to use the Menu Editor to change the NegotiatePosition property of your menu titles.

For a menu title that you want to keep intact, give it a NegotiatePosition from the following list, as shown in Figure 16-10:

- 0 - None
- 1 - Left
- 2 - Middle
- 3 - Right

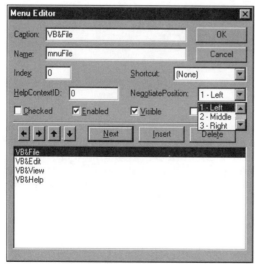

Figure 16-10:
Visual
BASIC's
Menu Editor
displaying
all the
acceptable
Negotiate-
Position
values.

For menu titles that you want the OLE server's menu titles to replace, set their NegotiatePosition properties to 0-None.

In Figure 16-9, the VBFile menu title has a NegotiatePosition value of 1-Left, so it appears to the far left of the menu bar. The VBEdit menu title has a NegotiatePosition value of 2-Middle, so it appears in the middle of the menu bar. The VBHelp menu title has a NegotiatePosition value of 3-Right, so it appears to the far right of the menu bar.

Two or more menu titles can have the same NegotiatePosition values.

Creating OLE Servers

OLE servers are nothing more than programs that provide objects for another program to use. Many OLE servers are complete programs that provide their own user interface (such as Microsoft Excel). However, OLE servers don't have to have a user interface at all and can exist solely to provide objects for another program.

The following example shows how to create a simple OLE server so you can understand the bare minimum of code necessary for creating an OLE server in Visual BASIC.

Visual BASIC 4.0 can create two types of OLE servers: In-Process and Out-of-Process servers. An In-Process server is actually a dynamic link library (DLL), while an Out-of-Process server is an executable (EXE) file. This example shows how to create an Out-of-Process (EXE) OLE server.

An OLE server provides objects for other programs to use. In Visual BASIC, objects are defined by a special file called a class module.

A class module defines an object and contains methods and properties. Methods perform actions on the object (class), and properties describe the characteristics of an object (class).

Writing an OLE server

The following example shows how to create a simple OLE server:

1. Load Visual BASIC.

2. Choose Tools⇨Options. An Options dialog box appears.

3. Click the Project tab, which is shown in Figure 16-11.

4. Click in the Startup Form list box and choose Sub Main.

5. Type **OLEObject** in the Project Name field.

6. Click the OLE Server radio button in the StartMode group.

7. Type **OLE Test** in the Application Description box, and click OK.

8. Choose Insert⇨Module. The Module1 code window appears.

9. Choose Insert⇨Procedure. An Insert Procedure dialog box appears.

10. Type **Main** in the Name box, click the Sub radio button, click the Public radio button, and click OK.

11. Choose Insert⇨Class Module. The Class1 code window appears.

12. Press F4 to display the Properties window, and change the following properties:

Property	*Value*
Instancing	2 - Creatable MultiUse
Public	True

13. Type the following in the Class1 code window:

```
Public TextString As String
Dim IntegerData As Integer
```

14. Choose Insert⇨Procedure. An Insert Procedure dialog box appears.

15. Type **Cubed** in the Name box, click the Function radio button, and click OK.

16. Modify the function as follows:

```
Public Function Cubed (X As Integer) As Integer
  Cubed = X * X * X
End Function
```

17. Choose Insert⇨Procedure. As shown in Figure 16-12, an Insert Procedure dialog box appears.

18. Type **Quantity** in the Name field, click the Property radio button, and click OK.

19. Modify the property as follows:

```
Public Property Get Quantity ()
  Quantity = IntegerData
End Property
```

20. Click in the Proc list box and choose Quantity [PropertyLet].

21. Modify the property as follows:

```
Public Property Let Quantity (vNewValue)
   IntegerData = vNewValue
End Property
```

22. Press Ctrl+F5 to choose the Start With Full Compile option. This compiles and runs your OLE server.

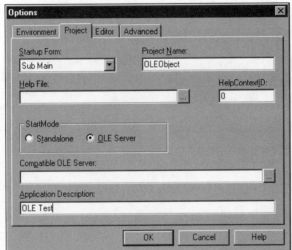

Figure 16-11:
The Project
tab in the
Options
dialog box.

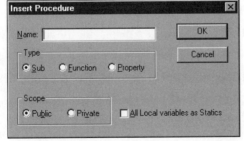

Figure 16-12:
The Insert
Procedure
dialog box.

Testing your OLE server

After you've created and successfully compiled your OLE server, you'll want to create a test program to verify that the OLE server actually works. The following example shows how to create this simple test program:

1. Load a second copy of Visual BASIC.

2. Draw a command button on the form.

3. Double-click the command button to open the code window.

4. Modify the event procedure as follows:

```
Private Sub Command1_Click()
' Declare a variable object
Dim OLEObject As Object

' Create that object
Set OLEObject = CreateObject("OLEObject.Class1")

' Use the object's Cubed method
MsgBox Str (OLEObject.Cubed(3))
MsgBox Str (OLEObject.Cubed(4))
MsgBox Str (OLEObject.Cubed(5))

' Change the object's properties
OLEOBject.Quantity = 99
MsgBox Str (OLEObject.Quantity)

OLEObject.TextString = "See? OLE actually works!"
MsgBox OLEObject.TextString
End Property
```

5. Press F5 to run the OLE test program.

6. Click the Command1 button. A Project1 dialog box appears, displaying the cube of 3, which is 27.

7. Click OK. A Project1 dialog box appears, displaying the cube of 4, which is 64.

8. Click OK. A Project1 dialog box appears, displaying the cube of 5, which is 125.

9. Click OK. A Project1 dialog box appears, displaying the number 99.

10. Click OK. A Project1 dialog box appears, displaying the message, "See? OLE actually works!"

11. Click OK.

12. Choose Run⇨End to stop the OLE test program.

13. Switch to the copy of Visual BASIC running your OLE server.

14. Choose Run⇨End to stop the OLE server program.

TECHNICAL STUFF

Registering your Visual BASIC OLE server

OLE works only as long as your Visual BASIC OLE program is properly registered in the Windows registry file. (We talk about registry specifics in Chapter 21.) Fortunately, Visual BASIC will automatically register your compiled program when you run it.

If you've compiled your Visual BASIC program into an EXE file, there are two ways you can install it on another computer and register it in the Windows registry file.

First, you can run your Visual BASIC program with the following command line parameter:

```
/ REGSERVER
```

Second (this is the easier way), you can use the Visual BASIC Setup Wizard to create an installation program for you. When a user installs a program created by the Visual BASIC Setup Wizard, the Setup Wizard automatically registers your Visual BASIC program in the Windows registry.

Test your newfound knowledge

1. What is the difference between Visual BASIC 4.0 and older versions of Visual BASIC (versions 3.0, 2.0, and 1.0)?

   a. The version numbers are different and imply that Microsoft is actually improving Visual BASIC (which justifies asking for more money).

   b. Visual BASIC 4.0 is only designed to help you write OS/2 programs, while older versions of Visual BASIC will only let you write CP/M-80 programs.

   c. Visual BASIC 4.0 lets you create OLE server and client programs. Older versions of Visual BASIC let you create only OLE client programs.

   d. By using any version of Visual BASIC, you can write your own operating system and help put Microsoft out of business for good.

2. Name the two types of OLE servers that Visual BASIC 4.0 can create.

   a. An In-Process server (DLL) and an Out-of-Process server (EXE).

   b. Visual BASIC can't create OLE servers. Everyone knows that Microsoft products never follow any standards that Microsoft creates.

   c. The names of the two types of OLE servers that Visual BASIC can create are Fred and Barney.

   d. Visual BASIC can create an OLE server, an OLE host, and an OLE chef for your wining and dining pleasure.

The 5th Wave — By Rich Tennant

"THE MANUFACTURERS OF A DATA ENCRYPTION PROGRAM THAT SCRAMBLES MESSAGES INTO A BRAINLESS MORASS OF INDECIPHERABLE CODE, HAS JUST FILED A 'LOOK AND FEEL' COPYRIGHT SUIT AGAINST OUR WORD PROCESSING PROGRAM."

Chapter 17

Writing OLE Programs with Delphi

●●

In This Chapter

▶ Using the Insert Object dialog box

▶ Using the Paste Special dialog box

▶ Adding in-place activation

●●

Delphi is Borland International's answer to Microsoft's Visual BASIC. Like Visual BASIC, Delphi is known as a Rapid Application Development (RAD) tool, which lets you design your program's user interface and then write commands to make that user interface do something useful. The main difference between Delphi and Visual BASIC is that Delphi uses Pascal for its commands while Visual BASIC uses BASIC.

Delphi comes in two versions: a 16-bit (Windows 3.1) version and a 32-bit (Windows 95) version. The 16-bit version of Delphi can only create programs that offer OLE 2 client capabilities. The 32-bit version of Delphi can create programs that offer both OLE 2 client and server capabilities.

This chapter focuses exclusively on the 16-bit version of Delphi. At the time of this writing, the 32-bit version of Delphi isn't available, although it might be available by the time you read this. Then again, considering the state of software development, the 32-bit version of Delphi may still be available *Real Soon Now*.

Using the Insert Object Dialog Box

The Insert Object dialog box is Delphi's way of embedding or linking whole files into a Delphi program. The following steps show you how to create a simple Delphi program that displays an Insert Object dialog box.

The following sample Delphi programs don't support in-place activation, which you'll learn how to add in a later section of this chapter.

1. Load Delphi.

2. Click the System tab on the Component palette.

3. Click the OleContainer icon and draw the OLE container on the form as shown in Figure 17-1.

4. Use the Object Inspector to change the AutoSize property of the OLE container to True.

5. Click the Standard tab on the Component palette and draw two buttons on the form.

6. Use the Object Inspector to change the caption of Button1 to **Use OLE** and its name to **OLEbutton**.

7. Use the Object Inspector to change the caption of Button2 to **Exit** and its name to **Exit**.

8. Double-click the Exit button to open the Code editor.

9. Type **Halt;** in the TForm1.ExitClick procedure, as shown in the following code:

```
procedure TForm1.ExitClick(Sender: TObject);
begin
  Halt;
end;
```

10. Add ToCtrl under the *uses* portion of the program as follows:

```
uses
    SysUtils, WinTypes, WinProcs, Messages, Classes, Graphics,
            Controls, Forms, Dialogs, StdCtrls, ToCtrl;
```

11. Press F12 to view the form again.

12. Double-click the Use OLE button to open the Code editor.

13. Type the following code in the TForm1.OLEbuttonClick procedure:

```
procedure TForm1.OLEbuttonClick(Sender: TObject);
var
  Info : Pointer;
begin
  if InsertOLEObjectDlg (Form1, 0, Info) then
    InitializeOLEObject (Info);
end;
```

14. Type the following procedure in the *implementation* portion of the program. (The following procedure should appear before the TForm1.OLEbuttonClick procedure you typed in step 13.):

```
procedure TForm1.InitializeOLEobject (Info:Pointer);
begin
  OLEContainer1.PInitInfo := Info;
  ReleaseOLEInitInfo (Info);
end;
```

15. Add the line, "procedure InitializeOLEobject (Info:Pointer);"—without the quotation marks—under the *type* section as follows:

```
type
  TForm1 = class(TForm)
    OleContainer1: TOleContainer;
    OLEbutton: TButton;
    Exit: TButton;
    procedure ExitClick(Sender: TObject);
    procedure InitializeOLEobject (Info:Pointer);
    procedure OLEbuttonClick(Sender: TObject);
```

Your OLE Delphi program is now ready to run.

OLE container   OLE container icon

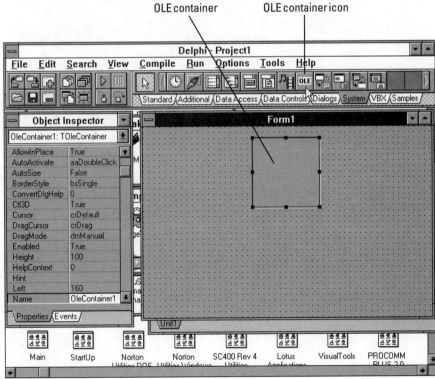

Figure 17-1:
The OLE
container
component.

Testing OLE embedding

Now you can test the OLE embedding capabilities of your Delphi program by following these steps:

1. Press F9 to run your program.

2. Click the Use OLE button. The Insert Object dialog box appears, as shown in Figure 17-2.

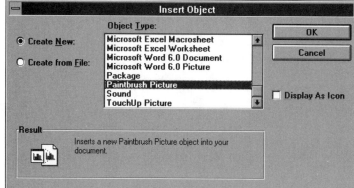

Figure 17-2:
The Insert
Object
dialog box.

3. Click the Create New radio button.

4. Choose Paintbrush Picture from the Object Type list box and click OK. As shown in Figure 17-3, a Microsoft Paintbrush (or Microsoft Paint) window appears.

5. Draw a picture. When you're done, choose File⇨Update.

6. Choose File⇨Exit & Return to. As shown in Figure 17-4, your Delphi program displays your drawing in the OLE container.

7. Click the Exit button to stop your Delphi program.

Testing OLE linking

Once you've created your Delphi program, you can test its OLE linking capabilities by following these steps:

1. Load Microsoft Paintbrush (or Microsoft Paint) and draw a picture.

2. Choose File⇨Save (or press Ctrl+S). A Save As dialog box appears.

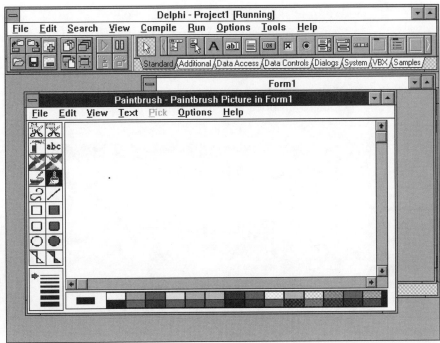

Figure 17-3:
The
Microsoft
Paintbrush
window.

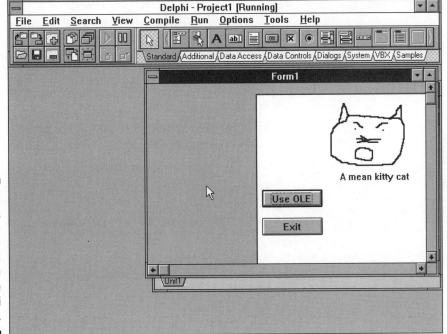

Figure 17-4:
A
Paintbrush
picture
embedded
in the
sample
Delphi
program.

3. Type a filename for your drawing and click OK.

4. Switch to Delphi and run your program by pressing F9.

5. Click the Use OLE button. The Insert Object dialog box appears (see Figure 17-2).

6. Click the Create from File radio button. The Insert Object dialog box changes its appearance as shown in Figure 17-5.

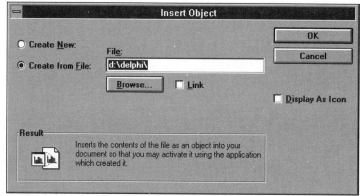

Figure 17-5:
The Insert
Object
dialog box,
ready to
create an
OLE link.

7. Select the Link check box.

8. Click the Browse button. A Browse dialog box appears.

9. Choose the filename (such as a Paintbrush file) that you want to link to your Delphi program, and click OK twice. Your Delphi program displays the linked file.

10. Switch to the program that created the file you chose in step 9 (such as Microsoft Paintbrush) and edit the file.

11. Switch back to your Delphi program to verify that the OLE link displays the changed file in your Delphi program.

12. Click the Exit button to stop your Delphi program.

Using the Paste Special Dialog Box

The drawback to using the Insert Object dialog box is that you must embed or link whole files, which can be like stuffing a whole pizza in your mouth just because you want to eat one slice of pepperoni.

As an alternative, Delphi lets you embed and link OLE objects that you've copied onto the clipboard. In this way, you can selectively embed or link portions of a file, rather than the whole file.

This sample Delphi program does not support in-place activation, which we'll discuss in a later section.

1. Load Delphi.

2. Click the System tab on the Component palette.

3. Click the OleContainer icon and draw the OLE container on the form (see Figure 17-1).

4. Use the Object Inspector to change the AutoSize property of the OLE container to True.

5. Click the Standard tab on the Component palette and draw two buttons on the form.

6. Use the Object Inspector to change the caption of Button1 to **Use OLE** and its name to **OLEbutton**.

7. Use the Object Inspector to change the caption of Button2 to **Exit** and its name to **Exit**.

8. Double-click the Exit button to open the Code editor.

9. Type **Halt;** in the TForm1.ExitClick procedure as follows:

```
procedure TForm1.ExitClick(Sender: TObject);
begin
  Halt;
end;
```

10. Add ToCtrl and BOLEDefs under the *uses* portion of the program as follows:

```
uses
    SysUtils, WinTypes, WinProcs, Messages, Classes, Graphics,
          Controls, Forms, Dialogs, StdCtrls, ToCtrl, BOLEDefs;
```

11. Press F12 to view the form again.

12. Double-click the Use OLE button to open the Code editor.

13. Type the following code in the TForm1.OLEbuttonClick procedure:

```
procedure TForm1.OLEbuttonClick(Sender: TObject);
var
  FEmbedClipFmt, FLinkClipFmt: Word;
  Fmts: array[0..1] of BOLEFormat;
  TheFormat: Word;
```

```
    TheHandle: THandle;
    TheInfo: Pointer;
begin
  FEmbedClipFmt := RegisterClipboardFormat('Embedded Object');
  FLinkClipFmt := RegisterClipboardFormat ('Link Source');
  Fmts[0].fmtId := FEmbedClipFmt;
  Fmts[0].fmtMedium := BOLEMediumCalc(FEmbedClipFmt);
  Fmts[0].fmtIsLinkable := False;
  StrPCopy (Fmts[0].fmtName, '%s');
  StrPCopy (Fmts[0].fmtResultName, '%s');
  Fmts[1].fmtId := FLinkClipFmt;
  Fmts[1].fmtMedium := BOLEMediumCalc(FLinkClipFmt);
  Fmts[1].fmtIsLinkable := True;
  StrPCopy (Fmts[1].fmtName, '%s');
  StrPCopy (Fmts[1].fmtResultName, '%s');
  if PasteSpecialEnabled(Self, Fmts) then
     if PasteSpecialDlg(Form1, Fmts, 0, TheFormat, TheHandle, TheInfo) then
        OLEContainer1.PInitInfo := TheInfo;
end;
```

Even though the preceding Delphi code looks daunting and a bit confusing, it simply tells your Delphi program how to paste OLE objects stored on the clipboard. (If you really want to know how each Delphi command works, do yourself a favor and get *Delphi For Dummies*, IDG Books Worldwide.)

Testing OLE embedding

Follow these steps to test your Delphi program's embedding capabilities:

1. Load Microsoft Paintbrush (or Microsoft Paint) and draw a picture.

2. Use the Selection tool to select part or all of your drawing.

3. Choose Edit⇨Copy (or press Ctrl+C).

4. Switch to Delphi and press F9 to run your program.

5. Click the Use OLE button. The Paste Special dialog box appears, as shown in Figure 17-6.

6. In the Object Type list box, choose Paintbrush Picture. Then, click OK. Your Delphi program displays the embedded OLE data.

7. Click the Exit button to stop your Delphi program.

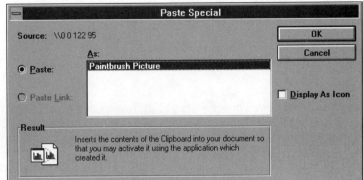

Testing OLE linking

After you've created your Delphi program, you can test its OLE linking capabilities by following these steps:

1. Load Microsoft Paintbrush (or Microsoft Paint) and draw a picture.

2. Choose File➪Save (or press Ctrl+S). A Save As dialog box appears.

3. Type a filename for your drawing and click OK.

4. Use the Selection tool to select part or all of your drawing.

5. Choose Edit➪Copy (or press Ctrl+C).

6. Switch to Delphi and run your program by pressing F9.

7. Click the Use OLE button. The Paste Special dialog box appears (see Figure 17-6).

8. Click the Paste Link radio button.

9. Choose Paintbrush Picture from the Object Type list box and click OK. Your Delphi program displays the linked OLE data.

10. Switch to the program that created the drawing (such as Microsoft Paintbrush) and edit the file.

11. Switch back to your Delphi program to verify that the OLE link displays the changed file in your Delphi program.

12. Click the Exit button to stop your Delphi program.

A program can use both the Insert Object and the Paste Special dialog boxes. The previous examples simply isolate the minimum amount of code necessary for using either type of dialog box.

Using In-Place Activation

An OLE 2 client program must support in-place activation, which lets you edit an embedded OLE object by replacing the client's menus with the OLE server's menus.

To allow for in-place activation within a Delphi program, your Delphi program must display pull-down menus. When you click on an embedded OLE object, the pull-down menus of the OLE server (such as Microsoft Excel) appear.

The OLE server can display its pull-down menus within a Delphi program in two ways:

✔ By replacing one or more titles on the Delphi program menu bar.

✔ By adding its own menu titles to the Delphi program menu bar.

Figure 17-7 shows a typical menu bar in a Delphi program. If an OLE server (such as Microsoft Excel) replaces the menu titles in the menu bar, the Delphi program menu bar changes as shown in Figure 17-8.

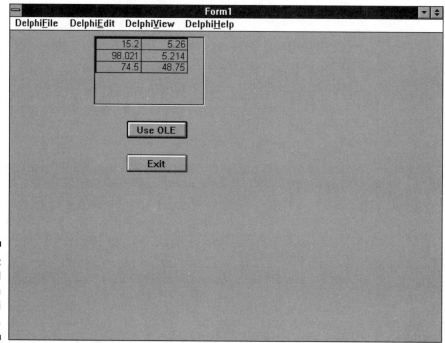

Figure 17-7:
A typical menu bar in a Delphi program.

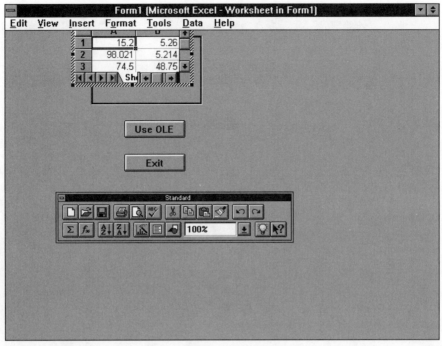

Figure 17-8:
Microsoft
Excel's
menu bar
wiping out
the entire
Delphi menu
bar.

In many cases, you may want to keep portions of your Delphi menu bar intact and just include the menu bar of the OLE server, as shown in Figure 17-9. For example, you won't want an OLE server (such as Microsoft Excel) to wipe out your Delphi program's File menu title because your Delphi program won't be able to save, print, or exit until the OLE server's menu bar goes away.

To keep your Delphi program's menu titles intact when the OLE server's menus appear, you have to use the Object Inspector to change the GroupIndex property of your menu titles:

  ✔ For a menu title that you want to keep intact, give it a GroupIndex value of 0, 2, 4, 6, or any number greater than 6.
  ✔ For menu titles that you want the OLE server's menu titles to replace, give them a GroupIndex value of 1, 3, or 5.

In Figure 17-9, the DelphiFile menu title has a GroupIndex value of 0, so it appears to the far left of the menu bar. If the DelphiFile menu title had a different GroupIndex value (such as 2), it would no longer appear to the far left of the menu bar.

Two or more menu titles can have the same GroupIndex value.

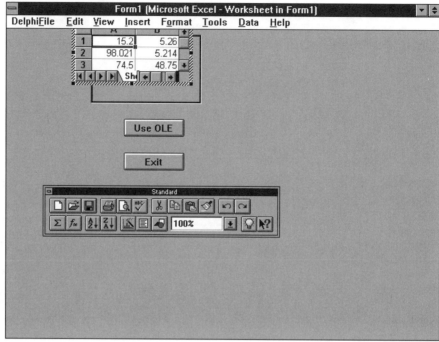

Test your newfound knowledge

1. What are the two differences between the 16-bit and the 32-bit versions of Delphi?

   a. The 32-bit version is twice as hard to learn as the 16-bit version.

   b. If Microsoft sold the 32-bit version of Delphi, everybody would have bought a copy one minute after midnight on the day of its introduction.

   c. There's no difference whatsoever because Windows 95 is still a 16-bit program at heart.

   d. The 16-bit version of Delphi can create only OLE client programs, while the 32-bit version can create both OLE client and server programs.

2. What is the difference between the Insert Object dialog box and the Paste Special dialog box?

   a. The Insert Object dialog box lets you link or embed whole files. The Paste Special dialog box lets you copy OLE objects to the clipboard before linking or embedding them into your program.

   b. The Insert Object dialog box inserts an object in the Paste Special dialog box, which glues an OLE object onto your computer screen.

   c. The Paste Special dialog box uses special paste to make sure your OLE objects stick where they are supposed to be.

   d. Both dialog boxes look like cute little rectangles that appear on your screen whenever something goes horribly wrong with your computer.

Chapter 18

Testing Your Application

• •

In This Chapter

▶ Understanding how computers break applications

▶ Finding bugs in your application

▶ Using proper computer communication techniques

• •

Computers have very simple minds. They always do exactly what you tell them to do, and that's a problem. A computer is a disaster waiting to happen because it's simply too stupid to know any better. If your computer could walk, you could tell it to jump off a cliff and it would happily do so.

That's only part of the problem. It's easy to believe the computer is smart when you see it perform math faster than any human. It's also easy to forget that the computer can't reason.

Has anyone ever teased you over a mix-up of words? The other person knew what you meant to say, even though it didn't come out right. A computer can't figure out what you *meant* to say, it only knows what you *did* say. That's why it's important to make sure that what you tell the computer is correct.

When an application fails to work, the computer doesn't understand what you meant to say. This doesn't mean the people who wrote the program didn't know what they were doing; it means the computer followed their instructions too well.

Testing an application allows you to find out whether the computer correctly follows the instructions you wrote. When it fails, you can tell the computer, "Hey stupid, do this, not that." Some people call this *bug fixing*, but it really comes down to computer fixing. Testing and bug fixing are two steps in learning to communicate effectively with your computer.

Initial Testing Makes Stronger Applications

Building an application is difficult; testing it is even harder. To find out whether it will work at all, you always have to test your application. When testing your applications, you have to remember three things:

- ✔ You never know what a user will try to do. The same stupidity that makes it easy for a computer to break your application also makes it easy for someone to use your application in ways you hadn't imagined.

- ✔ The more features the application offers, the more people will buy it. And if more people buy it, it'll get broken more often. A complex application does more, but it's also more difficult to test.

- ✔ An application never breaks in the manner you anticipated. The computer always finds a fault in the place you thought was safe. Always test everything as thoroughly as possible.

You can never completely test your application. Either your application won't work on someone's computer, or a user will mess it up by doing something totally unexpected. Application testers never run out of work because applications are never completely fixed.

Although you may run into problems trying to completely test an application before sending it to users, it's important to do the best job possible. For the best possible results in your testing efforts, follow these steps:

1. Divide the application into manageable pieces and test each piece. This first level of testing is known as *subsystem testing*.

2. Put the application back together and test it as a whole. This second level of testing is known as *system integration*.

3. Aggression becomes a major problem at this point. Running over the boss who points out a flaw that should have appeared during subsystem testing is mandatory.

4. Finally, perform *unexpected event testing*. This is the third level of testing. For example, what would happen to your database management system if the user pressed Ctrl+Alt+Delete in the middle of a transaction? That's an unexpected event, and your application has to know what to do if these occur.

5. Repeat the first four steps until one of two things happens: either you get the program working well enough that you can sell a few thousand copies to unsuspecting souls, or you get tired of the whole thing and give it up as a lost cause.

You can divide testing of a new application into three levels, each of which tests the application in a different way:

- ✔ Subsystem testing is like looking at the application through a microscope.
- ✔ System integration looks at the big picture.
- ✔ Unexpected event testing examines the application from the perspective of the dumb computer.

The following sections describe these levels of testing in more detail.

Subsystem testing

What's a subsystem? A subsystem is one piece of a program. As we discuss in Chapters 15 and 16, some programs use more than one screen. You can think of each screen as a separate module (or subsystem, as programmers call them).

A smart tester works with each screen separately, before moving on to the next one. Testing one screen at a time reduces the chance that something that was broken elsewhere will affect the current screen (a favorite trick of computers).

Subsystem testing also allows you and a partner to work on different parts of the application at the same time. You can test one subsystem while your partner writes another.

You can divide your application into even smaller pieces. Some people test their applications one button at a time. A subsystem can contain anything you want. The key to successful testing is making the pieces small enough to fully test.

A subsystem must be fully functional. In Visual BASIC, you can test a button or a data entry field, but you can't just test the logic that paints a funny picture on the button. Subsystem testing always looks at one piece of the program that can do something by itself.

Don't make your subsystems too large or too small. If you can't define a test procedure in ten steps or less, the subsystem is too big. If you have a hard time testing the subsystems without hiring additional help, the subsystems are too small.

System integration

Once you test all the pieces (subsystems) of an application, it's time to put them together. Programmers call this process *system integration*. It would be a lot clearer to say they put the application together, but then programming wouldn't seem so mysterious.

Although it seems obvious that an application should work once you've tested its separate pieces, this may not be the case. If you were giving someone directions to your office, you might tell them to walk straight, turn left, and then turn right. Although each piece of the puzzle works fine, finding your office depends on following the directions in the correct order. If the person rearranges the pieces and walks straight, turns left, walks straight, turns right, and then walks straight again, they'll walk into a wall.

Your application may have the same type of problem. The problem isn't with the pieces (which work fine individually). The problem lies with how the pieces work together. For example, if your OLE application asks an OLE server to provide a piece of information before you start the application that can provide it, your application will run into a wall.

System integration testing makes sure you have correctly assembled all the pieces of your application. You may not be able to test all the connections, but you can test the most important ones. Here are some simple steps you can follow for system integration testing:

1. Open the application. (If it doesn't open, your problems are just beginning.)

2. Open each of the menus and try each menu entry.

3. Test every button on every dialog box.

4. Open a file in your application. Create some data and perform a Copy command. Then, open a new document in your favorite word processor (which we hope supports OLE; if it doesn't, pick another application) and perform a Paste Special command. Make sure you actually created an OLE object in your word processor document.

5. Make some changes to the original file in your application (the server) and see if the changes appear in the pasted area of the client program.

6. Close the files in both programs.

7. Open an existing file in your word processor. Open a new document in your application. Copy the contents of the file in your word processor and do a Paste Special in your application.

8. Make some changes to the original file and verify that the changes appear in the pasted area of the file in your application.

9. Congratulations! You just checked the embedding capabilities of your application as both a client and a server.

10. Perform steps 4 through 9 again. This time, use the Paste Link command instead of Paste Special. Using the Paste Link command will test the linking capabilities of your application.

11. Perform steps 1 through 10 with a variety of applications. Make sure you test every available data type, even if you don't expect the user to use that data type with your application.

Unexpected events

The more complicated your application becomes, the harder it is to test all the interactions among all the pieces. One part of an application may change a condition that causes an application to fail, but only if the user follows a certain procedure. Even the best testing procedure can't test every possible combination of keystrokes a user can make. As a result, almost every application on your computer has a few bugs.

There's also another problem. The computer still can't think for itself. If a user tells it to do something, the computer will try to do it, even if it's impossible. For example, it's impossible for the computer to embed all of last year's sales receipts in a word processing document if that information could tax the memory limits of a mainframe.

An application usually provides little traps for detecting impossible tasks. The computer will know something is impossible only if the application tells it so.

To create these little traps, the programmer has to write code. In essence, this code tells the computer, "If a problem happens, here's how to fix it." But what if the programmer doesn't anticipate a certain problem? This type of problem is called an *unexpected event*.

Anything can be an unexpected event. A user turning off the machine during a file transfer is an unexpected event. Lighting striking the computer is also an unexpected event. Of course, some unexpected events are easier to test than others.

Unexpected event testing is fun. The programmer gets to think like a computer, which means the programmer gets to stop thinking. The following steps will give you some ideas about how to perform unexpected event testing:

1. Pick any set of keystrokes not listed on the menu. Pray that the application doesn't break when you try the key combination.

2. While the application stabilizes, wipe the sweat from your face. (During stabilization, an application updates its OLE links and then displays any new information. If the hourglass remains in place for more than a minute or two after any disk activity stops, the application is frozen.)

3. Reboot the computer when you realize the application is frozen.

4. Fix the bug and try the keystrokes again. Repeat this step until the application works.

5. Perform steps 1 through 4 for a variety of unexpected keystrokes.

6. Try to think of other unexpected things the user might try. Shutting off the computer while saving a file is a favorite user activity. Repeat steps 1 through 5 for each unexpected event.

Ask someone else to try to break your application. You'll be amazed at how quickly they can do it. Unexpected event testing always works best when it's performed by someone who didn't write the code.

Broken Applications

Even if you test your application completely, and then let someone else test it too, it will always break after you install it on the company network. Someone will always find a way to break your application. They probably won't even try all that hard to do it.

Feature-related errors

The computer seems to look for ways to misinterpret your application's instructions. For example, you might think there's only one way to link the information from your application to a word processing document. Because of the way the computer interprets instructions, your word processor will always come up with more than one way to do this.

For example, when I copy some graphics information from Paintbrush, Word for Windows gives me four ways to perform a Paste Special. What if the user decides to use the wrong option? Is your application broken? Not really. Did it do what it was supposed to do? Well, that's the object of much debate.

OLE 1 and other compatibility problems

Many people believe applications break solely because programmers didn't write the correct instructions for the computer. However, there are a number of other ways to break an application. You could break one application by adding a new capability to another program with which it interacts. Some people feel that OLE 1 compatible programs fall into this category.

You can embed the data from an OLE 1 compatible program into any application. However, if you double-click the embedded data, Windows won't open the application that created the data. Is the OLE 1 compatible program broken? In the strictest sense, the program is broken because it didn't open when you double-clicked its data. The program became broken when Microsoft (and other companies) came out with the OLE 2 standard, which allows you to open an application by double-clicking data created with that application.

Interactions with other applications

Another form of breakage involves problems with other programs. What would happen if someone installed a program that uses a DLL (dynamic link library) with the same name as one used by your application? This happens all the time under Windows (although Windows 95 does provide some new features that help to prevent this). Your application will look for some instructions it needs, and it might not find them.

INI file gotchas

A program can break in even more devious ways. To start up, many applications need INI files. These files contain settings with which applications configure themselves. What happens if a user erases the Windows directory, reinstalls Windows, and then simply creates a new Program Manager (Windows 3.x) or Explorer (Windows 95) entry for your application? The application won't start because the user deleted the INI file the application uses to configure itself. Will the user think the application is broken? Probably.

What about dueling programs? To make your application work correctly, you sometimes need to make an entry in WIN.INI or SYSTEM.INI. What if some other application needs to change the same entry? Your application won't work, and the user will think it's broken.

Memory-related errors

Under Windows, you're always faced with the problem of system resources and other memory constraints. Some users don't realize they must have enough system resources to run their application. To check resource availability from within the Windows 3.1 Program Manager, you can look at the Help⇨About dialog shown in Figure 18-1. Windows 95 provides a similar display. Just right-click the My Computer icon, select Properties from the menu that's displayed, and click the Performance tab. You'll see a dialog similar to the example in Figure 18-2.

Figure 18-1:
Always check to make sure you have enough memory and system resources left to run both applications required in an OLE application.

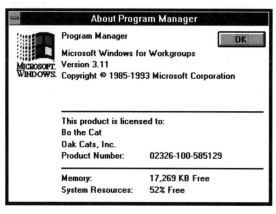

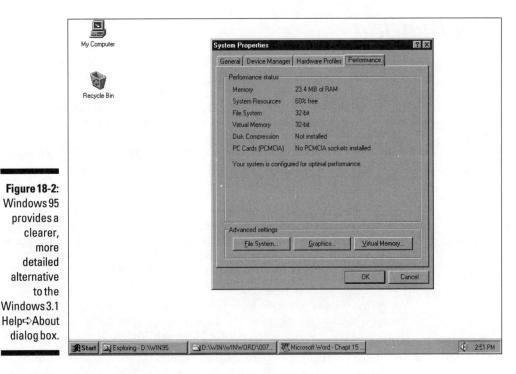

Figure 18-2:
Windows 95
provides a
clearer,
more
detailed
alternative
to the
Windows 3.1
Help⇨About
dialog box.

Fixing Broken Applications

The user-oriented definition of a broken application is one that operates in any
way other than as expected by the user. A broken program doesn't always
cause loss of data or some other catastrophe; it may just cause an inconve-
nience.

Now that you have a better idea what the user and the computer mean by
broken, let's take a look at what you can do about it. The following steps will
help you determine whether a program is really broken, or just a little bruised:

1. Ask whether the user installed the application from scratch after installing
   Windows.

2. Find out if the user installed any other applications after installing your
   application.

3. Verify that the user has the most recent version of your application.

4. Try to determine whether any other applications on the user's machine
   could conflict with yours.

5. Determine whether the user's computer has enough memory and other
   resources to run your application.

Bug Hunting

Bugs are problems that keep your OLE program from working correctly. Finding the problem areas within the OLE-specific portion of an application always means looking for other problem areas first. OLE involves two (or more) applications talking to each other. If either application contains major flaws, there's little chance they'll be able to communicate with each other.

Once you're sure you have two working applications, finding an OLE-specific problem is fairly easy. The following steps will help you find most OLE-related bugs:

1. Check the OLE capabilities of the other program — that is, the program with which your OLE application is communicating. If you want to check the OLE 2 capabilities of your application, the other program must support OLE 2. The other application also has to provide the services you need. You can't use a server application to check the server capabilities of your application; you need a client application to do that.

2. Verify that your application is properly registered in the registry. Make sure you can find it within the list of application types under HKEY_CLASSES_ROOT (see Chapter 14 for more details).

3. While you're in the registry, look for any conflicts in filename extensions. If another application uses the same filename extension as your application, the registry information you provide could be overwritten.

4. Check your source code to make certain you are using the correct calling syntax. The precise syntax varies by language and by the application you want to call. Look in Chapters 15 and 16 for examples.

Test your newfound knowledge

1. The three types of application testing are:

   a. Really a waste of time. As long as you get paid, who cares if the application is broken when you deliver it?

   b. Subsystem testing, system integration, and unexpected event testing.

   c. Something an intelligent programmer never performs. After all, the application is already perfect.

   d. A good way to waste an entire afternoon. The boss will think you're working, when you're really playing your fifth game of solitaire.

2. What is the purpose of unexpected event testing?

   a. It doesn't do anything.

   b. It allows you to check your application's response to unexpected events such as multiple keypresses.

   c. Application.

   d. It creates more problems than it solves, and it wastes a lot of the programmer's time.

The 5th Wave   By Rich Tennant

"HOLD ON, THAT'S NOT A SYNTAX ERROR, IT'S JUST A DONUT CRUMB ON THE SCREEN."

Chapter 19

What to Do When Things Go Wrong

$\bullet \bullet$

In This Chapter

▶ OLE and the Windows registry

▶ Fixing the Windows 95 registry

▶ Repairing broken OLE links

$\bullet \bullet$

*N*o matter which product you use, somewhere along the line you'll find a bug or something that just doesn't work right. This chapter provides some solutions to problems that many people experience when using OLE. These aren't necessarily the only solutions to these problems, but they are the ones that work most often.

Register that Application

OLE depends on one very important feature in Windows — the registry. It doesn't matter which version of Windows you use; OLE will always look to the registry as a source of information about your application. Unfortunately, the various versions of Windows rely on the registry in slightly different ways. In addition, each application uses a slightly different method for registering itself. Chapter 14 describes the registry from a programmer's point of view; this chapter describes the registry from the user's point of view.

So, what is the registry? Think of the registry as a phone book with more than the usual amount of information. Every time you need to do something with a file, Windows looks in its phone book to see who owns that file. Windows follows the same process as you do when you look for a business in the yellow pages. First, the registry looks for the type of application it needs; then, it finds the number of that business.

If Windows comes across a file that isn't registered, it usually displays some cryptic message that has nothing to do with the actual problem. For example, you might see a message indicating that Windows can't start the server application. What this usually means is that the registry entry for that application is missing. You should ask yourself the following questions when trying to eliminate everything but the registry as a possible source of the problem:

- Did you move the application? If so, you'll probably need to change any path statements, all INI files, and any registry entries to reflect the change. In most cases, it pays to install the application in the new location rather than simply move it.

- Have you installed any new applications on your system since the last time you tried to use OLE with this application? Some applications use the same file extensions and end up working against each other. In many cases, you'll find that the registry is corrupt, and you'll need to edit it to change it back to its original state.

- Which file extension are you using? Some people delight in using strange file extensions in place of the one an application expects. Windows uses the file extension to find the application in the registry. If you change a file extension — for example, from .DOC to .NEW — you'll prevent Windows from working correctly with your file.

- Did you move the file? OLE 2 can recover from some types of file moves, but it can't recover from all of them. Never move a file for an OLE 1 application, because you'll break the link required for using it within a compound document. (For more information, see Chapter 3).

Once you eliminate every other potential cause of problems, you need to use the registry editor to check the entries in your registry. Somewhere on your hard disk is a program called REGEDIT.EXE — a Windows utility that hides in either the SYSTEM or the WINDOWS directory. (The real reason why Microsoft hides REGEDIT is because it's a powerful editor that can significantly damage your system if you don't use it carefully. Chapter 21 describes how to use REGEDIT.)

Figure 19-1 shows the registry used by Windows 3.x. It actually looks like a telephone book, with a list of applications Windows can call. Each of these entries describes a different file type. Windows uses this information to determine how it should interact with the application that "owns" the file.

Looking at Figure 19-2, you can see that the Windows 95 registry is a lot more complex than the one provided with Windows 3.x. The reason is simple: Windows 95 does a lot more with its registry. In most cases, you can fix an OLE-related problem using the following procedure rather than the registry editor:

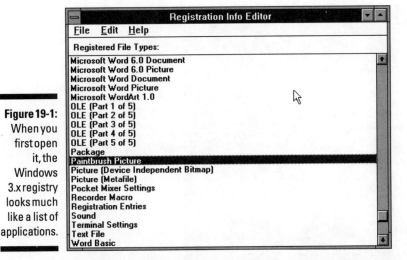

Figure 19-1:
When you
first open
it, the
Windows
3.x registry
looks much
like a list of
applications.

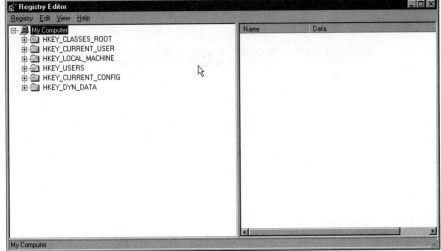

Figure 19-2:
The
Windows 95
registry is
extremely
complex
and very
susceptible
to damage.

1. Close the Registry Editor and open Explorer.

2. Open the Option dialog by choosing View⇨Options.

3. Click the File Types Tab to display the dialog box shown in Figure 19-3. Notice how similar this looks to the original Windows 3.x registry editor display shown in Figure 19-1.

4. Double-click the Paintbrush Picture entry if you're using Windows 3.x, or the Bitmap Image entry if you're using Windows 95. You should see a dialog box similar to the one in Figure 19-4 if you're using Windows 3.x, or Figure 19-5 if you're using Windows 95.

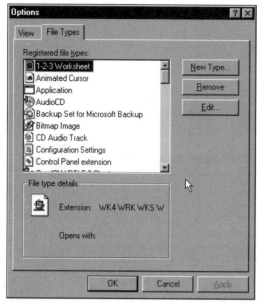

Figure 19-3:
Windows 95
provides this
Explorer
Options
dialog box
for changing
file
extension
entries. It
looks
remarkably
similar
to the
Windows 3.x
registry.

Figure 19-4:
Paintbrush
uses the
command
line method
for opening
an
application.

5. Close the Paintbrush Picture entry dialog box. If you have Word for
Windows or a similar high-end application, you can click one of its
entries. Figure 19-6 shows a typical Word for Windows entry when using
Windows 3.x. Figure 19-7 shows the same thing for Windows 95.

This dialog box shows the first kind of registry entry you should expect.
The application opens using a standard command line interface. The most
common method for opening an application under Windows is to provide
the application name and the name of the file you want to edit.

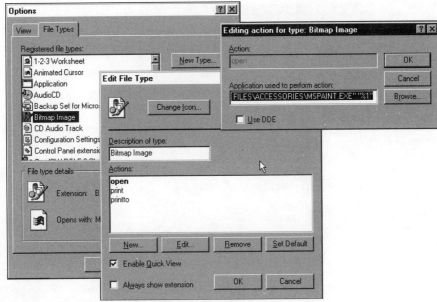

Figure 19-5:
This is the
Windows 95
version
of the
Paintbrush
file entry.

Figure 19-6:
Word for
Windows
uses the
DDE method
for opening
an
application.

6. Close the Option dialog box.

Notice that Word for Windows uses DDE (dynamic data exchange) to open a file. In this case, you need to know code words to make Word for Windows work. Most vendors document these code words somewhere in the user manual.

Figure 19-7:
This is the
Windows 95
version of
the Word for
Windows
file entry.

Now that you have some idea of how these entries look, you can probably fix or add any required entries for the applications that use OLE on your machine. Always check the vendor documentation to make sure you add the correct entry. This is especially important if the application requires a DDE entry.

Fixing a Broken Windows 95 Registry

There are numerous ways to break the registry. It's the glass jaw of the Windows 95 operating system. For example, no matter how careful you are, there's a good chance you'll make a mistake when editing the registry and Windows 95 won't boot the next time you use it. Problems can also be caused by old Windows 3.x applications that don't understand the Windows 95 registry.

Windows 3.x provided the WIN.INI and SYSTEM.INI files for configuration purposes. You could easily edit these files with any text editor, and boot your machine once you fixed the mistake. Unfortunately, Windows 95 doesn't store the registry as text but in a special format that looks like gibberish to any normal human.

Don't worry though, you can still overcome a registry error with relative ease by using the following steps. Windows 95 stores the previous copy of your registry in the USER.DA0 and SYSTEM.DA0 files. You can use these copies to recover from a registry error.

1. If you make a mistake while editing the registry, exit RegEdit immediately.

2. Shut down Windows 95.

3. Boot into DOS mode by pressing F8 during system boot. Windows 95 will display a menu with DOS mode as one of the entries. Do the same thing if you try to boot Windows 95 and it reports a registry error. Simply turn off the machine; don't allow Windows 95 to copy the error to your backup copies of the registry.

4. When you turn the system back on, boot into DOS mode instead of booting Windows 95.

5. Change directories to your Windows 95 main directory.

6. Make the SYSTEM.DA0, SYSTEM.DAT, USER.DA0, and USER.DAT files visible by using the ATTRIB utility with the -R, -H, and -S switches. (In other words, type **ATTRIB** *filename* **-R -H -S**.)

7. Copy the backup of your registry to the two original files (that is, SYSTEM.DA0 to SYSTEM.DAT and USER.DA0 to USER.DAT). This will restore your registry to its pre-edited state.

8. Restore the previous file attribute state by using the -R, -H, and -S switches of the ATTRIB utility.

Repairing Broken OLE Links

Broken OLE links can cause many problems when you depend on those links to automatically update your documents. Links may break in a number of ways, some of which are not obvious. When an application reports that it can't find a link anymore, the following list provides some ideas for figuring out what happened to the link:

- You moved the document by mistake.
- A colleague who can access your machine through a peer-to-peer network connection moved the file.
- Someone deleted the required file.
- The master document got corrupted.
- Someone renamed the file.
- You moved from Windows 3.x to Windows 95 and started using long filenames.
- A system configuration modification changed your drive lettering.

After you figure out the causes of link problems, it's fairly easy to fix most of them. Renaming or moving a file is a pretty easy way to fix the problem. But what happens if you move a file, create other master documents that depend on the location, and only then discover the problem?

Some programs — for example, Excel and Word for Windows — provide an easy method for fixing broken links. Figure 19-8 shows the Links dialog box for Excel under Windows 95. Notice that it includes a Change Source button. To change the source of a link, you simply click this button.

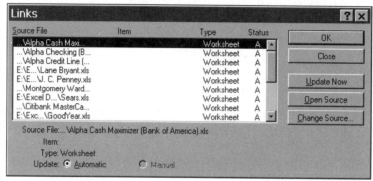

Figure 19-8:
The Links dialog box in Excel shows you the current location of a file link.

The Change Links dialog box shown in Figure 19-9 works just like the File Open dialog box you use for opening a file. Instead of opening a file though, it helps you reestablish contact with a moved or renamed file. All you need to do is move to the new location and double-click the required file.

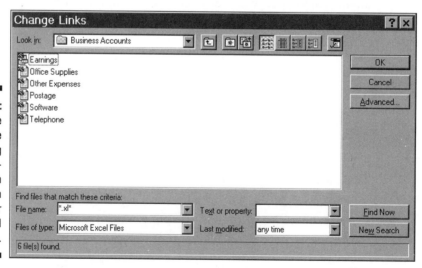

Figure 19-9:
You can use the Change Links dialog box to re-establish contact with a moved or renamed file.

Using the Change Source option with applications that provide it is one way to fix your problem. If your application doesn't provide this feature, you can still do a few things to get around the problem:

- ✔ Create a phantom document.
- ✔ Erase the old link and create a new one.
- ✔ Place a second copy of the document in the old location.

Creating a phantom document is probably the best and easiest way to fix a broken link. All you do is create a document with the original name in the original location. Then, you create a link from that new document to the original document. In other words, what your application really sees is a link to a linked document. The phantom document will only contain a link to the original document in its new location. This means your old and new documents will always stay up to date.

The other two options require little explanation. The second option on our list mimics the steps you used to create the original link. It works well if you have only a few documents, but it's time consuming if you have to change lots of documents. That's where the third option comes into play. You use it when there are too many documents to update. The problem with having two copies of your file lying around is that there's a good chance one of them will be out of date.

You can deal with master document corruption in several ways. A database application normally provides a repair utility. To recover your links, you simply run the repair utility. In many cases, the repair utility will do all the required work for you.

Of course, not every application is a database. Most programs allow you to maintain a backup copy of your document. A few programs even allow you to maintain more than one backup, but these are usually rare graphics applications that provide some form of version control. CAD programs often fall into the multiple-backup category. Maintaining a backup of your file consumes some disk space, but ensures that you have a good chance of recovering your master document if you experience some type of corruption.

The best defense against file corruption is a good backup. A backup may not get you back to the work you did yesterday (unless you made the backup yesterday), but it's better than starting from scratch. To avoid losing valuable data, always verify that your backup program is working correctly.

Test your newfound knowledge

1. If you make a mistake while editing the registry, you should

   a. Run around screaming at the top of your lungs.

   b. Immediately close the registry, boot into MS-DOS mode, and restore the registry from the backup that Windows 95 maintains.

   c. Blame the mistake on someone else.

   d. Consider running a Mack truck into your machine.

2. One of the ways to fix a broken OLE link is by

   a. Creating a phantom document that allows the older documents to access the data in its new location.

   b. Using a blowtorch to weld the broken connection.

   c. Sending it a get-well card.

   d. You can't fix a broken OLE link; you might as well start from scratch.

Part V
The Part of Tens

The 5th Wave   **By Rich Tennant**

In This Part...

*N*ow that you're an OLE guru, you may be wondering what to do until *MORE OLE For Dummies* appears on your favorite bookstore's shelves. Here are a few chapters of information you can use to make the most of your new-found OLE expertise. We look at some troubleshooting guidelines, a list of VBX and OCX add-ons for your favorite programming language, and a few bits of information that didn't quite fit anywhere else.

Chapter 20
Ten OLE Add-Ins for Visual BASIC

In This Chapter

▶ Adding OLE graphics capabilities

▶ OLE support in communications custom controls

▶ Graphs and charts that use OLE

▶ Hypertext tools with OLE support

▶ Creating great reports with OLE support

▶ Squashing OLE bugs

▶ Stuff that really didn't fit anywhere else

*N*ow that you have some idea of how you can use Visual BASIC to create an OLE-aware application, let's look at some of the tools available for making your job a bit easier. Each of the tools we describe in this chapter performs one or more specific OLE tasks, but none of them do everything. Some tools may sacrifice power for ease of use. You'll need to figure out which product can do everything you need it to do with the least amount of work.

Many products other than Visual BASIC support VBX and OCX add-ins — for example, Visual C++ and Access. There's also a good chance you'll find this support in other products, especially C++ compilers. For example, you'll find VBX support in Borland's Delphi product, which we discuss in Chapter 17.

This chapter isn't meant to provide an all-inclusive list of every OLE add-on for Visual BASIC. It will give you a good feel for what's available and some ideas of who to contact for additional controls.

Carefully check the specifications for your new custom control. Some vendors sell products that come in both VBX and OCX versions, while others sell them separately, usually selling the OCX version at a higher price.

All OCXs are not created equal

In most cases, you can use a VBX with any programming language that supports these controls. The only exceptions to this rule are when the VBX vendor fails to completely follow the Microsoft guidelines for creating the VBX, or your programming language uses Visual BASIC 1.0 controls and the VBX you want to use is designed for Visual BASIC 2.0. Needless to say, you'll have to try the VBX with your own program to see if it works.

OCXs aren't quite as easy to figure out until you learn one rule. Visual BASIC supports OCX controls in either bound or unbound mode. A bound control resides in the application. An unbound control resides outside the application.

Access and other programming languages don't support bound controls. In addition, you probably won't get the same level of support from Access for an OCX as you would from Visual BASIC. The reason is simple: When it comes to OCXs, Visual BASIC is a better container than Access.

Graphics and OLE

Windows speaks volumes about graphics. Everything about Windows is graphics-oriented. From the controls on a form to the images you edit, Windows is a graphical environment.

Graphics and OLE go hand in hand. Windows wouldn't be the product it is without this relationship. It stands to reason, then, that Visual BASIC should provide a programmer with all the tools needed for making OLE and graphics work in an application. Unfortunately, it falls a little short.

As an example of some of the problems you'll encounter, just try to access a 24-bit graphics image. You'll also find Visual BASIC's file format support lacking. Visual BASIC just doesn't allow you to access that Targa (TGA) image you captured last week.

Fortunately, some graphics-related VBXs out there also provide OLE support. The following paragraphs tell you all about them.

All prices in this chapter are current as of the time of writing. The prices may change without notice. All prices are list price for the product.

ImageKnife/VBX

Media Architects
1075 NW Murray Road, Suite 230
Portland, OR 97229-5501
Voice: (503) 297-5010
Fax: (503) 297-6744
$199.00

ImageKnife/VBX is a complex graphics VBX that supports the Microsoft Access Paintbrush Picture OLE Object format (whew!). It helps you acquire images using the TWAIN scanner interface. That's the same interface used by products such as CorelDRAW! Once you acquire an image, you can change its appearance and store it in either a file or a database.

ImageKnife supports a variety of file formats, including BMP, DIB, JPEG, GIF, PCX, TIFF, and TGA. You can also display those files as true-color (24-bit), Super VGA (8-bit), VGA (8-bit), or monochrome images.

The fancier graphic changes this product supports include rotating, mirroring, negation, sharpening, and matrix filtering. If that isn't enough, the product also allows you to perform image resizing, compositing, and masking for cropping and combining images. We'll just say it can do a lot of stuff and leave it at that.

Graphics Server SDK

Pinnacle Publishing, Inc.
P.O. Box 888
Kent, WA 98035-0888
Voice: (800) 231-1293
Fax: (206) 251-5057
$249.00

Graphics Server SDK is the full-fledged version of the runtime product included with Visual BASIC. Just like the runtime version, the server runs as an independent application outside your Visual BASIC application. However, this product provides a lot more than the runtime version does.

Graphics Server is an OLE 2 graphics primitive engine. It supports commands that draw circles or squares. You can use it to perform a variety of complex drawing tasks with products other than Visual BASIC, even those that don't support OLE directly (CA-Visual Objects is one of them).

If you don't want to work with graphics primitives, and a graph or a chart is your goal, you can use the included ChartBuilder product. This is the full-featured version of the Graph control included with Visual BASIC. All you need to do is tell ChartBuilder which data points you want to display and what type of graph or chart you want to use for displaying them. It takes care of all the details.

The features don't end there. You can also use Graphics Server SDK with products such as Microsoft Excel and Word for Windows. The new 2.5 version fully supports VBA.

Communicating with OLE

You may not immediately see a connection between OLE and communications, but there are several. One way you can use OLE in a communications program is the same as in any document. You can use it to combine text and graphics in a single message from multiple sources. For example, wouldn't it be nice to add a logo to your next fax over a fax modem? OLE can help you do just that.

Another form of communication is through the use of DDE. We talked about the standard DDE implementation in Chapters 10 and 14. A standard DDE command won't work over a network link, but there are ways of getting around the problem. Some Visual BASIC libraries do just that.

The following paragraphs tell you about communications products that fulfill a variety of communications needs. Unfortunately, we couldn't find a one-size-fits-all package, so you'll have to shop around for what you need. Remember: a communications package that sort of meets your needs is like a shoe that just barely fits; both are extremely uncomfortable.

Communications Library 3

MicroHelp
4359 Shallowford Ind. Parkway
Marietta, GA 30066
Voice: (800) 922-3383 or (404) 516-0899
Fax: (404) 516-1099
$149.00

Communications Library 3 is a general communications library. It supports five terminal emulations and eight file transfer protocols. You can use it at speeds up to 25.6 Kbps.

MicroHelp includes VBXs, DLLs, and 16- and 32-bit OCXs with this product. It provides OLE 2 support for all your file transfer needs. The library will support multiple communications ports (eight is the practical limit).

FaxMan

Data Techniques, Inc.
340 Bowditch Street, Suite 6
Burnsville, NC 28714
Voice: (800) 955-8015 or (714) 682-4111
Fax: (714) 682-0025

As its name implies, FaxMan will help you add fax capability to your application. It supports Class 1, Class 2, and Class 2.0 fax modems. One of the nicer features of this program is that you can chain several faxes together into one job. That means you could get all your faxes ready in the morning and send them that night when the rates are low.

Unlike most of the products in this chapter, FaxMan comes as a DLL, a VBX, or an OCX. That means you should be able to use it with just about any development environment in Windows, not just programming languages that support VBXs.

Other product features include a printer type interface from the user's perspective and a user-definable log. FaxMan also supports multiple fax modems on a single machine.

App-Link

Synergy Software Technologies, Inc.
159 Pearl Street
Essex Junction, VT 05452
Voice: (800) 294-8514 or (802) 879-8514
Fax: (802) 879-3754
$99.95

Communicating DDE commands over a network may seem like an impossible task, and it is unless you have help. Some products, such as LANtastic, provide this support as a built-in option. Other products, such as NetWare, don't.

App-Link helps you create DDE links over a network. Using a network DDE link would allow you to create an OLE connection between an application on one workstation and a different application on another workstation. Some magazines call this distributed processing, but that's such a nebulous and ill-used term that we'll avoid using it here.

So, how does App-Link get the job done? It uses something called a socket. If your network supports sockets (as both NetWare and Microsoft Network do), you can use this product. You'll probably want to talk with your network operating system vendor before you buy this product.

One of the nice features of App-Link is that it doesn't force you to use a specific message format. You can create user-defined data formats. This comes in handy for applications that support DDE but use a variety of data formats, such as database managers.

Graphs and OLE

Graphs and charts are the tools people use for comparing the current state of some value with its previous or future state. For example, you'll see graphs used to show how adding a new piece of machinery to the production area of a company has increased the number of units produced.

Another use of graphs and charts is for comparing two like items. For example, you'll see them used to describe the quarterly sales figures for a particular part of the company.

Suffice it to say then that including a graphing or charting capability in your program is one way to make it more useful. The following product can help you do just that. You may also want to take a look at the Graphics Server product in the "Graphics and OLE" section of this chapter.

Visio

Shapeware Corporation
520 Pike Street, Suite 1800
Seattle, WA 98101
Voice: (800) 446-3335
$199.00

If your application makes heavy use of flowcharts and network diagrams, Visio is probably the product you're looking for. This product provides a wide variety of presentation-quality flowchart symbols. All you need to do is provide a drawing window, and it takes care of the rest.

Visio supports both OLE 2 and VBA. You can use it as either an OLE client or a server. VBA support means you can use it with applications such as Microsoft Excel and Word for Windows.

OLE-Equipped Hypertext Tools

When looking at this product category, the first thing you have to know is what hypertext is. It's the capability of your program to make connections from one part of a file to another in a way that helps the user quickly find specific pieces of information. Windows Help uses this capability to move you from one spot to another in the help file based on the words you select.

HypertextManager

BrainTree, Ltd.
42-42 204th Street
Bayside, NY 11361
Voice: (800) 745-4645
Fax: (718) 224-4728
$89.00

You can use HypertextManager to create standard hypertext files. The OLE part comes in when you start using graphics in your hypertext files. For example, instead of providing a word for the user to click, you could have the user click an icon or a picture instead. You could even show a screenshot of an application and allow users to click the part of the screen for which they need help.

If you use the built-in help provided with Windows, you need to keep a copy of each graphic right with the HLP file. If you use the same graphic more than once, it must appear in the file each time you use it. Talk about a nightmare to fix when you want to change the graphic!

Using OLE to create a link to the graphics in your text file allows you to reduce the size of the file as well as change every occurrence of the graphic by changing one file. It also means you don't have to recompile the file every time you make a change, because the graphics exist outside the hypertext file.

ALLText HT/Pro

Bennet-Tec Information Systems
10 Steuben Drive
Jericho, NY 11753
Voice: (516) 433-6283
Fax: (516) 822-2679
CompuServe: 71201.1075
$350.00

ALLText HT/Pro is essentially a word processor with a little extra oomph. It includes hypertext support, embedded OLE 1 objects for graphics or other document embedding, RTF input and output, and data-aware support.

Rich text format (RTF) is the word processing format used by the Windows help compiler. Many word processors use this format as a means for exchanging data with other word processors. The data-aware support means ALLText includes the name of the application that created an object as part of the object.

ALLText HT/Pro supports embedded (not linked) OLE 1 objects such as bitmaps and spreadsheets. You can't see the object in its native form; all objects appear as icons in the word processing document. Double-clicking the object will launch the server application. ALLText does not provide OLE server support.

Creating OLE-Supported Reports

What good is having all the OLE support in your program if you can't use it when the user needs to print a report? Even though Visual BASIC provides a modicum of OLE support in reports, wouldn't it be nice if you had a report generation tool that worked with a wide variety of products?

The real problem with Visual BASIC and reports doesn't lie with OLE support alone; it lies with all the time it takes to create those reports. Other products fall down in this area, too. Ever try to get a really professional-looking report out of Delphi? The following product will help make your reports look as nice as (or even nicer than) what you see on-screen.

Crystal Reports Pro

Crystal Services
1050 West Pender Street, Suite 2200
Vancouver, B.C., Canada V6E-3S7
Voice: (800) 663-1244 or (604) 681-3435
$345.00

Crystal Reports Pro is a full-featured version of the product provided with Visual BASIC. It provides a two-pass report generator that allows you to include groups and cross-tabs in your report. It also provides a variety of data sorting methods. Most important, any of the fields in your report can contain OLE 1 or OLE 2 objects.

Other product features include a Print Preview window and a runtime engine. You can use the Crystal Reports Formula Editor to add calculated fields to your reports.

According to the vendor, you get all this functionality without a single line of code. Crystal Reports Pro converts the report picture you draw on-screen into a report on paper.

Squashing OLE Bugs

Anyone who has spent time with the Visual BASIC debugger will realize that it works well for simple programs, but lacks what it takes for squashing bugs in big projects. For example, how do you find and squash OLE-specific bugs in your programs?

The Visual BASIC debugger can help you look at the client or the server, but not both. The reason is simple: It only allows you to look at what the Visual BASIC program is doing. You can't see what happens when the program it calls takes over.

Another problem with the Visual BASIC debugger is that the information you receive doesn't survive system crashes. This isn't much of a problem until you run into a programming error that crashes the system before you can see what it is. You can't fix the problem because you don't know where it is, and you can't find it because you can't see it. (Talk about catch-22!)

The following product probably isn't perfect, but it will help you find specific types of OLE-related problems in your Visual BASIC programs. Unfortunately, this debugger is Visual BASIC specific, so you can't use it with other products such as Delphi.

PinPoint VB

Avanti Software, Inc.
385 Sherman Avenue, Unit 6
Palo Alto, CA 94306
Voice: (800) 758-7011
International: +1-415-329-8999
Fax: (415) 329-8722
CompuServe: 76260,266
$99.00

PinPoint uses logs to help you trace the activities of your Visual BASIC programs. This means you can find out what happened, even if a system crash prevents you from using a normal debugger. The traces cover both client and server activities, making PinPoint perfect for debugging both OLE and DDE projects.

Other product features include the capability to profile your programs. A profiler tells you how much time the program spends in each module. Knowing this information allows you to optimize the program for best performance.

Just in Case You Haven't Seen Enough

There were a few controls we couldn't quite fit into a pigeon hole. Consider them the free spirits of the Visual BASIC control world and a bonus to this list of ten. You'll have to read our description of each product to figure out what it does.

Custom Control Factory

Desaware
5 Town and Country Village, #790
San Jose, CA 95128
Voice: (408) 377-4770
Fax: (408) 371-3530
$48.00

Ever wonder what you would do if you couldn't find the custom control you needed? There is help, but it's not what you would call the ultimate level of help. Custom Control Factory will help you with a wide range of custom controls that don't quite fit a specific category (it's like attending a potluck supper, you never know what you're getting into until the dinner has started).

The OLE connection in this product is its DDE support. No, you can't use it to create a new object for your Visual BASIC application. However, you can use it to communicate better with another application. (Just take a look at the spreadsheet macro in Chapter 10 if you want an example of what DDE can do.)

Other product features include 256 and 24-bit color support for graphics and automatic 3D backgrounds. You'll also find image compression and some other graphics-related stuff thrown in for good measure. The package includes more than 50 custom controls of various types and sizes.

Rocket

SuccessWare 90, Inc.
27349 Jefferson Avenue
Temecula, CA 92590
Voice: (800) 683-1657 or (909) 699-9657
Fax: (909) 695-5679
CompuServe: Go SWARE
$249.00

Access users won't need Rocket; it adds database capability to your application. This VBX supports FoxPro, Clipper, and HiPer-Six index formats. Unlike a
standard Xbase DBF file, however, you get both variable length fields (VariField)
and BLOBs (supported through memo fields).

Speed is no problem with this product because it uses the Mach Six query
optimizer. A query optimizer takes your request as input and comes up with
the most efficient way possible to satisfy it. Rocket also comes with two
utility programs: Navigator (for database maintenance) and Filter-Builder (for
query maintenance).

NetPak Professional

Crescent
11 Bailey Avenue
Ridgefield, CT 06877-4505
Voice: (800) 352-2742 or (203) 438-5300
Fax: (203) 431-4626
$179.00

NetPak Professional doesn't actually address any OLE-specific needs, but we
included it for those of you who work with NetWare. Chapter 14 mentioned the
difficulties of working with OLE on a network, and this product addresses some
of those needs.

NetPak includes: NetWare 386 F2, bindery, communications, connection,
directory, message, print, TTS, and workstation functions (and other functions
too numerous to mention here).

The bottom line is that you would use NetPak to do things such as implement
security and monitor transactions. You could also add the capability to monitor
user connections so that your application would know if an OLE object is
available or not.

justButtons

Chrisalan Designs, Inc.
P.O. Box 775
815 Lambert Street
Wenatchee, WA 98807-0775
Voice: (509) 663-7770
Fax: (509) 662-5948
Standard Edition: $99.00
Developers Edition: $199.00
Professional Edition: $299.00

Every dialog box you'll ever see contains at least one button: OK. You could probably say the same thing about windows; they contain buttons. Using buttons helps make Windows programs a lot easier to use. Of course, programming those buttons can take a lot of developer time.

You can use justButtons to reduce the amount of time it takes to create buttons. The functions in this package include Command Line, Memo, Control Panel Applet, WinFile, and Talking Time.

All the buttons are OLE 2 compliant. You can even use drag and drop with your new buttons. A button scheduler allows you to attach timed events to a button or even wake up the button at a specific time.

Chapter 21

Ten OLE Topics that Didn't Fit Anywhere Else

● ●

In This Chapter

▶ Becoming an OLE programming junky

▶ Working with OLE and the Windows 95 registry

▶ Using OLE with VBA

● ●

*O*LE is such a monstrously complicated topic that this book can introduce you to only the basics. We didn't want to leave you thirsting for more information, so we put some more advanced odds and ends in here. This chapter offers some ideas on how to advance your knowledge of OLE, uncover the hidden secrets within the Windows 95 registry, and understand how the new Visual BASIC for Applications (VBA) language might affect you in the future.

Getting Even Deeper into OLE Programming

Some of you won't be satisfied with the OLE features in a product such as Delphi or Visual BASIC. If so, there are a few ways to improve your applications' capabilities. The easiest way is by using a third-party library — in most cases, an add-on product for Delphi or Visual BASIC in the form of an OCX or a VBX. Programming in a lower-level language (C and C++ are the most common) is the other route that people commonly take.

If you must insist on learning to write OLE programs in C or C++, you'll need to get a few programming tools first. Most of them aren't very expensive (at least for programming tools), but they are quite complex, so don't even think about going to sleep for the next six months if you get them:

✔ A C or C++ compiler

✔ The Microsoft OLE Software Development Kit (SDK)

✔ The Microsoft Windows SDK

✔ A book that explains how to use OLE with C and C++

C and C++ compilers

To write an OLE-enhanced program or a DLL (dynamic link library), you must have a C or C++ compiler such as Microsoft Visual C++, version 2.0 or higher. This compiler must have all the tools you'll need for writing a complete application. The current version of Microsoft Visual C++ does just that. On the other hand, if you don't particularly like Microsoft and would rather eat worms than buy their product, you could always buy Borland's C++ compiler (version 4.5 or higher). Symantec C++ is also a good choice because it uses a licensed copy of the Microsoft Foundation Classes (MFC). Whichever compiler you choose, it will cost you about $400.

The Microsoft OLE SDK

There's no way to avoid buying Microsoft's OLE SDK if you want to write OLE-compliant programs. If you want the most detailed information available on OLE, you need this toolkit. Not only does it contain all the OLE specifications, it provides example code and other aids to help you develop OLE-enabled applications. An OLE SDK will run you about $50. You can order it directly from Microsoft by calling 800-227-4679.

The Microsoft Windows SDK

Choosing the right Windows SDK is one of the trickier pieces of the OLE programming puzzle. You need to get the SDK that applies to the version of Windows for which you are developing applications. The Windows SDK includes special versions of some of the Windows operating system files, which can help you debug your applications. Without these special files, life becomes difficult, and programming even harder. The Windows SDK will cost you about $220. You can order it directly from Microsoft by calling 800-227-4679.

A book that explains how to use OLE with C and C++

OLE is a complex topic. There's no way you'll learn to write a program that uses OLE under C++ without a lot of time, patience, and research. Make sure you get a back brace before lifting your new book for the first time.

Once you get all these nifty items together, you can spend the next two days loading them onto your machine (after you take off all your game programs, of course). After you get the software loaded, get out your OLE book and go for it.

Peering Inside the Windows 95 Registry

Some of you may be wondering what a registry is or why you should care about it. There's no way we can briefly describe the Windows 95 registry. Think of it as the Windows version of a closet, everything gets stuffed in there. In the following sections, we'll take you inside the Windows 95 registry, paying particular attention to the OLE-specific entries.

The following sections contain lots of technical information. If you only want to know registry usage information, you can safely avoid any sections of the chapter that are marked with a technical stuff icon. Programmers will want to pay special attention to the sections, "OLE 1 entries in the registry" and "OLE 2 entries in the registry."

The Windows 95 registry is far more complex than the one you may have seen when using Windows 3.x. In fact, most people never saw the registry when using Windows 3.x, because it contained only some file association information and the barest examples of OLE-specific entries. The fact that very few people even used OLE under Windows 3.x only made things worse. Believe it or not, most people don't even know there's a registry in Windows 3.x.

The new Windows 95 registry format incorporates a lot more than just a few file associations and a little OLE thrown in for good measure. It includes everything in both the SYSTEM.INI and WIN.INI files as well as many new entries that make Windows 95 a lot easier to use. Microsoft probably threw the kitchen sink in there somewhere, too; you'll never be quite sure what to expect when you look in the registry. One thing is certain: Windows 95 is totally dependent on the registry. If your registry gets damaged, Windows 95 won't work.

Think of the registry as the place where Windows 95 hides its deepest, darkest secrets that only programmers are supposed to know. It would be nice if the registry really worked this way, but it doesn't. We have to dig around in there, too. For example, you can't adjust some color settings without resorting to changing the registry settings directly. Some people have complained that they can't rename their Recycle Bin without using the registry. In essence, the registry is a database of settings, configuration information, instructions for application programs, and a lot of other neat stuff that no one except Microsoft has figured what to do with yet.

Learning the registry lingo

The first thing you need to learn is that the registry is a database in a constant state of disorder. The contents of the registry can change second-by-second. Some programs only store settings here, but others, such as the System Monitor utility, also store data in the registry. Every time you change the color of your screen, install a new program, or add a new piece of hardware, the change shows up in the registry.

We'll provide an overview of the registry that will help you find things in this madman's paradise, but don't be surprised if you run into a few misplaced or missing entries from time to time. If that happens, take a deep breath and count to at least 20 before you look at the registry again. Because the registry is responsible for managing every aspect of Windows, you can ill afford to contaminate it in any way. Unlike Windows 3.x, you cannot simply reboot DOS to fix an error in judgment. Changes to the registry are usually very permanent and very hard to fix.

A *key* is the basic building block of the registry. It's helpful to think of the registry as a book. Every chapter title, section, subsection, and paragraph heading is a key. The keys organize the registry and make it a little easier to understand.

For example, if you see a key with a .TXT extension, you know the information under that key pertains to the text file type. You might see the same subkeys under any number of main keys. For example, both the .TXT and the .BMP file associations have a ShellNew subkey.

A *value* is something that's attached to a key and defines the key. Think of a value as a paragraph of descriptive text in a book. Keys organize the information contained in values. The values are the content you read. The registry uses three different kinds of values:

- ✔ String
- ✔ Binary
- ✔ DWORD

A string value is English-like text. It could describe a major key or provide some type of configuration value. String values are the ones you'll modify most often, because they're the ones you can read and understand. A string value always appears in quotes "like this" so you can easily identify it. For example, you might see a string value of "Paint.Picture" for the BMP key. (We'll tell you exactly what this means later on in the chapter.)

A binary value is a string of 1s and 0s. These values are always used to configure a program or Windows 95 itself. Most programs use binary values for something known as a flag. A flag tells the program whether something is off or on, just like a light switch in your house. If the light switch is in the off position (0), you know the light is off. If it's in the on position (1), you know the light is on. You will find binary values used to tell Windows 95 things like if you have a sound board installed or the volume level for your CD-ROM drive.

It almost never pays to touch a binary value unless you know precisely what that value does. Many applications set their flags as part of the start-up process. Binary values are also used when a DWORD value is too short to hold some piece of configuration information.

A DWORD value is two 16-bit words — that is, a double word. Programs use DWORD values to tell Windows how to configure something. For example, a program might use a DWORD value to tell Windows which color its background should be or how many client windows it needs for displaying data. If you have adequate documentation about a particular program, you can usually modify the DWORD values to make a permanent change in the way the program works. However, it's always easier to use standard program configuration methods — for example, the Setup program provided with Microsoft products — instead of directly manipulating DWORD values in the registry.

Adding the Registry Editor to the Start menu

Now that you know the terminology of the registry, let's look at how you can edit registry information. You can't use a word processor or a hex editor to change the registry. Instead, Microsoft provides a special tool called the Registry Editor (or RegEdit for short) for modifying the registry. To keep people from accidentally destroying their Windows installation, Microsoft keeps RegEdit hidden in the main Windows directory.

Let's begin our registry adventure by adding RegEdit to the Start menu. The following procedure is the same one you've probably used before to add other programs. It's important to keep the RegEdit utility handy while we go through the rest of this section.

1. Right-click the Taskbar, and then select Properties from the Context menu that's displayed. Select the Start Menu Programs page. You should see the Taskbar Properties dialog box shown in Figure 21-1.

2. Click the Add ... button. You'll see the Create Shortcut dialog box shown in Figure 21-2.

3. Enter the location of your main Windows directory (normally WINDOWS or WIN95) and REGEDIT.EXE, as shown in Figure 21-2. You could also click the Browse button to find REGEDIT.EXE using the standard File Open dialog box used by Windows applications.

4. Click Next. You will see the Select Program Folder dialog box shown in Figure 21-3. This dialog box allows you to select the location for the RegEdit icon on the Start menu.

5. Select a location for RegEdit. The Accessories folder (highlighted in Figure 21-3) is a good place for it.

6. Click Next. You'll see the Select a Title for the Program dialog box shown in Figure 21-4.

7. Enter a descriptive name. You could name the program Registry Editor or RegEdit (as shown in the figure). Any descriptive name is fine.

8. Click Finish to complete the process. Your Start menu now has a shortcut to the Registry Editor.

9. Click Cancel to get rid of the Taskbar Properties dialog box.

Figure 21-1:
The Start Menu Programs page of the Taskbar Properties dialog box allows you to add a new program to the Start menu.

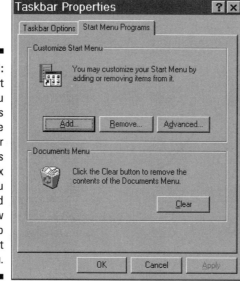

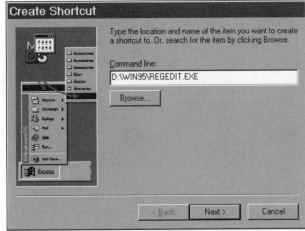

Figure 21-2:
The Create Shortcut dialog box lets you tell Windows 95 which application you want to add to the Start menu.

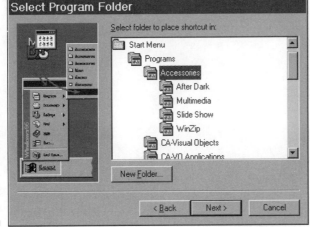

Figure 21-3:
Use this dialog box to select a location for the RegEdit shortcut.

An overview of the registry

Once you get the Registry Editor installed, you can start taking a look at what the registry itself has to offer. You may want to start RegEdit right now by using the shortcut you added to the Start menu. Figure 21-5 shows how the registry looks when you first start RegEdit.

As shown in Figure 21-5, there are two panes. The pane on the left holds the keys, or the outline of our book. The pane on the right lists the values — that is, the contents of our book.

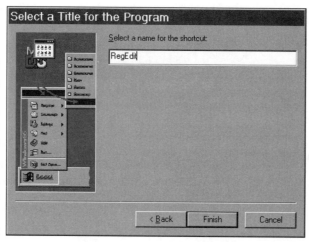

Figure 21-4:
The Select a
Title for the
Program
dialog box
allows you
to select a
name for
your
application.

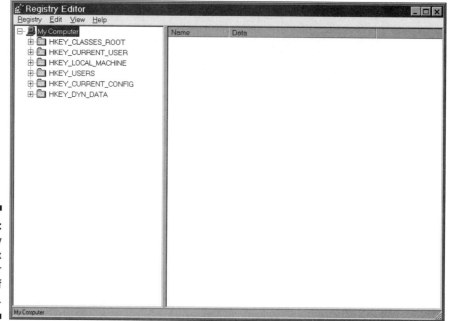

Figure 21-5:
The registry
contains six
main keys or
categories of
information.

As you can see, there are six keys under the My Computer key. You could view these six keys as categories of registry entries. In fact, throughout the rest of this chapter we'll refer to them as registry categories. Another way to look at them would be as chapters in a book. Each chapter relates to the book as a whole, but contains different types of information.

Don't let the long and confusing category names intimidate you. Microsoft uses them to keep people from checking out the registry. They probably figure that the long names will scare all but the most stubborn users away from their private domain.

As described in the following paragraphs, each registry category serves a different purpose. Here are the six registry categories:

- ✔ HKEY_CLASSES_ROOT
- ✔ HKEY_CURRENT_USER
- ✔ HKEY_LOCAL_MACHINE
- ✔ HKEY_USERS
- ✔ HKEY_CURRENT_CONFIG
- ✔ HKEY_DYN_DATA

File association and OLE entries

You will find two types of entries in the HKEY_CLASSES_ROOT category. The first key type is a file association like the ones you created using the File Manager in Windows 3.x. Think of all the three-character file extensions you used under DOS — for example, DOC and TXT. Windows 95 still uses them to differentiate one file type from another. Windows 95 also uses them to associate each file type with a specific action. For example, even though you can't do anything with a file that uses the DLL extension, it appears in this list because Windows 95 needs to associate DLLs with an executable file type.

The second entry type is the association itself. The file extension entries normally associate a data file with an application, or an executable file with a specific Windows 95 function. Below the association key are entries for the menus you see when you right-click an entry in Explorer. It also contains keys that determine what type of icon to display, and other parameters associated with a particular file type. We'll look at these entries in more detail later in this chapter.

Current user configuration and environment settings

The HKEY_CURRENT_USER category contains lots of user configuration and environment settings for your machine. These settings tell Windows 95 how to configure the desktop and the keyboard as well as the color settings and the configuration of the Start menu. All the user-specific settings appear in this category.

The settings you find in the HKEY_CURRENT_USER category are those for the current user — that is, the one who's currently logged on to the machine. This information is different from all the user configuration entries in other parts of the registry. This category contains dynamic settings; the other user-related categories contain static information. When a user starts Windows 95, the registry copies that user's entries from the HKEY_USERS category into HKEY_CURRENT_USER. Then, when that user shuts down Windows 95, the registry updates the appropriate entries in HKEY_USERS.

Hardware configuration entries

The HKEY_LOCAL_MACHINE category centers its attention on the machine hardware. This information includes the drivers and configuration information required to run the hardware. Every piece of hardware appears somewhere in this section of the registry, even if that hardware uses real-mode drivers. (A real-mode driver is a DOS driver that you have to add to the CONFIG.SYS file.) If a piece of hardware doesn't appear here, Windows 95 can't use it.

This category also contains all the Plug and Play information about your machine, and provides a complete listing of the device drivers and their revision level. This section may even contain the revision information for the hardware itself. For example, there's a distinct difference between a Pro Audio Spectrum 16+ Revision C sound board and the Revision D version of that same board. Windows 95 stores that difference in the registry.

This category does contain some software-specific information. For example, a 32-bit application will store the location of its Setup and Format Table (SFT) here. This is a file an application uses during installation, although some applications also use it during setup modification. Applications such as Word for Windows 95 store all their setup information in SFT tables. However, this is the limit of the software information for this category. The only application information you'll see here is global, configuration-specific information, such as the SFT.

Permanent user configuration and environment settings

The HKEY_USERS category contains a static listing of all the users of this particular registry file. Each user entry contains a complete copy of all the information found in HKEY_CURRENT_USER. It never pays to edit any of the information you find in this category. However, you can use this category for reference purposes. You don't want to edit these entries because none of your changes will take effect until the next time the user logs on to Windows 95. In other words, you really don't know what effect your changes will have until you reboot the machine. In addition, changing the settings for the current user is a waste of time because Windows 95 will overwrite the new data with the data contained in HKEY_CURRENT_USER during log-out or shutdown.

Graphics device interface (GDI) settings

The HKEY_CURRENT_CONFIG category is the simplest part of the registry. It contains two major keys: Display and System. Essentially, the GDI (graphics device interface) module of Windows 95 uses these entries to configure the display and the printer. The Display key has two subkeys: Fonts and Settings. The Fonts subkey determines which fonts Windows 95 uses for general display purposes. These are the raster (nonTrueType) fonts Windows 95 displays when you get a choice of which font to use for icons or other purposes.

The Settings subkey contains the current display resolution and the number of bits per pixel. The bits-per-pixel value determines the number of colors available. For example, 4 bits per pixel provides 16 colors, and 8 bits per pixel provides 256 colors. The three fonts listed as values under this key are the default fonts used for icons and application menus. You can change all the settings under this key using the Settings tab of the Properties for Display dialog box found in the Control Panel.

System status and performance settings

The final category, HKEY_DYN_DATA, contains two subkeys: Config Manager and PerfStats. You can monitor the status of the Config Manager key using the Device Manager. The PerfStats key values appear as statistics in the System Monitor utility display.

In a nutshell

As you can see from this description, the registry contains a lot of information. In addition to configuring your machine, it acts as a storage place for application settings and even the score of your last game of FreeCell. It would be difficult at best to tell you about everything in the registry because every machine is different. The contents of the registry are affected as much by which software you install as by which hardware you have and how you configure both hardware and software for your personal tastes. The following list does provide some general categories of information you should expect to see:

- ✔ File associations
- ✔ OLE settings
- ✔ Hardware configuration
- ✔ Software configuration
- ✔ Network configuration
- ✔ Windows settings (the entries you used to find WIN.INI and SYSTEM.INI)
- ✔ Dynamic data storage (such as the current level of processor activity)
- ✔ Static data storage (for example, the score for your last game of FreeCell)
- ✔ Software installation information

We haven't even begun to scratch the surface on what the registry actually contains. This overview simply lets you see the registry as a whole so that you have some idea of how all the pieces fit together. Many books on the market can give you an in-depth description of each category we've just introduced. For the rest of this chapter, we'll concentrate on the OLE-specific sections of the registry.

The registry uses a hierarchical format. In other words, it looks just like the outline for a book. Whenever you see a plus sign next to a registry key, you know there are other subkeys below it in the hierarchy. These subkeys always provide more details about the key you're examining. You can always expand a key to show its subkeys by clicking the plus sign. Click the minus sign next to a key to remove unneeded levels of detail.

Taking a closer look at the registry and OLE

OLE programmers will be most interested in the HKEY_CLASSES_ROOT category. Figure 21-6 provides a good view of the two main key types you'll find in this category. As you can see, the first type of key uses a file extension as a name (the .ZIP key shown in Figure 21-6 is a good example). The second type of key contains descriptions of those file extensions as names (the 123Worksheet key shown in Figure 21-6 is a good example).

The simplest way to look at these two key types is that Windows looks up the first type to see which application "owns" a particular file extension. Windows then looks at the description of that file extension to find out how to interact with the application that owns it. As we'll soon see, the picture gets a little more complex when you start examining these keys in greater detail.

Windows 95 doesn't limit you to three-character file extensions. You can create associations for file extensions of just about any length. For example, if you don't like using .DOC as the extension for Word for Windows files, you can change it to something better — for example, .My Stuff. The only thing Windows 95 looks for is a final period in the filename. Anything after the final period in a filename is a file extension.

Now, it's time to take a look at one of the file extension subkeys. Click the plus sign next to HKEY_CLASSES_ROOT and you'll see a list of file extensions. Select the .BMP file extension and click the plus sign next to it. Your display should look similar to the example in Figure 21-7.

The .BMP file extension has a default value of Paint.Picture and a subkey called ShellNew. (For additional information on which task this subkey performs, see the section, "Special shell extension subkeys," later in this chapter.) Most file extensions will include only a default value. Some also will add a ShellNew or other subkeys. Right now, we're interested in the default value.

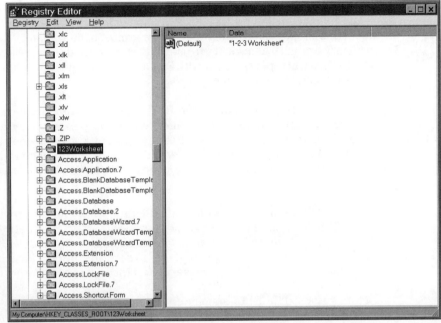

Figure 21-6:
The HKEY_
CLASSES_
ROOT
category is
divided into
two main
informational
areas.

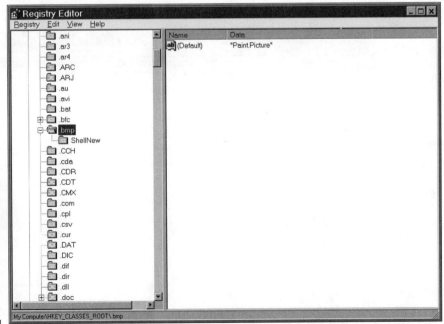

Figure 21-7:
The .BMP
file
extension
key contains
one value
and a single
subkey.

The default value of the file extension key tells Windows 95 where to look in the second part of the HKEY_CLASSES_ROOT category for additional information about this file extension. Every file extension must have a default value or the system will crash when you try to use that extension. (At the very least, Windows 95 will report an error with Explorer or any other application you try to use to look at that file extension.)

We saw that the default value for the .BMP file extension is Paint.Picture. Notice that there's a period between Paint and Picture. This period is very important because Windows 95 needs it to find the correct entry in the second half of the registry. Make sure you always observe little details like this when you edit the registry. The placement and types of symbols you use in a value or a key are as important as the text.

If you open the entire hierarchy for Paint.Picture, you should see something like Figure 21-8. The Paint.Picture key describes the file association between .BMP and Microsoft Paint, and it contains some other important Windows 3.x information. All of these entries work together to describe the OLE 1 entries for a particular file type. We'll take a closer look at these entries in the next section.

Before we look at the OLE1-specific entries, let's look at the Shell subkey of Paint.Picture. These entries tell Explorer what kinds of actions it can perform with this particular file type and how to perform them. You add these entries when you define a new file association in Explorer using the Options⇨View

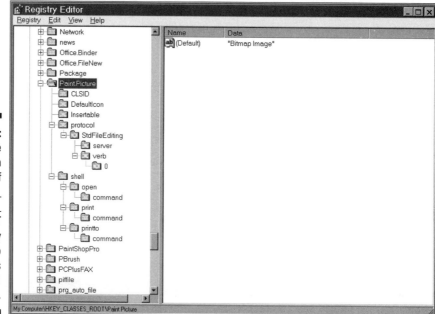

Figure 21-8:
The file association section of the HKEY_ CLASSES_ ROOT category also contains OLE 1 information.

command. Our Paint.Picture association defines three actions: open, print, and print to. If you right-click any .BMP file, you'll find those same three actions in the Context menu.

There are two types of Explorer entries. Figure 21-8 shows the first type, in which you open or print a file using an application's command line parameters. The other format, shown in Figure 21-9, relies on DDE to get the job done.

DDE is the predecessor to OLE, and, to a certain extent, OLE still relies on DDE. The spreadsheet macro example in Chapter 10 shows how DDE allows you to automatically create OLE links to another document.

Let's take a look at the Open command. We start by telling Explorer which application to use and where it is located. That's the value contained in the command key. The ddeexec key value appears in Figure 21-9. It looks much like the DDE macro we created in Chapter 10. This one tells Word for Windows to open a file.

Below the ddeexec key are application and topic keys. These two keys tell Word for Windows who's performing the DDE action and how they're doing it. In this case, you'll find that WinWord is the application and it's performing the system-related action of opening a file.

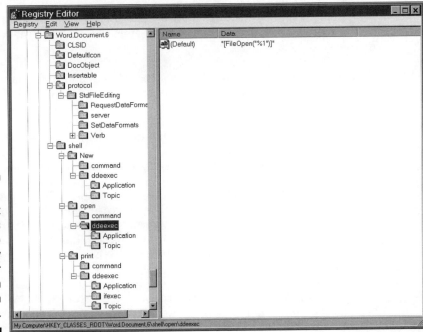

Figure 21-9:
Microsoft Word uses DDE to automatically open files or print them from Explorer.

Part of the file association information is to define an icon for that file type. The DefaultIcon key value always contains the name of an application, a DLL, or an icon file. For example, the Word.Document.6 file association key uses E:\MSOFFICE\WINWORD\WINWORD.EXE,1 as the DefaultIcon value. The 1 after the comma tells Windows to use the first icon it finds in that application as the icon for the .DOC file extension.

Special shell extension subkeys

Some file extensions — for example, .BMP — provide a Shell*X* subkey (see Figure 21-7). In the case of .BMP and .TXT, the standard subkey is ShellNew (the most common key). The term Shell*X* means shell extension. Think of a shell extension as an automated method for doing something like opening an existing document or creating a new one under Windows 95. When you right-click on the Desktop and look at the New option on the context menu that's displayed, all the file types listed are the result of shell extensions.

Even though ShellNew is the most common type of shell extension, various other shell extensions are available. Microsoft Word for Windows 95 adds quite a few shell extensions to the .DOC file extension key. You'll find up to four subkeys if you have Word for Windows installed on your machine (Shell, Word.Document.6, WordDocument, and Wordpad.Document.1).Other vendors will probably follow Microsoft's example. The number of shell extensions you see is limited only by your application vendor. For example, Microsoft Excel provides no less than three different shell extension entries for the .XLS file extension.

There's also another Windows 95-specific shell extension. If you manually add QuickView capability to a particular file extension, you'll see a QuickView key for that file extension in the registry.

A shell extension is a means for adding file- or application-specific OLE capabilities to Windows 95. Only an application that supports OLE 2 extensions can place a Shell*X* key in the registry; don't add one of these keys on your own. When you see this key, you know the application provides some type of extended OLE-related functionality. You'll see one example of this extended functionality when you double-click a shortcut to a data file that no longer exists. An application with the ShellNew shell extension will ask if you want to create a new file of the same type. (If you look at the values associated with ShellNew, there's always a NullFile entry that tells the shell extension which type of file to create.)

You can use the behavior of ShellNew to overcome a problem that Windows 95 has with some older applications. A few older applications don't register themselves correctly, so their file type won't appear as part of the New option on the context menu even though the application supports this capability. By following these steps, you can use the shell extension behavior to create new files as if the context menu entry did exist:

1. Create a temporary file.

2. Place a shortcut to it on your Desktop.

3. Erase the temporary file. (Make certain the application provides a ShellNew shell extension before you do this.)

Whenever you double-click the shortcut, your application will create a new file. This behavior also works if you place the file shortcut in the Start menu folder.

Windows 95 also provides you with a few generic shell extensions. For example, the * extension has a generic Shell*X* subkey. Below this, you'll see a PropertySheetHandler key and a 128-digit key that looks like some kind of secret code. In fact, the 128-digit value *is* a secret code. It's a reference identifier for the DLL (a type of application) that takes care of the * extension. You'll find this key under the CLSID key. (CLSID stands for *class identifier*.)

The secret code is for the "OLE Docfile Property Page." Looking at the value of the next key will tell you it exists in DOCPROP.DLL. This DLL provides the dialog box that asks which application you want to use to open a file when no registry entry is associated with that extension.

OLE 1 entries in the registry

At a minimum, almost every application that supports OLE will provide some type of OLE 1 support. The OLE 1 entries appear with the file association entries in the second half of the HKEY_CLASSES_ROOT category. An application could make quite a few different entries in this category. The problem is that different applications don't all make the same entries.

The types of OLE 1 entries an application makes in the registry depend on the capabilities the programmer builds into the DLL for that application. The following list tells you which entries a program could make. However, not every application will create every entry in this list. By examining the entries an application makes, you can learn a lot about the capabilities that application provides.

✔ CLSID — Even though it appears in the OLE 1 section, this is actually part of the OLE 2 entry. It's a pointer to a subkey you'll find under the CLSID (class identifier) key of the HKEY_CLASSES_ROOT category. C programmers use a special application to generate this 128-digit magic number. If you look for this number under the My Computer | HKEY_CLASSES_ROOT | CLSID key (as we'll do in the next section), you'll find the OLE 2 entries for this file association.

- Insertable — You won't usually see any value associated with this key. A blank value means Windows can place this file association in the Insert Object (or equivalent) dialog box provided by many applications — for example, Word for Windows. For various reasons, some OLE 1 objects aren't insertable.

- Protocol — This is a header key. (Think of it as a heading in a book — that is, a means for grouping related information in one place.) Below this key, you'll find all the standard actions this OLE 1 application can perform. In most cases, the only supported function is a standard file edit (StdFileEditing).

- StdFileEditing — This key is another header, and it appears under the Protocol key. It's the heading for all the keys that define a particular action. In this case, we're defining standard file editing. The things we need to define include: RequestDataFormats, Server, SetDataFormats, and Verb. The Verb key defines some verbs (action words) for the server. In this case, the Edit verb tells Word for Windows that you want to edit a document. The two data format entries tell Word for Windows which data formats to use for a particular document.

- Server — This key always tells Windows which application it should use to service an OLE 1 request. The Server key in my registry uses a value of E:\MSOFFICE\WINWORD\WINWORD.EXE for the Word.Document.6 file association (your registry might use a different path). This tells Windows precisely where the OLE server is located (although the server could also be a DLL). The string always includes the application's name, extension, and path.

If you ever run into a situation in which your OLE links worked yesterday but won't work today, check the Server value to make certain the path matches the application's location.

- Verb — Several verbs are associated with an OLE 1 object. Each verb defines a specific action the server will perform. This key doesn't have a value associated with it; its sole purpose is to organize actual verb entries. A client application can use only the verbs that are defined for a specific server. The following list tells you which verbs you will normally find:

    - 3 = Hide, 0, 1 — This verb allows the client application to hide the server window. The first number following the verb is a menu flag. A menu flag tells Windows 95 to display this item on the Object menu when the user right-clicks an object. You normally set this flag to 0. The second number is the verb flag. It specifies the precedence — in other words, the order — of this flag. Hide, Open, or Show normally take precedence over editing. In other words, those are the things that will happen first if the user double-clicks an object.

    - 2 = Open, 0, 1 — This verb allows the client to open the server in a separate window rather than allow it to take over the client window.

- 1 = Show, 0, 1 — A client would use this verb to display the server window in its preferred state. The whole idea of a state can be quite complex. If you think of it as the way the window looks, you'll have a pretty good idea of what to expect from a user's point of view.

- 0 = &Edit, 0, 2 — Every server provides this verb. It allows the client to call the server to edit the object.

- 1 = &Play, 0, 3 — You'll see this verb only when you're looking at some form of multimedia object.

✔ RequestDataFormats — This entry allows the server to define which data formats it supports for retrieval purposes.

✔ SetDataFormats — This entry allows the server to define which data formats it supports for storage purposes.

You will probably find other application-specific OLE 1 entries in this section of the registry. These entries represent the common, documented entries that a vendor is supposed to support. Of course, a vendor can add other verbs or features to an application. This is especially true with multimedia programs for which the only verbs are edit and play. A vendor may want to create a special Show or Record entry for a particular multimedia application.

OLE 2 entries in the registry

To qualify for Microsoft's seal of approval, every Windows 95-specific application needs to support OLE 2. It wouldn't do for Microsoft to make it easy for vendors to add this support. After all, what good is a seal that's easy to get? With that in mind, Microsoft came up with the magic number and the convoluted entry scheme we see in the Windows registry.

Figure 21-10 shows the OLE 2 entries for our Word.Document.6 file association. Of course, the big problem is how we got to this point. If you remember from your OLE 1 entry reading, there was a CLSID key. That key contained a 128-digit magic number.

When you look under the CLSID key in the HKEY_CLASSES_ROOT category of the registry, you'll find a long list of 128-digit magic numbers. All you need to do is match the magic number you find in the OLE 1 entry for your file association with one of the magic numbers under this key. Confused yet? We thought so.

Refer to Figure 21-10 as you read through the following list of OLE 2 entries in the registry. As with the OLE 1 entries, this list contains the common, documented, OLE 2 entries. A vendor could add other entries to support special program features.

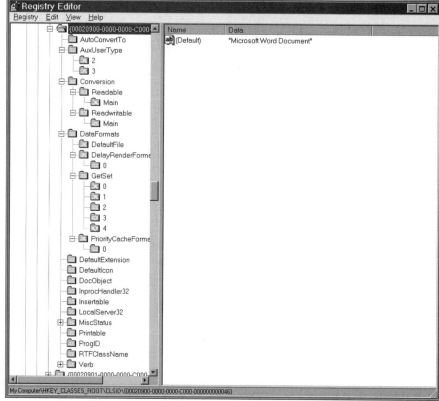

✔ AuxUserType — This key is a heading for the following user type keys:

- 2 — The 2 AuxUserType always contains the short name for the application. A client can use this name in a list box to identify the object's owner.

- 3 — This key contains the full name of the application that created the object. Like the 2 key, a client could use the 3 key value to provide an English application name for the object.

✔ DataFormats — This key is a heading for the following data format keys:

- GetSet — This key is a subheading for all the data formats the server can store and retrieve. For example, an OLE server such as Word for Windows would support DOC, RTF, and standard text formats. Its OLE 2 entries would reflect this fact. Each entry below this one defines a specific format type.

- • n = format, aspect, medium, flag — Each key contains a different format. The format argument contains the type of format as a string. You might find some as easy to read as "Rich Text Format" or as cryptic as "Embed_Source." An OLE client displays this string when you select the format you want to use for performing a Paste Special command. Aspect tells the client which display orientation the object supports. This usually means portrait and/or landscape. You will usually find a value of 1 here for portrait. Medium contains the supported format as a computer-readable number. Flag tells the client whether this is a get (1), set (2), or both (3) format. A get format allows you to get the data. A set format allows you to change (write) the data.

- ✔ DefaultFile — This entry works much like GetSet, except it identifies the default file format for this particular object.

- ✔ DefaultExtension — This is the default file extension for a particular file type. If you type a filename without the extension when using the Insert Object command, Windows assumes this extension. However, Windows won't stop you from assigning a different file extension to specific files. (This appears to be a new key specifically designed for Windows 95 use.)

- ✔ DefaultIcon — The value of this key tells the client which application icon to use when displaying the object as an icon.

- ✔ InProcHandler or InProcHandler32 — This key contains the name of the in-process handler. A handler is a special program that helps two programs communicate. Unless the application provides its own OLE 2 handler, this is usually OLE2.DLL or OLE32.DLL. A 32-bit application uses the InProcHandler32 entry.

- ✔ Insertable — Normally, you won't see any value associated with this key. A blank value means Windows can place this file association in the Insert Object (or equivalent) dialog box provided by many applications — for example, Word for Windows. For various reasons, some OLE 2 objects aren't insertable.

- ✔ LocalServer or LocalServer32 — Every OLE 2 object must have a server. This key contains the name of the server on the local machine. Because OLE 2 doesn't support RPCs (remote procedure calls), you'll always need a local server. The registry uses the LocalServer32 key for 32-bit applications.

- ✔ MiscStatus — This key contains the default status value for all data format aspects (such as portrait or landscape). For example, a value of 2 here means that users can see an object only in icon form when they insert it into a compound document. A value of 1 tells OLE that the server must perform special processing every time the user resizes the box holding the object.

- ProgID — The program identifier is a pointer to the file association for this class identifier. The file association is always a character string of some sort. It's the same string you look for when you try to find the file association that goes with a file extension in the HKEY_CLASSES_ROOT category. For example, the ProgID value for a .DOC file association is Word.Document.6. That's the same value we've used throughout this chapter for explanation purposes.

- Verb — Several verbs are associated with an OLE 2 object. Each verb defines a specific action the server will perform. This key doesn't have a value associated with it; its sole purpose is to organize actual verb entries. A client application can use only the verbs that are defined for a specific server. We already looked at all the available verbs in the OLE 1 section of this chapter.

- InProcServer — This is a special form of OLE server. Instead of calling the application that created the object, the client calls a DLL to handle any necessary display or editing functions. This has the advantage of speed; calling a DLL is faster than calling the executable file. However, the programmer has to do a lot more coding to make this kind of interface work.

- TreatAs — When this key is present, it contains the CLSID for another file format. The client can treat the current file format like the specified file format. For example, if you looked at the Paintbrush Picture OLE 2 entry, you would find a TreatAs value with the same 128-digit value as a Bitmap Image. This tells you that Windows 95 uses the same application to service Paintbrush Picture files as it does for Bitmap Image files. A little more research would tell you that the OLE 2 server for Paintbrush Pictures is Microsoft Paint.

- AutoTreatAs — This key forces the client to treat the current file format the same way it would treat the file format specified by the CLSID. From the user's perspective, it works just like the TreatAs entry.

- AutoConvert or AutoConvertTo — Some objects' context menus contain a Convert option. This key allows you to automatically convert the current file format to the one identified by CLSID. For example, Word for Windows allows you to convert many types of data to a format that it specifically supports. This conversion process changes the embedded or linked object into a Word for Windows object. In other words, it changes the data into something that Word might have created itself.

- Conversion or Convertible — This key defines the Conversion option of the OLE Object menu. There are two levels of subkeys. The first level tells which action to perform: Readable or Writable. The second level contains a list of readable or writable file conversion formats. For example, you'll find that Word for Windows supports several formats, including Word Document. The number of conversion format entries is determined by the number of file filters you install for the application. For example, if you install WordPerfect file support in Word for Windows, you'll find an entry for it here. Remember though that these are OLE 2 entries. Even though one application supports another application's file format as part of a Save As option, it might not support that format for OLE purposes.

✔ Interfaces — This key contains a list of interfaces supported by the server. The value for this key will eventually contain the names of other ways of accessing the OLE server (other than from the local machine), but no applications currently support this. For example, this entry could contain the types of network protocols the application supports.

Future Shock — OLE and VBA

Most applications don't provide any support for VBA as a programming language, and some may never support it. Programs from Lotus will use a BASIC-like language called LotusScript, while programs from Novell will use their own universal macro language that might be called PerfectScript. However, more and more applications are providing support for VBA as an interface by opening their internal macro language for outside use. (LotusScript is actually VBA-compatible to a great extent.)

To get a better idea of how this affects you, consider what it would be like to drive an application by remote control. You could do everything you would normally do with the application, but you wouldn't have to do it directly. For example, you could process all the data needed from your spreadsheet to complete a report from within your word processor.

Macros give us this capability right now. All you need to do is open the application and run the macro. However, what if you have several documents linked together and you need to control the application from a centralized point? For example, what if your report contains a graph from Corel Chart, some spreadsheet data from Excel, and a few items from your Access database. Now, imagine that Corel Chart also needs the information from the Excel spreadsheet before it can update your graph. Using VBA would allow you to call Excel first, update the spreadsheet, pass that data on to Corel Chart, and then retrieve the updated graph. As you can see, you could control all of the required updates from your word processor using VBA.

As a programming language, VBA will allow you to perform the same tasks you would normally perform with a macro, but from another application. Think of VBA as a remote control for all the applications on your system. You don't have to be a programming genius to use this capability; the only requirement is that you know how to write a macro in each of the applications you want to link.

Many programs already support VBA, but not as fully as you might expect. For example, some Corel Systems offerings allow you to perform a limited number of file-related tasks, but no drawing-related tasks. This means you could automatically update the contents of a drawing or even add a new one to your current document, but you could not modify that drawing in any way.

Other applications, such as Microsoft Word for Windows, provide full access to all their features through VBA. You could conceivably write a book (or any other task you wanted to perform) through another application that supported VBA as a language.

Think of the ways you could combine VBA and OLE to make "smart" documents. For example, it might be possible to program your spreadsheet to automatically generate your monthly reports using a graphing package and your presentation graphics program. You could even vary formats within the document depending on the value of specific numbers. The number of ways you could use VBA is probably limitless. Now, we just have to wait for vendors to implement it.

Glossary

Binary Large Object (BLOB) A special field in a database table that accepts objects such as bitmaps, sounds, or text as input. This field type is normally associated with the OLE capabilities of a DBMS, but some third-party products make it possible to add BLOB support to older database file formats such as the Xbase DBF file format. BLOB fields always imply OLE client support by the DBMS.

bitmap A file or OLE object containing the binary representation of a graphic image in raster format. Each pixel on the display is represented as one entry in the file. The size of the entry depends on the number of colors the image supports. Common sizes include monochrome (1-bit), VGA (4-bits), SVGA (8-bits), and true color (24-bits).

BLOB (See Binary Large Object)

CAD (See Computer-Aided Design)

client When used in the OLE sense of the word, an application that receives data or services from another application.

client/server A method of networking that relies on a file server as a central repository for data. The file server acts as the server for a workstation (or client). This term is also used in regard to OLE. In OLE terms, the client is the application requesting data, while the server is the application providing data.

compound document A special form of file containing one or more OLE objects. Each object can consist of text, graphics, sound, or other classes of information and contributes to the document as a whole. The compound document is also referred to as a container. The new Binder document in Microsoft Office 95 is actually an OLE compound document.

Computer-Aided Design (CAD) A special type of graphics program used for creating, printing, storing, and editing architectural, electrical, mechanical, or other forms of engineering drawings. CAD programs normally provide precise measuring capabilities and libraries of predefined objects such as sinks, desks, resistors, and gears.

Database Management System (See DBMS)

DBMS (Database Management System) A collection of tables, forms, queries, reports, and other data elements. It acts as a central processing point for data accessed by one or more users. Most DBMSs (except free-form or text-based) rely on a system of tables for storing information. Each table contains records (rows) consisting of separate data fields (columns). Common DBMSs include Access, Paradox, dBASE, and FileMaker Pro.

DDE (Dynamic Data Exchange) The capability for cutting data found in one application and pasting it into another application — for example, cutting a graphics image created by a paint program and pasting it into a word processing document. Once pasted, the data doesn't reflect changes made to it by the originating application. DDE is the predecessor to OLE.

DDE macro A method of manipulating data found in one application (the server) from within another application (the client). The macro sends commands to the server application, which places the requested data on the Windows clipboard. The client application can retrieve this data for its own use.

DLL (Dynamic Link Library) One form of Windows executable files. DLLs normally contain one or more common executable functions, such as a File Open dialog box. A program loads the DLL and requests specific services from it. Using DLLs promotes code sharing in high-level operating systems such as Windows and OS/2.

document-centric A method for managing information that relies on OLE to create the links between a document and its originating application. The file associations under Windows 3.x were a simple form of this data management approach; they allowed a user to open a document by double-clicking it. OLE 2 allows better management by providing additional commands such as print and convert. Windows 95 uses a document-centric approach to information management.

Dynamic Data Exchange (See DDE)

Dynamic Link Library (See DLL)

embedding Placing a copy of the contents of an OLE object within the compound document. Contrast this with linking, in which the object remains outside the container.

file conversion The capability of an OLE 2 compatible application to change an object into a native format document. For example, Word for Windows can convert an MS Paint object to a native format bitmap.

Graphical User Interface (See GUI)

GUI (Graphical User Interface) A system of icons and graphic images that replace the character mode menu system used by many machines. The GUI can reside on top of another operating system (such as DOS or UNIX) or as part of the operating system itself (such as OS/2 or Windows NT). Advantages of a GUI are ease of use and high-resolution graphics. Disadvantages are higher workstation hardware requirements and lower performance compared to a similar system using a character mode interface.

hatching A set of diagonal lines used to designate an object in a compound document. Hatching is used for a variety of purposes. Most applications use it to show which object is active. See Chapters 10 and 14 for further details.

icon A symbol used for graphically representing the purpose and/or function of an application or a file. For example, text files might appear as sheets of paper, with the name of the file below the icon. Applications designed for the environment or operating system usually appear with a special icon depicting the vendor's or the product's logo. Icons normally appear as part of a GUI environment or operating system such as Windows or OS/2.

Light Remote Procedure Calls (LRPC) One of several methods for accessing data within another application. LRPC only work on the current workstation. If you have a Freelance Graphics chart embedded in a WordPerfect document and you double-click the Freelance Graphics chart, OLE looks for a copy of Freelance Graphics on your computer. If you don't have a copy of Freelance Graphics, OLE is dumbfounded and won't let you edit the embedded Freelance Graphics chart. Future versions of OLE promise to use Remote Procedure Call (RPC) technology, which means that OLE can search across a network for the programs it needs.

linking The process of creating a pointer to a file on disk within a compound document (container). The pointer tells the client application which file to use; the data itself stays on disk. Contrast this with embedding, in which the data contained in the OLE object becomes part of the compound document.

LRPC (See Light Remote Procedure Calls)

macros A form of programming that records keystrokes and other program-related tasks to a file on disk or within the current document. Most applications provide a macro recorder that records the keystrokes and mouse clicks you make. This means you don't even have to write them in most cases. Macros are especially popular in spreadsheets. Most macros use some form of DDE to complete OLE-related tasks.

modem An electronic device used to connect computers and terminals over the telephone lines. A modem can be internal (a card fitting into an expansion slot and connecting directly into the phone jack) or external (a separate box directly connecting your telephone to a serial port on your PC).

nested objects The capability of some OLE 2 objects to act as both an information source and a container for holding other objects. Nesting allows several layers of objects within one compound document.

object When used in the OLE sense of the word, a representation of all or part of a graphic, text, sound, or other data file within a compound document. An object retains its original format and properties. The client application must call on the server application to change or manipulate the object.

Object Data Manager A specialized database found within drafting and drawing programs. It allows the user to create lists of objects and arrange them in specific ways. See Chapter 8 for more details.

Object Linking and Embedding (See OLE)

OCX (OLE Custom eXtension) A special form of VBX designed to make adding OLE capabilities to an application easier for the programmer. Essentially, an OCX is a DLL with an added programmer and OLE interface.

ODBC (Open Database Connectivity) One of several methods for exchanging data between DBMSs. ODBC normally relies on SQL to translate DBMS-specific commands from the client into a generic language. The ODBC agent on the server translates these SQL requests into server-specific commands.

OLE (Object Linking and Embedding) The successor to DDE, OLE allows two programs to exchange information. OLE provides two methods of exchange: linking and embedding. The client application creates a compound document containing one or more OLE objects. Whenever an object requires service, the client sends a message to the originating application (the server). The server fulfills the request, and then unloads itself from memory if it isn't needed. There are currently two versions of OLE: OLE 1 and OLE 2. See Chapters 1 and 14 for more details.

OLE Custom eXtension (See OCX)

Open Database Connectivity (See ODBC)

RAD (Rapid Application Development) A tool that lets you design your program's user interface and then write commands to make that user interface do something useful. Visual BASIC and Delphi are both examples of RAD programs.

Rapid Application Development (See RAD)

raster graphic A file format that contains one entry for each pixel in the bitmap. All entries are precisely the same size, usually 1-, 4-, 8-, or 24-bits. Raster graphic files are also called bitmaps because they map the color of each pixel on the image canvas. Contrast this with vector graphics that depend on math equations to define an image rather than storing its representation as a bitmap.

Remote Procedure Calls (RPC) One of several methods for accessing data within another application. RPC is designed to look for the application first on the local workstation, and then across the network at the applications stored on other workstations. If you have a Freelance Graphics chart embedded in a WordPerfect document and you double-click the Freelance Graphics chart, OLE looks for a copy of Freelance Graphics on your computer. If you don't have a copy of Freelance Graphics, OLE becomes dumbfounded and won't let you edit the embedded Freelance Graphics chart. RPCs will allow OLE to hunt out the programs it needs across a network.

RPC (See Remote Procedure Calls)

SDK (Software Development Kit) A special add-on to an operating system or an application that describes how to access its internal features. For example, an SDK for Windows would show how to create a File Open dialog box. Programmers use an SDK to learn how to access special Windows components such as OLE.

Software Development Kit (See SDK)

SOM (See System Object Model)

SQL (Structured Query Language) Most DBMSs use this language to exchange information. Some also use it as their native language. SQL provides a method for requesting information from the DBMS. It defines which table or tables to use, what information to get from the table, and how to sort that information.

Structured Query Language (See SQL)

System Object Model (SOM) An alternative object standard from IBM used with OS/2. The Workplace Shell uses SOM in place of OLE to create objects. See Chapter 1 for further details.

VBA (See Visual BASIC for Applications)

VBA interface The set of functions and commands an application makes available to other applications for the purpose of exchanging data.

VBX (Visual BASIC eXtension) A special form of DLL that contains functions as well as a programmer interface. The DLL part of the VBX accepts requests from an application for specific services such as opening a file. The programmer interface portion appears on the toolbar of a program such as Visual BASIC as a button. Clicking the button creates one instance of that particular type of control.

vector graphic A method of defining graphics based on mathematical equations. The application using the vector graphic must create a bitmap using the data points found within the vector graphic file. Contrast this with raster graphic files, which contain one entry for each pixel in the bitmap.

Visual BASIC eXtension (See VBX)

Visual BASIC for Applications (VBA) A new scripting language standard from Microsoft designed to replace DDE. It uses functions and commands that a server application makes available to a client application to exchange data.

Index

• *Symbols* •

+ (plus sign), 141, 185, 187
- (minus sign), 282
16-bit programming
  DLLs and, 80
  VBX components and, 42
  version of Delphi, 223
  Visual BASIC and, 207
32-bit programming
  DLLs and, 80
  VBX components and, 42
  version of Delphi, 223
  Visual BASIC and, 207

• *A* •

Access, 124, 175, 184
  compatibility with, ensuring, 42–43
  database form, adding a bitmap
    to, 128–131
  DDE and, 177
  form macros and, 134–144
  object properties and, 131–132
  simple object macros and, 142–144
  typical table in, 126
  VBX/OCX components and, 259
Access BASIC, 143, 159, 175, 177,
    184, 191–206
  forms and, 193–194, 202–205

macros and, 193–194
Accessories group, 60
actions, standard, 180–182
activation, in-place, 14–15, 52, 54
  adding, 214–217
  Delphi and, 223, 232–234
  Excel and, 117, 148
activation techniques, 183–184
Active mode, 179, 180
Add Below button, 160
ADDRESS table, 154
Add Selected Fields button, 94
AI (Adobe Illustrator), 91
AllText HT/Pro, 265–266
Alt+Tab (display spreadsheets), 113
Alt+Tab (reselect TurboCAD), 100
animation, 81, 104
Apple Computer, 16, 32
application-based languages,
    reasons to use, 73
Application Description box, 218
App-Link, 263–264
Arial font type, 88, 113
ASCII files, 169
As Is list box, 67
associations, file, 279, 281, 284–287,
    289–290
ATTRIB, 253

audience, for your programs, 172
AutoActivate event, 133
AutoConvert key, 292
AutoConvertTo key, 292
AUTOEXEC.BAT, 169
automation, OLE. *See also* VBA (Visual BASIC for Applications)
  CorelDRAW! and, 93
  DBMSs and, 119–122
  definition of, 15–16, 54, 71–80
  macros and, 72–77
  spreadsheets and, 119, 120–122
AutoSize property, 224, 229
AutoTreatAs key, 292
AuxUserType key, 290
availability, of programming tools, 172
Avanti Software, 267–268

• B •

Back Color property, 204
backup systems, 255
BASIC, 73, 164
  as a high-level language, 171
  Visual BASIC and, 223
  Word for Windows and, 159
batch files, 169
Bennet-Tec Information Systems, 265–266
beta format (video format), 42
binary values, in the registry, 274–275

bitmap(s), 61, 83, 126. *See also* graphics; raster graphics
  in Access BASIC tables, 200
  adding, to forms/reports, 124, 128–131
  adding, to spreadsheets, 112, 117
  converting raster graphics into, 102
  DBMSs and, 124, 126
  definition of, 295
  files, in the registry, 274–275, 283–287
  inserting, into Word documents, 74–77, 150–151
  linking, 63
  manipulating, with form macros, 133–142
Blank Database radio button, 134
BLOBs (binary large objects), 124, 126, 129, 191
  definition of, 295
  object frames and, comparison of, 130
BMP files (listed by name). *See also* bitmaps
  BREAD.BMP, 135
  DAIRY.BMP, 135
  FRUIT.BMP, 135
  LEAVES.BMP, 74–77, 83, 87, 94, 121
  MEAT.BMP, 135
  SWEETS.BMP, 200–201
  VEGETABLE.BMP, 135
bookmarks, 116, 122

Borland International, 16, 73, 126

Bound Object Frame control, 130–131

BrainTree, 265

BREAD.BMP, 135

Browse button, 63, 87, 94, 160, 211, 228

Browse dialog box, 63, 211, 228

bug(s). *See also* errors; testing

add-ins for handling, 267–268

fatware and, 40

fixing, testing as, 235

hunting for, 244

buttons

Add Below button, 160

Add Selected Fields button, 94

Browse button, 63, 87, 94, 160, 211, 228

Create New Field button, 94

Exit button, 209, 214, 224, 230, 231

Form View button, 127–128, 197, 205

Get Data button, 152

Insert Data button, 156

Menus button, 160

Object Data Manager button, 94, 97

Options button, 153

Save button, 198

Stop button, 160

Table AutoFormat button, 156

Use OLE button, 209, 211, 213, 214, 224, 228, 231

• C •

C (programming language), 170, 175

learning, 271–273

as a low-level language, 171, 172, 271–272

MFC classes and, 80, 272

C++ (programming language), 1–2

learning, 271–273

as a low-level language, 172, 271–272

VBX components and, 42

CAD (computer-aided design), 81, 91. *See also* graphics

architectural drawings and, 82, 92

attaching descriptive data to objects with, 97

basic description of, 82, 295

chart programs and, 105

fixing broken links and, 255

OLE scripts and, 103–104

specialized server methods and, 100–103

calling syntax, 244

capabilities, OLE

of charting programs, 107

of forms, maximizing, 202–205

identifying, 45–56

of paint programs, 50–52, 83–86

types of, 46–47

Category combo box, 134, 138–139, 142, 196, 202

CA-Visual Objects, 124

CDR (CorelDRAW!) files, 91

CGM (computer graphics metafile) files, 91

Change Category macro, 142–144, 196

Change Links dialog box, 254

Change Source pushbutton, 254–255

Change What Menu field, 160

ChartBuilder, 262

charting programs
add-ins for, 264
basic description of, 104–108
checking the capabilities of, 107
as clients, 177
CorelCHART, 82, 104–108, 293
design of, for static presentations, 110

Choose Builder dialog, 140

Chrisalan Designs, 270

Claris Works, 10

class(es)
identifiers, 186–188, 287, 289
MFC (Microsoft Foundation Classes), 80, 272
modules, definition of objects by, 217

Class1 code window, 218

client(s)
basic code for, in DLLs, 79
basic description of, 20–26, 176, 295
charting programs and, 105, 106
DBMSs as, 124
how servers work with, 24–26

types of OLE capabilities and, 46–50

clip art, 104, 112

clipboard
copying bitmaps to, 128
copying charts to, 107
copying scripts to, 103–104

CLSID (class identifier) key, 186–187, 287, 289

cmdExit_Click(), 208, 212

cmdOLE_Click(), 208, 212

Code editor, 224, 229

color, in forms, 204

Color dialog box, 204

Columnar Form Wizard, 127

Combo Box tool, 138

Combo Box Wizard, 138

CommandButton control, 208, 212

command line interface, using, 177–178

communications programs, 262–264
App-Link, 263–264
Communications Library 3, 262–263

compatibility. *See also* capabilities, OLE
ensuring, 42–43, 241
testing and, 241
Windows 3.1 and, 45
Windows 95 and, 45

Component palette, 224, 229

compound documents
definition of, 10, 295

programming modes and, 178–179

sharing, 28–29

system resources and, 28

Config manager, 281

CONFIG.SYS, 280

containers. *See* compound documents

context menus

basic description of, 147–149

DBMSs and, 126–127

lack of edit/open options in, 158

shell extension subkeys and, 286

word processors and, 147–149, 151

Control Panel, 281

conversion

basic description of, 54, 296

embedding vs., 30

registry key for, 292

as a standard action, 181

Conversion key, 292

Convertible key, 292

Copy action, 182

Copy⇨Paste Special method, 146

CorelCHART, 82, 104–108, 293

CorelDRAW!, 103

attaching descriptive data to objects with, 97

client/server services provided by, 177

CorelDRAW.CorelDRAWApp5 and, 186, 187

interface documentation and, 93

macros and, 82, 92

special OLE capabilities in, 93–94

using, basic description of, 91–98

VBA and, 92–93, 104

Version 4.0, 94

CorelShow, 92

CP/M-80, 221

CP/M-86, 37

Create from File radio button, 87, 94

Create from File tab, 74

Create New Field button, 94

Create New radio button, 209

Create Shortcut dialog box, 276–277

Crescent, 269

Crystal Reports Pro, 266

Crystal Services, 266

Ctrl+Alt+Del, 236–237

Ctrl+C (Edit⇨Copy), 60, 63, 67, 213, 214, 230, 231

Ctrl+F5 (Start With Full Compile), 218

Ctrl+S (File⇨Save), 60, 63, 67, 211, 214, 226, 231

cursor position, inserting pictures at, 150

Custom Control Factory, 268

Customize dialog box, 160

custom programs. *See also* automation, OLE

basic description of, 40–42

fatware and, 40–41

making your own applications, 41–42

Cut action, 182

• D •

DAIRY.BMP, 135

Database dialog box, 135, 137, 152, 154, 156, 194, 196, 198, 203–204

databases. *See also* DBMSs (database management systems)

DataFormats key, 290

Data Properties control, 131

Data Sources dialog box, 125

dBASE, 42, 123–124, 133

DBMSs (database management systems). *See also* FoxPro; dBASE

basic description of, 123–144, 296

editing pictures and, 143

engines and, 123

forms and, 128–131

macros and, 131–144, 158–165

mailing lists and, 146, 151–158

objects within, basic description of, 125–127

programming and, 191, 192

reports and, 128–131

word processing and, 158–165

DDE (Dynamic Data Exchange), 10–11, 116, 120

the command line interface and, 177

communications programs and, 262–264

Custom Control Factory and, 268

DDE-EXECUTE command and, 73, 121, 122

definition of, 296

macros, 120–122, 142

methods, vs. ODBC, 157

OLE as a better version of, 37

Word for Windows and, 251–252

ddeexec key, 285

DDE_LINK1, 122

DefaultExtension key, 291

DefaultFile key, 291

DefaultIcon key, 291

Delete pushbutton, 74

deleting, macros from style sheets, 74

Delphi

potential Borland counterpart to, 73

VBX components and, 42, 259

writing OLE programs with, 223–234

Delrina, 50–51

Desaware, 268

design mode, definition of, 128

Design View, 134, 137, 142

Device Manager, 281

diagonal lines (hatching), 118, 297

dialog boxes, adding, 161–165. *See also* dialog boxes (listed by name)

dialog boxes (listed by name)

Browse dialog box, 63, 211, 228

Change Links dialog box, 254

Color dialog box, 204

Create Shortcut dialog box, 276–277

Customize dialog box, 160

Database dialog box, 135, 137, 152, 154, 156, 194, 196, 198, 203–204

Data Sources dialog box, 125

Expression Builder dialog box, 140, 141

File Open dialog box, 83, 163, 254, 276

Insert Data dialog box, 157–158

Insert Object dialog box, 50–51, 57–58, 61–64, 94, 112–113, 116–118, 126, 200, 207–211, 214, 223–228, 231

Insert Picture dialog box, 150–151

Insert Procedure dialog box, 203, 218, 220

Links dialog box, 113, 115, 254

Macro dialog box, 74, 140, 142, 159–160

New Button dialog box, 161

New Category dialog box, 200

Object Data dialog box, 95, 97

Object dialog box, 65–66

Open Data Source dialog box, 153

Option dialog box, 249–251

Options dialog box, 121, 217–218, 219

Paste Special dialog box, 50, 67–68, 84–87, 113, 211–214, 228–231

Project1 dialog box, 220

Properties dialog box, 139, 140, 142, 196

Query Options dialog box, 154–155

Record dialog box, 159

Save As dialog box, 60, 63, 67, 211, 214, 226, 231

Select a Title for the Program dialog box, 278

Select Program Folder dialog box, 276

Dialog Editor, 161–165

DIR command, 169

DLLs (dynamic link libraries)

basic description of, 296

compilers and, 272

DOCPROP.DLL, 287

file extension for, 279

MFCOLEUI.DLL, 80

OLE2CONV.DLL, 79

OLE2DISP.DLL, 79

OLE2.DLL, 79, 291

OLE2NLS.DLL, 79

OLE32.DLL, 291

OLECLI.DLL, 78, 79, 80

OLE-specific, basic description of, 78–80

OLESRV.DLL, 78, 79, 80

registry and, 150, 287

shell extension subkeys and, 287

testing and, 241

VBX/OCX components and, 42

as Visual BASIC In-Process servers, 217, 221

document(s). *See also* documents, compound

(continued)

document(s) *(continued)*
  -centric computing, definition of,
    16–17, 296
  phantom, creating, 255
  templates, 41
documents, compound
  definition of, 10, 295
  programming modes and, 178–179
  sharing, 28–29
  system resources and, 28
Documents⇨Page Layout, 88
"domino effect," 31
DOS (Disk Operating System)
  -based programs, 43, 45
  DIR command, 169
  determining OLE capabilities
    and, 46
  macros and, 133
  mode, booting in, 253, 274
  spreadsheets and, 110
drag-and-drop support, 54
drawing programs, 81. *See also*
    CorelDRAW!; graphics
  special OLE capabilities in, 93–94
  using, basic description of, 91–98
DWORD values, 274–275

• *E* •

Edit action, 180–182
Edit menu, 106, 107
  Edit⇨Copy, 60, 63, 67, 83, 87, 100,
    113, 128, 213, 214, 230, 231
Edit⇨Copy Special, 100
Edit⇨Insert, 47, 49
Edit⇨Insert Object, 50, 57–58, 94,
    110–111, 118
Edit⇨Links, 113
Edit⇨Paste Link, 47–48, 60, 113
Edit⇨Paste Special, 47–48, 50, 67,
    83–84, 87, 100, 113, 128–129, 150
editors
  Code editor, 224, 229
  Dialog Editor, 161–165
  Field Editor, 94, 96
  Menu Editor, 215
  REGEDIT (registry editor), 185,
    248, 252, 275–277
Edit pushbutton, 74
eight-track cartridges, 42
embedding
  advantages/disadvantages of,
    13–14
  basic description of, 10, 12–15,
    112–118, 296
  vs. file conversion, 30
  in-place editing and, 14–15
  linking and, differences between, 39
  memory requirements for, 25
  with Microsoft Office, 65–68
  testing, 209–210, 213, 226–228,
    230–231
end-of-paragraph mark, 114
engines, DBMS, 123
environment settings, 279–280, 281
equations, graphics as a series of, 91

errors. *See also* bugs; testing
  feature-related, 240–241
  file access, 192
  file search, 87
  macro recording, 77
  memory-related, 242–243
  registry, 252–253
  sounds, adding, 128
Event page, 140
Event Properties control, 131–132
event(s). *See also* events (listed
  by name)
  testing, unexpected, 236–237,
    239–240
  tracking, 191–192
events (listed by name). *See*
  also events
  Auto Activate event, 133
  On Change event, 142
  On Click event, 198, 202, 204
  On Current event, 140, 196
  On Dbl Click event, 198, 201
  On Got Focus event, 198
Excel. *See also* spreadsheets
  client/server programs and, 22–23
  compatibility with, ensuring,
    42–43
  customizing applications and, 41
  determining OLE capabilities and,
    50–51
  Edit menu, 110–111
  embedding spreadsheets and,
    112–118

  fixing broken links and, 254–256
  in-place editing and, 52–53, 215,
    232–234
  linking spreadsheets data and,
    112–115
  macros and, 120–122
  memory requirements for, 28
  OLE automation and, 120–122
  shell extension subkeys and, 286
  testing OLE links and, 214
  updating files and, 39
  VBA and, 293
EXE files
  compiling Visual BASIC programs
    into, 221
  converting macro programs
    into, 159
  as Out-of-Process servers, 217, 221
EXE files (listed by name)
  GDI.EXE, 28
  KRNL386.EXE, 28
  REGEDIT.EXE, 185, 248, 276
  USER.EXE, 28
Exit button, 209, 214, 224, 230, 231
exiting
  Delphi, 230, 231
  Visual BASIC, 209, 214
Explorer, 241, 249–250
  file association and, 279
  Options dialog, 121
  registry and, 284–285
  View Options dialog, 87

Export Filename command, 93
Expression Builder dialog box, 140, 141
Expression field, 141
extensibility, 173

• F •

fatware, 40
FaxMan, 263
Field Editor, 94, 96
fields
  Change What Menu field, 160
  definition of, 126
  Expression field, 141
  Name field, 218
  Position in Menu field, 160
  Preview field, 156
  Project Name field, 218
  Record Macro Name field, 160
  Source field, 84
file(s). *See also* file extensions
  association, 279, 281, 284–287, 289–290
  conversion, 30, 54, 191, 292, 296
  corruption, 255
  -names, long, 253
  read-only, 192
file extensions. *See also* file extensions (listed by type)
  changing, with the Explorer, 249–250
  in the registry, 244, 248, 282–286

searching for applications associated with, 87
file extensions (listed by type)
  BAT, 169
  BMP, 283–285, 286
  DLL, 279
  DOC, 279, 283, 285
  TXT, 274, 279, 286
  XLS, 286
File menu, 215, 233
  File⇨Edit, 58, 118, 162, 209
  File⇨Open, 83, 128
  File⇨Page Setup, 88
  File⇨Save, 60, 63, 67, 211, 214, 226, 231
  File⇨Update, 58, 101, 118
File Open dialog box, 83, 163, 254, 276
File radio button, 63, 228
File Types list box, 152
File Types tab, 249
File Types table, 198
filter criteria, selecting, 154
flags
  definition of, 184
  OLEMISC_ACTIVATEWHENVISIBLE flag, 184
  OLEMISC_INSIDEOUT flag, 184
flexibility, 172–173
font(s)
  Arial, 88, 113

registry settings for, 281

for spreadsheets data, 113

types, of logo text, 88

Food Group combo box, 141, 204

Food Group control, 205

Food Inventory Control 1, 139, 140–142, 203

Food Inventory Control 2, 196, 198, 200, 203–205

Food Itemizer table, 135–138

Food Picture control, 141–142, 198, 200, 202, 205

Food Select 1 query, 135, 136, 137

Food Types table, 135–142, 194–198

form(s)

    Access BASIC and, 193–194, 202–205

    adding bitmaps to, 124, 128–131

    capabilities of, maximizing, 202–205

    DBMSs and, 124, 128–131

    macros, 134–144

Format⇨Paragraph, 88

Format Properties control, 131

Form Properties dialog, 196

Forms tab, 137

Form View button, 127–128, 197, 205

Form Wizard, 137

FoxPro, 124, 125

FreeCell, 281

Freelance Graphics, 31–32

FRM files, 133

front end, accessing DBMS engines through, 123

FRUIT.BMP, 135

Function radio button, 218

• G •

GDI (graphics device interface), 28, 280–281

GDI.EXE, 28

Get Data button, 152

Got Focus property, 132

grammar checkers, 17, 41

graphics. *See also* bitmaps; CAD (computer-aided design); charting programs; paint programs

    adding, to forms/reports, 124, 128–131

    adding, to spreadsheets, 110, 115

    adding, to word processing documents, 74–77, 150–151

    advanced OLE for, 99–108

    basic description of, 81–98

    client/server services provided by, 177

    clip art, 104, 112

    the Graphics Server SDK and, 261–262

    hatching and, 118, 297

    modules, customizing applications and, 41

    specialized server methods and, 99–103

    Visual BASIC and, 260–262

graphs, add-ins for, 264

Grisham, John, 26

GroupIndex property, 233

GUI (graphical user interface), 10, 297

• H •

hard disk(s)

  basic requirements for OLE, 27, 28–30

  customizing applications and, 40, 41

  space, taken up by Microsoft's overview of OLE specification, 175

hardware configuration entries, in the registry, 280, 281

hatching (diagonal lines), 118, 297

Height property, 139

help

  macros and, 73

  word processing format used for, 266

Help⇨About Dialog, 242–243

high-level languages, basic description of, 171

HiJaak, 50–51

HKEY_CLASSES_ROOT, 185–186, 187, 244, 278, 282–289

HKEY_CURRENT_CONFIG, 278, 280–281

HKEY_CURRENT_USER, 278–280

HKEY_DYN_DATA, 278, 281

HKEY_LOCAL_MACHINE, 278, 280

HKEY_USERS, 278, 280

HyperAccess, 50–51

Hypertext manager, 265

hypertext tools, OLE-equipped, 265–266

• I •

IBM (International Business Machines)

  multiplatform support and, 32

  SOM (System Object Model), 16, 299

icon drawing, 81, 82. *See also* graphics

Image control, 130

ImageKnife/VBX, 261

implementation, portions of programs, 224

Import Filename command, 93

Inactive mode, 178–179

INI files, problems with, 241, 248

in-place activation/editing, 14–15, 52, 54

  adding, 214–217

  Delphi and, 223, 232–234

  Excel and, 117, 148

InProcHandler key, 291

InProcServer key, 292

Insertable key, 288, 291

Insert Data as Field check box, 157

Insert Data button, 156

Insert Data dialog box, 157–158

Insert menu
 Insert⇨Class Module, 218
 Insert⇨Database, 152
 Insert⇨Module, 218
 Insert⇨New Object, 87
 Insert⇨Object, 47, 49–50, 61–65, 74, 110–111, 121, 128, 150, 159–160
 Insert⇨Picture, 150
 Insert⇨Procedure, 203, 218
 Insert⇨Sound, 161, 163
 Insert⇨Sound File, 158–165
Insert Object dialog box, 50–51, 57–58, 61–64, 94, 112–113, 116–118, 126, 200, 207–211, 214, 223–228, 231
Insert⇨Object method, 146
Insert Picture dialog box, 150–151
Insert Procedure dialog box, 203, 218, 220
InsertSoundObject macro, 162
inside-outside activation technique, 183–184
installation, the registry and, 185, 275, 281
Instancing property, 218
interactions with other applications, testing, 241
integrated programs, 10
integrity, of tables, 158
Interfaces key, 293
Item⇨Button, 161
Item⇨Text Box, 161

•J•
justButtons, 270

•K•
keys, registry
 AutoConvert key, 292
 AutoConvertTo key, 292
 AutoTreatAs key, 292
 AuxUserType key, 290
 CLSID key, 186–188, 287, 289
 Conversion key, 292
 Convertible key, 292
 DataFormats key, 290
 ddeexec key, 285
 DefaultExtension key, 291
 DefaultFile key, 291
 DefaultIcon key, 291
 HKEY_CLASSES_ROOT key, 185–186, 187, 244, 278, 282–289
 HKEY_CURRENT_CONFIG key, 278, 280–281
 HKEY_CURRENT_USER key, 278–280
 HKEY_DYN_DATA key, 278, 281
 HKEY_LOCAL_MACHINE key, 278, 280
 HKEY_USERS key, 278, 280
 InProcHandler key, 291
 InProcServer key, 292
 Insertable key, 288, 291
 Interfaces key, 293

(continued)

keys, registry *(continued)*
  LocalServer key, 291
  MiscStatus key, 291
  My Computer key, 278
  Paint.Picture key, 283–285
  PerfStats key, 281
  ProgID key, 292
  PropertySheetHandler key, 287
  Protocol key, 288
  QuickView key, 286
  ShellNew subkey, 274, 283, 286–287
  StdFileEditing key, 288
  TreatAs key, 292
  Verb key, 288, 292
  ZIP key, 282–283
KRNL386.EXE, 28
keystroke combinations
  Alt+Tab (display spreadsheets), 113
  Alt+Tab (reselect TurboCAD), 100
  Ctrl+Alt+Del, 236–237
  Ctrl+C (Edit⇨Copy), 60, 63, 67, 213, 214, 230, 231
  Ctrl+F5 (Start With Full Compile), 218
  Ctrl+S (File⇨Save), 60, 63, 67, 211, 214, 226, 231

• *L* •

LAUNCH command, 121
learning curves, for learning about macros vs. programming, 173
LEAVES.BMP, 74–77, 83, 87, 94, 121

LINK-ASSIGN command, 122
Link check box, 63, 150, 201, 228
LINK-CREATE macro command, 122
linking
  advantages/disadvantages of, 12–13, 14
  basic description of, 10, 12–14, 39, 297
  client/server programs and, 24–25, 47
  embedding and, differences between, 39
  logos, 86–91
  Paint graphics, 60, 63–64, 87–88
  repairing broken OLE links, 253–256
  spreadsheet data, 67, 112–115
  testing, 211–214, 226–228, 231–232
Links dialog box, 113, 115, 254
Link to File check box, 160
LocalServer key, 291
locking mechanisms, 192
logos
  inserting, with macros, 72, 78
  linking, 86, 87–91
  using paint programs for, 83
Lotus 1-2-3, 16, 50–51, 109, 170. *See also* spreadsheets
  application-based languages and, 73
  determining OLE capabilities and, 46
  Edit menu, 110–111

embedding spreadsheets data and, 112–118

linking spreadsheets data and, 112–115

macros and, 118–119, 120–122

OLE automation and, 120–122

as a server, 176

system resources and, 27, 28, 40

LotusScript, 73, 293

low-level languages, basic description of, 171, 172

LRPC (Lightweight Remote Procedure Call), 17, 31, 297

• *M* •

Macintosh, 32. *See also* Apple Computer

macro(s), 20, 91

Access BASIC and, 193–194

advanced tasks performed by, 72

basic description of, 71–77, 99, 297

Change Category macro, 142–144, 196

charting programs and, 105

CorelDRAW! and, 82, 92

DBMSs and, 124, 131–144

DDE, 116, 120–122, 146, 285, 296

deciding when to use, 172–173

DLLs and, 79–90

editing, 77–78

as a form of programming, 169–171

InsertSoundObject macro, 162

LINK-CREATE macro command, 122

OLE automation and, 120–122

OLE-specific files and, 78–80

planning, 77

programming languages vs., 172–173

scripts and, comparison of, 103

shells, 160, 162

simple form, creating, 133–142

simple object, creating, 142–144

spreadsheets and, 116, 118–119

testing, 78

word processors and, 146

Macro Builder entry, 140

Macro dialog box, 74, 140, 142, 159–160

mail merge, 146, 151, 170–171

MEAT.BMP, 135

Media Architects, 261

memory. *See also* hard disks

the limitations of OLE and, 27–30

programs which manage, 29

RAM (random-access memory), 28–29

-related errors, 242–243

requirements for embedding, 25

shortages, using a notepad as a client in the case of, 176

menu(s). *See also* specific menus

customizing applications and, 41

edit action and, 181–182

in-place activation and, 214–217, 232–234

Menu Editor, 215

Menus button, 160

methods

basic description of, 20–21

class modules and, 217

Copy⇨Paste Special method, 146

Insert⇨Object method, 146

specialized server, 99–103

MFC (Microsoft Foundation Classes), 80, 272

MFCOLEUI.DLL, 80

MicroHelp, 262–263

microprocessors, 27

Microsoft

Office, 43, 65–68

OLE Software Development Kit (SDK), 272–273

Publisher, 22–23

Schedule+, 65

Windows Software Development Kit (SDK), 272

Works, 10

minus sign (-), 282

MiscStatus key, 291

Module tab, 203

MS-DOS, 37, 43. *See also* DOS (Disk Operating System)

multiplatform support, lack of, 32

My Computer icon, 242–243

My Computer key, 278

• N •

Name field, 218

Name property, 139

NegotiatePosition properties, 215–216

nested objects, 54, 298

NetPak Professional, 269

network support, lack of, for OLE, 31–32

New Button dialog box, 161

New Category dialog box, 200

New Category form, 198

New pushbutton, 135

New table, 198

NLS (National Language Support), 79

NotePad, 145, 176

command line interface and, 177

registry and, 186

Novell, 16, 73, 120

• O •

object(s)

attaching descriptive data to, 97

basic description of, 20–21, 298

converting, from linked to embedded, 25

in DBMSs, 124–127

definition of, by class modules, 217

frames, 130–131

nested, 54, 298

properties, 131–133

in spreadsheets, 112–118

in word processing documents, 146–150

Object Data dialog box, 95, 97

Object Data Manager button, 94, 97

Object Data menu, 94, 96

Object Data Roll-up, 94

Object dialog box, 65–66

Object Inspector, 224, 229

Object Type list box, 58, 61, 65, 209, 213, 230, 231

Object Type scroll box, 50

OCXs (OLE Custom eXtensions), 42, 259–260, 263, 298

ODBC (Open Database Connectivity), 125, 153
  basic description of, 298
  DDE vs., 157

OLE2CONV.DLL, 79

OLE2DISP.DLL, 79

OLE2.DLL, 79, 291

OLE2NLS.DLL, 79

OLE2.REG, 79

OLE32.DLL, 291

OLE automation. See also VBA (Visual BASIC for Applications)
  CorelDRAW! and, 93
  DBMSs and, 119–122
  definition of, 15–16, 54, 71–80
  macros and, 72–77
  spreadsheets and, 119, 120–122

OLECLI.DLL, 78, 79, 80

OLEConnect entry, 74, 75

OLEContainer icon, 224, 229

OLE_LINKX bookmark, 116

OLEMISC_ACTIVATEWHENVISIBLE flag, 184

OLEMISC_INSIDEOUT flag, 184

OLE Server radio button, 218

OLESRV.DLL, 78, 79, 80

OLE Version 1.0
  as a better version of DDE, 37
  DLLs and, 80
  entries in the registry, 287–289
  file moves and, 248
  in-place activation/editing and, 15
  OLE capabilities and, 46, 51–55, 241
  open programming mode and, 179
  software publishers and, 30
  standard actions and, 181, 182
  updating objects from, 181

OLE Version 2.0
  DDE and, 120
  DLLs and, 80
  entries in the registry, 289–293
  file moves and, 248
  in-place activation/editing and, 15, 148, 232–234
  LRPC and, 17, 31
  OLE automation and, 120
  OLE capabilities and, 46, 51–55, 241
  the single-user standard and, 31–32
  standard actions and, 181, 182
  testing and, 244
  updating objects from Version 1.0 to, 181

OLE.WK4, 118

On Change event, 142

On Click event, 198, 202, 204

On Current event, 140, 196

On Dbl Click event, 198, 201

On Got Focus event, 198

Open action, 180–182

Open Data Source dialog box, 153

OpenDoc, 16, 32

Open Filename command, 93

Open mode, 179, 180–181

Option dialog box, 249–251

Options button, 153

Options dialog box, 121, 217–218, 219

OS/2, 16, 43

outside-in plus inside-out preferred, 183

• P •

Paint (Windows 95)

enhancing spreadsheets with, 110, 117, 118

file associations and, 285

form macros and, 135–144

interface documentation and, 93

macros and, 74–77

objects, in Access tables, 128–131, 197, 200

objects, context menu for, 147

objects, inserting, into Word, 74–77

OLE capabilities of, assessing, 50, 83–84, 87

testing linking/embedding and, 209–214, 226–228, 230–232

using OLE with, basic example of, 60–64

Paintbrush

enhancing spreadsheets with, 110, 118

feature-related errors and, 240

file entry, in the registry, 249–250

macros and, 82

objects, inserting, into Access, 128–131

objects, inserting, into WordPad, 87–91

OLE capabilities of, assessing, 50, 51–52, 83, 84–86

testing linking/embedding and, 209–214, 226–228, 230–232

using OLE with, basic example of, 57–60

Paint.Picture key, 283–285

paint programs. *See also* Paint (Windows 95); Paintbrush

basic description of, 81, 83–91

OLE capabilities of, assessing, 50–52, 83–86

Paradox for Windows, 126

paragraph, end-of, mark for, 114

Paragraph⇨Centered, 88

Pascal

Delphi and, 223

as a high-level language, 171

Paste Link radio button, 67, 88, 100, 214, 231

Paste Special dialog box, 50, 67–68, 84–87, 113, 211–214, 228–231

PCX (Zsoft Paintbrush) files, 83, 126, 150

Pentium processor, 109

PerfectScript, 293

PerfStats key, 281

phantom documents, creating, 255

Picture property, 140

Picture tool, 138

Picture Type property, 139

Pinnacle Publishing, 261

PinPoint VB, 267–268

pixels, raster graphics and, 91

Play action, 182

Plug 'n Play, 280

plus sign (+), 141, 185, 187

pointers, basic description of, 20

Position in Menu field, 160

PowerBuilder, 42

PowerPoint, 42–43, 82

Preview field, 156

Print Filename command, 93

printing

  with Notepad applications, 176, 177

  using a command line switch, 178

Print method, 20

Proc list box, 218

ProgID key, 292

Program Manager, testing and, 241, 242

programming

  16-bit, 42, 80, 207, 223

  32-bit, 42, 80, 207, 223

  with Access BASIC, 175, 177, 184, 191–206

  activation techniques and, 183–184

  the command line interface and, 177–178

  deciding what to program, 175–178

  with Delphi, 223–234

  good, twelve steps to, 187–189

  in-depth topics, 271–273

  languages, deciding when to use, 172–173

  modes, four OLE, 178–182

  principles for OLE, 175–190

  reasons for, 169–174

  registering your program, 185–187, 221, 247–252

  standard actions, 180–182

  with Visual BASIC, 173, 175–177, 184, 207–222

  writing the OLE portion of your program, 187–189

Project1 dialog box, 220

Project Name field, 218

Project tab, 217–218, 219

properties. *See also* properties (listed by name)

  class modules and, 217

  DBMS object, 131–133

  definition of, 20

properties (listed by name)
AutoSize property, 224, 229
Back Color property, 204
Got Focus property, 132
GroupIndex property, 233
Height property, 139
Instancing property, 218
Name property, 139
Picture property, 140
Picture Type property, 139
Public property, 218
Record Source property, 196
Size Mode property, 139, 196
Source Doc property, 130
Source Item property, 131
Special Effects property, 204, 205
Value property, 141
Width property, 139
Properties dialog box, 139, 140,
142, 196
Properties window, 208, 218
Property radio button, 218
PropertySheetHandler key, 287
Protocol key, 288
Public property, 218

• *Q* •

Quattro Pro, 28, 109. *See also*
spreadsheets
queries
Access BASIC and, 193–194
creating tables and, 134, 135

inserting databases and, 157–158
Query Options dialog box, 154–155
QuickView key, 286
Quit command, 93

• *R* •

RAD (Rapid Application Development). *See* Delphi; Visual BASIC
basic description of, 298
Delphi as a form of, 223
radio buttons
Blank Database radio button, 134
Create from File radio button, 87, 94
Create New radio button, 209
File radio button, 63, 228
Function radio button, 218
OLE Server radio button, 218
Paste Link radio button, 67, 88,
100, 214, 231
Property radio button, 218
RAM (random-access memory),
28–29
raster graphics
charting programs and, 105
converting vector graphics into,
100–103
definition of, 83, 299
support for, in drawing programs, 91
read-only status, 192
read-write status, 192
real estate software, 41
Record dialog box, 159
Record Macro dialog, 74

Record macro Name field, 160

Record pushbutton, 74

Record Source property, 196

records, definition of, 126

Recycle Bin, 274

Redo action, 182

REGEDIT, 185, 248, 252, 275–277

REGEDIT.EXE, 185, 248, 276

registry, 79, 117, 150. *See also* keys, registry; REGEDIT

  basic description of, 247, 273–294

  DDE macros and, 122

  environment settings, 279–280, 281

  file extensions in, 244, 248, 282–286

  file association and, 279, 281, 284–286, 287, 289–290

  flags and, 184

  hardware configuration entries, 280, 281

  installation and, 185, 275, 281

  OLE Version 1.0 entries in, 287–289

  OLE Version 2.0 entries in, 289–293

  performance settings, 281

  problems with, fixing, 252–253

  registering programs with, 185–187, 221, 247–252

  system status settings, 281

  taking a closer look at, 282–286

  terminology, 274–275

  user configuration settings, 279–280, 281

  Windows 95, 185, 249–253, 273–294

reports

  adding bitmaps to, 124, 128–131

  OLE-supported, creating, 266–267

RequestDataFormats, 289

reusability, 172

Rocket, 269

RPC (Remote Procedure Call), 17, 32, 291, 299

RTF (rich text format), 266, 291

rules, validation, 193

Run⇨Compile Loaded Modules, 200, 204

Run⇨End, 220

run-time, definition of, 128, 184

• S •

Save As dialog box, 60, 63, 67, 211, 214, 226, 231

Save button, 198

Save tool, 134–135, 139, 142

Schedule, 42–43, 65

Scissors tool, 60

scripting, 91, 92. *See also* VBA (Visual BASIC for Applications)

  CAD and, 103–104

  definition of, 103

SDKs (Software Development Kits)

  basic description of, 299

  Graphics Server Software Development Kit, 261–262

  OLE Software Development Kit, 272–273

Windows Software Development Kit, 272

search-and-replace commands, 170

Select a Title for the Program dialog box, 278

Selected mode, 178–179, 180

Select Fields tab, 155

Selection tools, 63, 83, 87, 213

Select Method check box, 152

Select Program Folder dialog box, 276

server(s)

  basic code for, in DLLs, 79

  basic description of, 20–26, 176

  charting programs and, 105, 106

  DBMSs as, 124

  how clients work with, 24–26

  in-place activation/editing and, 214–217, 232–234

  In-Process/Out-of-Process, 217–221

  methods, specialized, 99–103

  registering, 221

  testing, 219–220

  two types of, in Visual BASIC, 217

  types of OLE capabilities and, 46–47, 50–51

  writing, with Visual BASIC, 217–221

SetDataFormats, 289

Setup Wizard, 185, 221

SetValue, 140–141

SFT (Setup and Format Table), 280

Shapeware Corporation, 264

sharing data, basic description of, 37–39

ShellNew subkey, 274, 283, 286–287

shrinking applications, to a manageable size, 40–42

single-click procedures, 202

single-user standard, problem of, 31–32

Size Mode property, 139, 196

sizing

  images, vector graphics and, 91

  logos, to match headers, 88

slide show applications, 92, 104

SOM (System Object Model), 16, 299

Sort Records tab, 155

sound(s)

  alarm, 128

  CorelShow and, 92

  objects, DLLs for, 80

  objects, macros for, 158–165

  WAV format for, 126, 148–149

Source Doc property, 130

Source field, 84

Source Item property, 131

Special Effect property, 204, 205

spell checkers, 17, 41

spreadsheets. *See also* Excel; Lotus-1-2-3; charting programs; Quattro Pro

  basic description of, 109–122

  CorelShow and, 92

  DDE and, 10–11

embedding, inside a Word document, 65–66

embedding data in, 112–118

linking, 67, 112–116

macros and, 116, 118–119

OLE automation and, 120–122

as servers, 176

SQL (Structured Query Language), 125, 157–158, 299

Standard tab, 224, 229

Start menu, adding RegEdit to, 275–277

StartMode group, 218

Startup Form list box, 218

StdFileEditing key, 288

stock market software, 41

Stop button, 160

string values, 274–275

stylesheets, 170

SuccessWare90, 269

SWEETS.BMP, 200–201

switch between inside-out through-out and outside-in throughout, 184

switches, 177–178, 253

Symantec C++, 272

symbols
+ (plus sign), 141, 185, 187
- (minus sign), 282

Synergy Software Technologies, 263

SYSTEM.DA0, 252–253

SYSTEM directory, 80, 81, 185, 248

SYSTEM.INI, 241, 252, 273, 281

system integration testing, 236–239

system resources. *See also* hard disk; memory
the limitations of OLE and, 27–30

maximizing, 29

testing and, 242

System tab, 229

• T •

table(s)
Access BASIC and, 193–205

adding OLE objects to, 198–201

changing the contents of, 194–201

creating, 134–137

maintaining the integrity of, 158

modifying OLE objects in, 194–198

Table AutoFormat button, 156

Table View, 127

templates, document, 41

testing
broken applications and, 240–243

initial, advantages of, 236–240

linking/embedding, 209–214, 226–228, 230–232

overview of, 235–246

servers, 219–220

subsystem, 236–238

system integration, 236–239

unexpected event, 236–237, 239–240

Text Properties action, 182

TForm1.ExitClick, 224, 229

TForm1.OLEbuttonClick, 224, 229

TGA files, 260

TIF (tagged image format) files, 83

time, taken up by programming vs. macro recording, 172

Toggle Field Codes option, 157

tool(s). *See also* toolbars; toolbox
  Combo Box tool, 138
  Picture tool, 138
  Save tool, 134–135, 139, 142
  Scissors tool, 60
  Selection tools, 63, 83, 87, 213

toolbar(s)
  customizing applications and, 41
  edit action and, 181–182

toolboxes
  provided with DBMS frames, 130–131
  Visual BASIC, 208, 212

Tools⇨Macro, 74, 159, 162

Tools⇨Macro⇨Record, 118

Tools⇨Macro⇨Show Transcript, 118

Tools⇨Options, 217

tracking events, 191–192

TreatAs key, 292

TTS (NetWare Transaction Tracking System), 191–192

TurboCAD, 100–103

• *U* •

UCSD Pascal, 37

UFOs (Unidentified Flying Objects), 25, 52

Unbound Object Frame control, 130, 197

Undo action, 182

unexpected event testing, 236–237, 239–240

Update Field option, 157

Update Links option, 151

Use OLE button, 209, 211, 213, 214, 224, 228, 231

user configuration settings, 279–280, 281

USER.DA0, 252–253

USER.DAT, 253

USER.EXE, 28

• *V* •

validation rules, 193

Value property, 141

VBA (Visual BASIC for Applications), 72–73, 159, 271, 293–294
  basic description of, 300
  CorelDRAW! and, 82, 92–93
  DBMSs and, 124

VBEdit menu, 217

VBFile menu title, 217

VBXs (Visual Basic eXtensions), 42
  basic description of, 259–263, 300
  graphics-related, 260–262
  ImageKnife/VBX, 261

vector graphics
  basic description of, 91, 300
  charting programs and, 105

converting raster graphics into, 100–103

VEGETABLE.BMP, 135

Ventura Publisher, 176

Verb key, 288, 292

Version 1.0 (OLE)

  as a better version of DDE, 37

  DLLs and, 80

  entries in the registry, 287–289

  file moves and, 248

  in-place activation/editing and, 15

  OLE capabilities and, 46, 51–55, 241

  open programming mode and, 179

  software publishers and, 30

  standard actions and, 181, 182

  updating objects from, 181

Version 2.0 (OLE)

  DDE and, 120

  DLLs and, 80

  entries in the registry, 289–293

  file moves and, 248

  in-place activation/editing and, 15, 148, 232–234

  LRPC and, 17, 31

  OLE automation and, 120

  OLE capabilities and, 46, 51–55, 241

  the single-user standard and, 31–32

  standard actions and, 181, 182

  testing and, 244

updating objects from Version 1.0 to, 181

videocassette formats, 42

video clips, editing, 149–150

View⇨Field Codes, 74

View⇨Field List, 196

View⇨Options, 87, 249

Views option, 153

VisiCalc, 109

Visio, 264

Visual BASIC, 1, 175–177, 207–222

  activation techniques and, 184, 214–217

  communications programs and, 262

  creating OLE servers with, 217–221

  DDE and, 177

  debugger, 267–268

  extensibility and, 173

  graphics and, 260–262

  learning to write programs with, 173

  menus, 214–217

  OLE-specific files and, 79

  Setup Wizard, 185, 221

  subsystem testing and, 237

  ten OLE add-ins for, 259–270

  testing with, 209–214

  Version 1.0, 207, 221, 260

  Version 2.0, 207, 221, 260

  Version 3.0, 207, 221

  Version 4.0, 207, 217, 221

Visual C++, 259, 272

VxD (virtual device drivers), 150

• W •

WAV (sound) files, 126, 148–149
Width property, 139
WIN32S, 80
WIN.INI, 241, 252, 273, 281
WinComm Pro, 50–51
Windows 3.0, 2
Windows 3.1, 2, 42, 57–60
  compatibility issues and, 45
  determining OLE capabilities and,
    46, 50
  DLLs and, 80
  lack of a drawing program in, 91
Windows 3.x, 87, 147
  DBMSs and, 127
  Paintbrush provided with, 83
  registry and, 185, 248–249, 273
  upgrading from, 253
Windows 95, 2, 37, 45, 60–64. *See
    also* Paint (Windows 95)
  additional OLE support provided
    by, 87
  determining OLE capabilities
    and, 47
  displaying context menus in, 147
  lack of a drawing program in, 91
  long filenames in, 253
  OLE-specific files and, 80
  registry, 185, 249–253, 273–294
  specialized server methods
    and, 100

VBX components and, 42
  Visual BASIC and, 207
WINDOWS directory, 185, 248, 275
Windows NT
  determining OLE capabilities
    and, 47
  OLE Version 2.0 and, 37
  REGEDIT and, 185
Wizards
  Columnar Form Wizard, 127
  Combo Box Wizard, 138
  Form Wizard, 137
  Setup Wizard, 185, 221
WMF (Windows metafile) format, 150
Word for Windows. *See also* word
    processors
  client/server programs and,
    22–23, 176
  compatibility with, ensuring,
    42–43
  database OLE feature, 152–158
  DDE and, 121–122, 177, 251, 285
  determining OLE capabilities and,
    46, 50–51
  Dialog Editor, 161–165
  DOC file format, 279, 283, 285
  document-centric computing
    and, 17
  embedding spreadsheets in, 65–66
  extensibility and, 173
  feature-related errors and, 240
  fixing broken links and, 254–256

form of BASIC provided by, 159

in-place editing and, 52–53

inserting graphics into, 74–77, 93, 150–151

linking spreadsheets to, 67, 112–116

macros and, 74–77, 158–165

memory requirements for, 27–28

menu system of, 159

OCX components and, 42

OLE automation and, 121

registry and, 250–252, 288, 290, 293

sharing compound documents and, 29

system resources and, 27–28

testing links and, 214

updating files and, 39

using different versions of, 29

VBA and, 294

WordPad, 87, 145. *See also* word processors

client support, 84

inserting pictures in, 60–64, 150–151

interface documentation and, 93

linking Paintbrush objects to, 87–91

specialized server methods and, 100–103

WordPerfect, 31, 293. *See also* word processors

customizing applications and, 40, 41

document-centric computing and, 17

memory requirements for, 28, 40

OCX components and, 42

word processors. *See also* Word for Windows; WordPerfect

client/server services provided by, 176

DBMSs and, 124

definition of, 145

inserting databases into, 151–158

inserting pictures into, 74–77, 93, 150–151

macros and, 158–165

mail merge and, 146, 151, 170–171

spreadsheets links and, 67, 112–116

text, adding, to forms/reports, 124

using, overview of, 145–165

Write, 84, 145. *See also* word processors

inserting pictures in, 57–60, 150–151

linking Paintbrush objects to, 60, 87–91

specialized server methods and, 100–103

• Z •

ZIP key, 282–283

The Fun & Easy Way™ to learn about computers and more!

Windows® 3.11 For Dummies,® 3rd Edition
by Andy Rathbone
ISBN: 1-56884-370-4
$16.95 USA/
$22.95 Canada
SUPER STAR

Mutual Funds For Dummies™
by Eric Tyson
ISBN: 1-56884-226-0
$16.99 USA/
$22.99 Canada
SUPER STAR

DOS For Dummies,® 2nd Edition
by Dan Gookin
ISBN: 1-878058-75-4
$16.95 USA/
$22.95 Canada
SUPER STAR

The Internet For Dummies,® 2nd Edition
by John Levine & Carol Baroudi
ISBN: 1-56884-222-8
$19.99 USA/
$26.99 Canada

Personal Finance For Dummies™
by Eric Tyson
ISBN: 1-56884-150-7
$16.95 USA/
$22.95 Canada
SUPER STAR

PCs For Dummies,® 3rd Edition
by Dan Gookin & Andy Rathbone
ISBN: 1-56884-904-4
$16.99 USA/
$22.99 Canada

Macs® For Dummies,® 3rd Edition
by David Pogue
ISBN: 1-56884-239-2
$19.99 USA/
$26.99 Canada

The SAT® I For Dummies™
by Suzee Vlk
ISBN: 1-56884-213-9
$14.99 USA/
$20.99 Canada
SUPER STAR

Here's a complete listing of IDG Books' ...For Dummies® titles

Title	Author	ISBN	Price
DATABASE			
Access 2 For Dummies®	by Scott Palmer	ISBN: 1-56884-090-X	$19.95 USA/$26.95 Canada
Access Programming For Dummies®	by Rob Krumm	ISBN: 1-56884-091-8	$19.95 USA/$26.95 Canada
Approach 3 For Windows® For Dummies®	by Doug Lowe	ISBN: 1-56884-233-3	$19.99 USA/$26.99 Canada
dBASE For DOS For Dummies®	by Scott Palmer & Michael Stabler	ISBN: 1-56884-188-4	$19.95 USA/$26.95 Canada
dBASE For Windows® For Dummies®	by Scott Palmer	ISBN: 1-56884-179-5	$19.95 USA/$26.95 Canada
dBASE 5 For Windows® Programming For Dummies®	by Ted Coombs & Jason Coombs	ISBN: 1-56884-215-5	$19.99 USA/$26.99 Canada
FoxPro 2.6 For Windows® For Dummies®	by John Kaufeld	ISBN: 1-56884-187-6	$19.95 USA/$26.95 Canada
Paradox 5 For Windows® For Dummies®	by John Kaufeld	ISBN: 1-56884-185-X	$19.95 USA/$26.95 Canada
DESKTOP PUBLISHING/ILLUSTRATION/GRAPHICS			
CorelDRAW! 5 For Dummies®	by Deke McClelland	ISBN: 1-56884-157-4	$19.95 USA/$26.95 Canada
CorelDRAW! For Dummies®	by Deke McClelland	ISBN: 1-56884-042-X	$19.95 USA/$26.95 Canada
Desktop Publishing & Design For Dummies®	by Roger C. Parker	ISBN: 1-56884-234-1	$19.99 USA/$26.99 Canada
Harvard Graphics 2 For Windows® For Dummies®	by Roger C. Parker	ISBN: 1-56884-092-6	$19.95 USA/$26.95 Canada
PageMaker 5 For Macs® For Dummies®	by Galen Gruman & Deke McClelland	ISBN: 1-56884-178-7	$19.95 USA/$26.95 Canada
PageMaker 5 For Windows® For Dummies®	by Deke McClelland & Galen Gruman	ISBN: 1-56884-160-4	$19.95 USA/$26.95 Canada
Photoshop 3 For Macs® For Dummies®	by Deke McClelland	ISBN: 1-56884-208-2	$19.99 USA/$26.99 Canada
QuarkXPress 3.3 For Dummies®	by Galen Gruman & Barbara Assadi	ISBN: 1-56884-217-1	$19.99 USA/$26.99 Canada
FINANCE/PERSONAL FINANCE/TEST TAKING REFERENCE			
Everyday Math For Dummies™	by Charles Seiter	ISBN: 1-56884-248-1	$14.99 USA/$22.99 Canada
Personal Finance For Dummies™ For Canadians	by Eric Tyson & Tony Martin	ISBN: 1-56884-378-X	$18.99 USA/$24.99 Canada
QuickBooks 3 For Dummies®	by Stephen L. Nelson	ISBN: 1-56884-227-9	$19.99 USA/$26.99 Canada
Quicken 8 For DOS For Dummies,® 2nd Edition	by Stephen L. Nelson	ISBN: 1-56884-210-4	$19.95 USA/$26.95 Canada
Quicken 5 For Macs® For Dummies®	by Stephen L. Nelson	ISBN: 1-56884-211-2	$19.95 USA/$26.95 Canada
Quicken 4 For Windows® For Dummies,® 2nd Edition	by Stephen L. Nelson	ISBN: 1-56884-209-0	$19.95 USA/$26.95 Canada
Taxes For Dummies,™ 1995 Edition	by Eric Tyson & David J. Silverman	ISBN: 1-56884-220-1	$14.99 USA/$20.99 Canada
The GMAT® For Dummies™	by Suzee Vlk, Series Editor	ISBN: 1-56884-376-3	$14.99 USA/$20.99 Canada
The GRE® For Dummies™	by Suzee Vlk, Series Editor	ISBN: 1-56884-375-5	$14.99 USA/$20.99 Canada
Time Management For Dummies™	by Jeffrey J. Mayer	ISBN: 1-56884-360-7	$16.99 USA/$22.99 Canada
TurboTax For Windows® For Dummies®	by Gail A. Helsel, CPA	ISBN: 1-56884-228-7	$19.99 USA/$26.99 Canada
GROUPWARE/INTEGRATED			
ClarisWorks For Macs® For Dummies®	by Frank Higgins	ISBN: 1-56884-363-1	$19.99 USA/$26.99 Canada
Lotus Notes For Dummies®	by Pat Freeland & Stephen Londergan	ISBN: 1-56884-212-0	$19.95 USA/$26.95 Canada
Microsoft® Office 4 For Windows® For Dummies®	by Roger C. Parker	ISBN: 1-56884-183-3	$19.95 USA/$26.95 Canada
Microsoft® Works 3 For Windows® For Dummies®	by David C. Kay	ISBN: 1-56884-214-7	$19.99 USA/$26.99 Canada
SmartSuite 3 For Dummies®	by Jan Weingarten & John Weingarten	ISBN: 1-56884-367-4	$19.99 USA/$26.99 Canada
INTERNET/COMMUNICATIONS/NETWORKING			
America Online® For Dummies,® 2nd Edition	by John Kaufeld	ISBN: 1-56884-933-8	$19.99 USA/$26.99 Canada
CompuServe For Dummies,® 2nd Edition	by Wallace Wang	ISBN: 1-56884-937-0	$19.99 USA/$26.99 Canada
Modems For Dummies,® 2nd Edition	by Tina Rathbone	ISBN: 1-56884-223-6	$19.99 USA/$26.99 Canada
MORE Internet For Dummies®	by John R. Levine & Margaret Levine Young	ISBN: 1-56884-164-7	$19.95 USA/$26.95 Canada
MORE Modems & On-line Services For Dummies®	by Tina Rathbone	ISBN: 1-56884-365-8	$19.99 USA/$26.99 Canada
Mosaic For Dummies,® Windows Edition	by David Angell & Brent Heslop	ISBN: 1-56884-242-2	$19.99 USA/$26.99 Canada
NetWare For Dummies,® 2nd Edition	by Ed Tittel, Deni Connor & Earl Follis	ISBN: 1-56884-369-0	$19.99 USA/$26.99 Canada
Networking For Dummies®	by Doug Lowe	ISBN: 1-56884-079-9	$19.95 USA/$26.95 Canada
PROCOMM PLUS 2 For Windows® For Dummies®	by Wallace Wang	ISBN: 1-56884-219-8	$19.99 USA/$26.99 Canada
TCP/IP For Dummies®	by Marshall Wilensky & Candace Leiden	ISBN: 1-56884-241-4	$19.99 USA/$26.99 Canada

The Internet For Macs® For Dummies® 2nd Edition	by Charles Seiter	ISBN: 1-56884-371-2	$19.99 USA/$26.99 Canada
The Internet For Macs® For Dummies® Starter Kit	by Charles Seiter	ISBN: 1-56884-244-9	$29.99 USA/$39.99 Canada
The Internet For Macs® For Dummies® Starter Kit Bestseller Edition	by Charles Seiter	ISBN: 1-56884-245-7	$39.99 USA/$54.99 Canada
The Internet For Windows® For Dummies® Starter Kit	by John R. Levine & Margaret Levine Young	ISBN: 1-56884-237-6	$34.99 USA/$44.99 Canada
The Internet For Windows® For Dummies® Starter Kit, Bestseller Edition	by John R. Levine & Margaret Levine Young	ISBN: 1-56884-246-5	$39.99 USA/$54.99 Canada

MACINTOSH

Mac® Programming For Dummies®	by Dan Parks Sydow	ISBN: 1-56884-173-6	$19.95 USA/$26.95 Canada
Macintosh® System 7.5 For Dummies®	by Bob LeVitus	ISBN: 1-56884-197-3	$19.95 USA/$26.95 Canada
MORE Macs® For Dummies®	by David Pogue	ISBN: 1-56884-087-X	$19.95 USA/$26.95 Canada
PageMaker 5 For Macs® For Dummies®	by Galen Gruman & Deke McClelland	ISBN: 1-56884-178-7	$19.95 USA/$26.95 Canada
QuarkXPress 3.3 For Dummies®	by Galen Gruman & Barbara Assadi	ISBN: 1-56884-217-1	$19.95 USA/$26.99 Canada
Upgrading and Fixing Macs® For Dummies®	by Kearney Rietmann & Frank Higgins	ISBN: 1-56884-189-2	$19.95 USA/$26.95 Canada

MULTIMEDIA

Multimedia & CD-ROMs For Dummies® 2nd Edition	by Andy Rathbone	ISBN: 1-56884-907-9	$19.99 USA/$26.99 Canada
Multimedia & CD-ROMs For Dummies® Interactive Multimedia Value Pack, 2nd Edition	by Andy Rathbone	ISBN: 1-56884-909-5	$29.99 USA/$39.99 Canada

OPERATING SYSTEMS:

DOS

MORE DOS For Dummies®	by Dan Gookin	ISBN: 1-56884-046-2	$19.95 USA/$26.95 Canada
OS/2® Warp For Dummies® 2nd Edition	by Andy Rathbone	ISBN: 1-56884-205-8	$19.99 USA/$26.99 Canada

UNIX

MORE UNIX® For Dummies®	by John R. Levine & Margaret Levine Young	ISBN: 1-56884-361-5	$19.99 USA/$26.99 Canada
UNIX® For Dummies®	by John R. Levine & Margaret Levine Young	ISBN: 1-878058-58-4	$19.95 USA/$26.95 Canada

WINDOWS

MORE Windows® For Dummies® 2nd Edition	by Andy Rathbone	ISBN: 1-56884-048-9	$19.95 USA/$26.95 Canada
Windows® 95 For Dummies®	by Andy Rathbone	ISBN: 1-56884-240-6	$19.99 USA/$26.99 Canada

PCS/HARDWARE

Illustrated Computer Dictionary For Dummies® 2nd Edition	by Dan Gookin & Wallace Wang	ISBN: 1-56884-218-X	$12.95 USA/$16.95 Canada
Upgrading and Fixing PCs For Dummies® 2nd Edition	by Andy Rathbone	ISBN: 1-56884-903-6	$19.99 USA/$26.99 Canada

PRESENTATION/AUTOCAD

AutoCAD For Dummies®	by Bud Smith	ISBN: 1-56884-191-4	$19.95 USA/$26.95 Canada
PowerPoint 4 For Windows® For Dummies®	by Doug Lowe	ISBN: 1-56884-161-2	$16.99 USA/$22.99 Canada

PROGRAMMING

Borland C++ For Dummies®	by Michael Hyman	ISBN: 1-56884-162-0	$19.95 USA/$26.95 Canada
C For Dummies® Volume 1	by Dan Gookin	ISBN: 1-878058-78-9	$19.95 USA/$26.95 Canada
C++ For Dummies®	by Stephen R. Davis	ISBN: 1-56884-163-9	$19.95 USA/$26.95 Canada
Delphi Programming For Dummies®	by Neil Rubenking	ISBN: 1-56884-200-7	$19.99 USA/$26.99 Canada
Mac® Programming For Dummies®	by Dan Parks Sydow	ISBN: 1-56884-173-6	$19.95 USA/$26.95 Canada
PowerBuilder 4 Programming For Dummies®	by Ted Coombs & Jason Coombs	ISBN: 1-56884-325-9	$19.99 USA/$26.99 Canada
QBasic Programming For Dummies®	by Douglas Hergert	ISBN: 1-56884-093-4	$19.95 USA/$26.95 Canada
Visual Basic 3 For Dummies®	by Wallace Wang	ISBN: 1-56884-076-4	$19.95 USA/$26.95 Canada
Visual Basic "X" For Dummies®	by Wallace Wang	ISBN: 1-56884-230-9	$19.99 USA/$26.99 Canada
Visual C++ 2 For Dummies®	by Michael Hyman & Bob Arnson	ISBN: 1-56884-328-3	$19.99 USA/$26.99 Canada
Windows® 95 Programming For Dummies®	by S. Randy Davis	ISBN: 1-56884-327-5	$19.99 USA/$26.99 Canada

SPREADSHEET

1-2-3 For Dummies®	by Greg Harvey	ISBN: 1-878058-60-6	$16.95 USA/$22.95 Canada
1-2-3 For Windows® 5 For Dummies® 2nd Edition	by John Walkenbach	ISBN: 1-56884-216-3	$16.95 USA/$22.95 Canada
Excel 5 For Macs® For Dummies®	by Greg Harvey	ISBN: 1-56884-186-8	$19.95 USA/$26.95 Canada
Excel For Dummies® 2nd Edition	by Greg Harvey	ISBN: 1-56884-050-0	$16.95 USA/$22.95 Canada
MORE 1-2-3 For DOS For Dummies®	by John Weingarten	ISBN: 1-56884-224-4	$19.99 USA/$26.99 Canada
MORE Excel 5 For Windows® For Dummies®	by Greg Harvey	ISBN: 1-56884-207-4	$19.95 USA/$26.95 Canada
Quattro Pro 6 For Windows® For Dummies®	by John Walkenbach	ISBN: 1-56884-174-4	$19.95 USA/$26.95 Canada
Quattro Pro For DOS For Dummies®	by John Walkenbach	ISBN: 1-56884-023-3	$16.95 USA/$22.95 Canada

UTILITIES

Norton Utilities 8 For Dummies®	by Beth Slick	ISBN: 1-56884-166-3	$19.95 USA/$26.95 Canada

VCRS/CAMCORDERS

VCRs & Camcorders For Dummies™	by Gordon McComb & Andy Rathbone	ISBN: 1-56884-229-5	$14.99 USA/$20.99 Canada

WORD PROCESSING

Ami Pro For Dummies®	by Jim Meade	ISBN: 1-56884-049-7	$19.95 USA/$26.95 Canada
MORE Word For Windows® 6 For Dummies®	by Doug Lowe	ISBN: 1-56884-165-5	$19.95 USA/$26.95 Canada
MORE WordPerfect® 6 For Windows® For Dummies®	by Margaret Levine Young & David C. Kay	ISBN: 1-56884-206-6	$19.95 USA/$26.95 Canada
MORE WordPerfect® 6 For DOS For Dummies®	by Wallace Wang, edited by Dan Gookin	ISBN: 1-56884-047-0	$19.95 USA/$26.95 Canada
Word 6 For Macs® For Dummies®	by Dan Gookin	ISBN: 1-56884-190-6	$19.95 USA/$26.95 Canada
Word For Windows® 6 For Dummies®	by Dan Gookin	ISBN: 1-56884-075-6	$16.95 USA/$22.95 Canada
Word For Windows® For Dummies®	by Dan Gookin & Ray Werner	ISBN: 1-878058-86-X	$16.95 USA/$22.95 Canada
WordPerfect® 6 For DOS For Dummies®	by Dan Gookin	ISBN: 1-878058-77-0	$16.95 USA/$22.95 Canada
WordPerfect® 6.1 For Windows® For Dummies® 2nd Edition	by Margaret Levine Young & David Kay	ISBN: 1-56884-243-0	$16.95 USA/$22.95 Canada
WordPerfect® For Dummies®	by Dan Gookin	ISBN: 1-878058-52-5	$16.95 USA/$22.95 Canada

Fun, Fast, & Cheap!™

 **NEW!**

 **NEW!** **SUPER STAR**

 **SUPER STAR**

The Internet For Macs® For Dummies® Quick Reference
by Charles Seiter

ISBN: 1-56884-967-2
$9.99 USA/$12.99 Canada

Windows® 95 For Dummies® Quick Reference
by Greg Harvey

ISBN: 1-56884-964-8
$9.99 USA/$12.99 Canada

Photoshop 3 For Macs® For Dummies® Quick Reference
by Deke McClelland

ISBN: 1-56884-968-0
$9.99 USA/$12.99 Canada

WordPerfect® For DOS For Dummies® Quick Reference
by Greg Harvey

ISBN: 1-56884-009-8
$8.95 USA/$12.95 Canada

Title	Author	ISBN	Price
DATABASE			
Access 2 For Dummies® Quick Reference	by Stuart J. Stuple	ISBN: 1-56884-167-1	$8.95 USA/$11.95 Canada
dBASE 5 For DOS For Dummies® Quick Reference	by Barrie Sosinsky	ISBN: 1-56884-954-0	$9.99 USA/$12.99 Canada
dBASE 5 For Windows® For Dummies® Quick Reference	by Stuart J. Stuple	ISBN: 1-56884-953-2	$9.99 USA/$12.99 Canada
Paradox 5 For Windows® For Dummies® Quick Reference	by Scott Palmer	ISBN: 1-56884-960-5	$9.99 USA/$12.99 Canada
DESKTOP PUBLISHING/ILLUSTRATION/GRAPHICS			
CorelDRAW! 5 For Dummies® Quick Reference	by Raymond E. Werner	ISBN: 1-56884-952-4	$9.99 USA/$12.99 Canada
Harvard Graphics For Windows® For Dummies® Quick Reference	by Raymond E. Werner	ISBN: 1-56884-962-1	$9.99 USA/$12.99 Canada
Photoshop 3 For Macs® For Dummies® Quick Reference	by Deke McClelland	ISBN: 1-56884-968-0	$9.99 USA/$12.99 Canada
FINANCE/PERSONAL FINANCE			
Quicken 4 For Windows® For Dummies® Quick Reference	by Stephen L. Nelson	ISBN: 1-56884-950-8	$9.95 USA/$12.95 Canada
GROUPWARE/INTEGRATED			
Microsoft® Office 4 For Windows® For Dummies® Quick Reference	by Doug Lowe	ISBN: 1-56884-958-3	$9.99 USA/$12.99 Canada
Microsoft® Works 3 For Windows® For Dummies® Quick Reference	by Michael Partington	ISBN: 1-56884-959-1	$9.99 USA/$12.99 Canada
INTERNET/COMMUNICATIONS/NETWORKING			
The Internet For Dummies® Quick Reference	by John R. Levine & Margaret Levine Young	ISBN: 1-56884-168-X	$8.95 USA/$11.95 Canada
MACINTOSH			
Macintosh® System 7.5 For Dummies® Quick Reference	by Stuart J. Stuple	ISBN: 1-56884-956-7	$9.99 USA/$12.99 Canada
OPERATING SYSTEMS:			
DOS			
DOS For Dummies® Quick Reference	by Greg Harvey	ISBN: 1-56884-007-1	$8.95 USA/$11.95 Canada
UNIX			
UNIX® For Dummies® Quick Reference	by John R. Levine & Margaret Levine Young	ISBN: 1-56884-094-2	$8.95 USA/$11.95 Canada
WINDOWS			
Windows® 3.1 For Dummies® Quick Reference, 2nd Edition	by Greg Harvey	ISBN: 1-56884-951-6	$8.95 USA/$11.95 Canada
PCs/HARDWARE			
Memory Management For Dummies® Quick Reference	by Doug Lowe	ISBN: 1-56884-362-3	$9.99 USA/$12.99 Canada
PRESENTATION/AUTOCAD			
AutoCAD For Dummies® Quick Reference	by Ellen Finkelstein	ISBN: 1-56884-198-1	$9.99 USA/$12.99 Canada
SPREADSHEET			
1-2-3 For Dummies® Quick Reference	by John Walkenbach	ISBN: 1-56884-027-6	$8.95 USA/$11.95 Canada
1-2-3 For Windows® 5 For Dummies® Quick Reference	by John Walkenbach	ISBN: 1-56884-957-5	$9.95 USA/$12.95 Canada
Excel For Windows® For Dummies® Quick Reference, 2nd Edition	by John Walkenbach	ISBN: 1-56884-096-9	$8.95 USA/$11.95 Canada
Quattro Pro 6 For Windows® For Dummies® Quick Reference	by Stuart J. Stuple	ISBN: 1-56884-172-8	$9.95 USA/$12.95 Canada
WORD PROCESSING			
Word For Windows® 6 For Dummies® Quick Reference	by George Lynch	ISBN: 1-56884-095-0	$8.95 USA/$11.95 Canada
Word For Windows® For Dummies® Quick Reference	by George Lynch	ISBN: 1-56884-029-2	$8.95 USA/$11.95 Canada
WordPerfect® 6.1 For Windows® For Dummies® Quick Reference, 2nd Edition	by Greg Harvey	ISBN: 1-56884-966-4	$9.99 USA/$12.99/Canada

10/31/95

"A lot easier to use than the book Excel gives you!"

Lisa Schmeckpeper, New Berlin, WI, on PC World Excel 5 For Windows Handbook

Official Hayes Modem Communications Companion
by Caroline M. Halliday

ISBN: 1-56884-072-1
$29.95 USA/$39.95 Canada
Includes software.

1,001 Komputer Answers from Kim Komando
by Kim Komando

ISBN: 1-56884-460-3
$29.99 USA/$39.99 Canada
Includes software.

PC World DOS 6 Handbook, 2nd Edition
by John Socha, Clint Hicks, & Devra Hall

ISBN: 1-878058-79-7
$34.95 USA/$44.95 Canada
Includes software.

PC World Word For Windows® 6 Handbook
by Brent Heslop & David Angell

ISBN: 1-56884-054-3
$34.95 USA/$44.95 Canada
Includes software.

PC World Microsoft® Access 2 Bible, 2nd Edition
by Cary N. Prague & Michael R. Irwin

ISBN: 1-56884-086-1
$39.95 USA/$52.95 Canada
Includes software.

PC World Excel 5 For Windows® Handbook, 2nd Edition
by John Walkenbach & Dave Maguiness

ISBN: 1-56884-056-X
$34.95 USA/$44.95 Canada
Includes software.

PC World WordPerfect® 6 Handbook
by Greg Harvey

ISBN: 1-878058-80-0
$34.95 USA/$44.95 Canada
Includes software.

QuarkXPress For Windows® Designer Handbook
by Barbara Assadi & Galen Gruman

ISBN: 1-878058-45-2
$29.95 USA/$39.95 Canada

Official XTree Companion, 3rd Edition
by Beth Slick

ISBN: 1-878058-57-6
$19.95 USA/$26.95 Canada

PC World DOS 6 Command Reference and Problem Solver
by John Socha & Devra Hall

ISBN: 1-56884-055-1
$24.95 USA/$32.95 Canada

Client/Server Strategies™: A Survival Guide for Corporate Reengineers
by David Vaskevitch

ISBN: 1-56884-064-0
$29.95 USA/$39.95 Canada

"PC World Word For Windows 6 Handbook is very easy to follow with lots of 'hands on' examples. The 'Task at a Glance' is very helpful!"

Jacqueline Martens, Tacoma, WA

"Thanks for publishing this book! It's the best money I've spent this year!"

Robert D. Templeton, Ft. Worth, TX, on MORE Windows 3.1 SECRETS

Microsoft and Windows are registered trademarks of Microsoft Corporation. WordPerfect is a registered trademark of Novell. ----STRATEGIES and the IDG Books Worldwide logos are trademarks under exclusive license to IDG Books Worldwide, Inc., from International Data Group, Inc.

scholastic requests & educational orders please
ducational Sales, at 1. 800. 434. 2086

FOR MORE INFO OR TO ORDER, PLEASE CALL ▶ 800 762 2974

For volume discounts & special orders please call
Tony Real, Special Sales, at 415. 655. 3048

Macworld® Mac® & Power Mac SECRETS™, 2nd Edition
by David Pogue & Joseph Schorr

This is the definitive Mac reference for those who want to become power users! Includes three disks with 9MB of software!

WINNERS 1994-95 TECHNICAL PUBLICATIONS AND ART COMPETITIONS OF THE SOCIETY FOR TECHNICAL COMMUNICATION

ISBN: 1-56884-175-2
$39.95 USA/$54.95 Canada

Includes 3 disks chock full of software.

NEWBRIDGE BOOK CLUB SELECTION

Macworld® Mac® FAQs™
by David Pogue

Written by the hottest Macintosh author around, David Pogue, Macworld Mac FAQs gives users the ultimate Mac reference. Hundreds of Mac questions and answers side-by-side, right at your fingertips, and organized into six easy-to-reference sections with lots of sidebars and diagrams.

ISBN: 1-56884-480-8
$19.99 USA/$26.99 Canada

Macworld® System 7.5 Bible, 3rd Edition
by Lon Poole

ISBN: 1-56884-098-5
$29.95 USA/$39.95 Canada

NATIONAL BESTSELLER!

Macworld® ClarisWorks 3.0 Companion, 3rd Edition
by Steven A. Schwartz

ISBN: 1-56884-481-6
$24.99 USA/$34.99 Canada

NATIONAL BESTSELLER!

Macworld® Complete Mac® Handbook Plus Interactive CD, 3rd Edition
by Jim Heid

ISBN: 1-56884-192-2
$39.95 USA/$54.95 Canada

Includes an interactive CD-ROM.

NEWBRIDGE BOOK CLUB SELECTION

BM BC SPRIN CHOICE H

Macworld® Ultimate Mac® CD-ROM
by Jim Heid

ISBN: 1-56884-477-8
$19.99 USA/$26.99 Canada

CD-ROM includes version 2.0 of QuickTime, and over 65 MB of the best shareware, freeware, fonts, sounds, and more!

Macworld® Networking Bible, 2nd Edition
by Dave Kosiur & Joel M. Snyder

ISBN: 1-56884-194-9
$29.95 USA/$39.95 Canada

Macworld® Photoshop 3 Bible, 2nd Edition
by Deke McClelland

ISBN: 1-56884-158-2
$39.95 USA/$54.95 Canada

Includes stunning CD-ROM with add-ons, digitized photos and more.

WINNERS 1994- TECHNICAL PUBLICATION AND ART COMPETITION OF THE SOCIE FOR TECHNICAL COMMUNICATI

NEW!

Macworld® Photoshop 2.5 Bible
by Deke McClelland

ISBN: 1-56884-022-5
$29.95 USA/$39.95 Canada

NATIONAL BESTSELLER!

Macworld® FreeHand 4 Bible
by Deke McClelland

ISBN: 1-56884-170-1
$29.95 USA/$39.95 Canada

Macworld® Illustrator 5.0/5.5 Bible
by Ted Alspach

ISBN: 1-56884-097-7
$39.95 USA/$54.95 Canada

Includes CD-ROM with QuickTime tutorials.

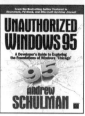

ORDER FORM

Order Center: **(800) 762-2974** *(8 a.m.–6 p.m., EST, weekdays)*

Quantity	ISBN	Title	Price	Total

Shipping & Handling Charges

	Description	First book	Each additional book	Total
Domestic	Normal	$4.50	$1.50	$
	Two Day Air	$8.50	$2.50	$
	Overnight	$18.00	$3.00	$
International	Surface	$8.00	$8.00	$
	Airmail	$16.00	$16.00	$
	DHL Air	$17.00	$17.00	$

*For large quantities call for shipping & handling charges.
**Prices are subject to change without notice.

Ship to:

Name _____

Company _____

Address _____

City/State/Zip _____

Daytime Phone _____

Payment: □ Check to IDG Books Worldwide (US Funds Only)

□ VISA   □ MasterCard   □ American Express

Card # _____ Expires _____

Signature _____

Subtotal _____

CA residents add
applicable sales tax _____

IN, MA, and MD
residents add
5% sales tax _____

IL residents add
6.25% sales tax _____

RI residents add
7% sales tax _____

TX residents add
8.25% sales tax _____

Shipping _____

Total _____

Please send this order form to:

IDG Books Worldwide, Inc.
7260 Shadeland Station, Suite 100
Indianapolis, IN 46256

Allow up to 3 weeks for delivery.
Thank you!

IDG BOOKS WORLDWIDE REGISTRATION CARD

Title of this book: OLE For Dummies

My overall rating of this book: ❏ Very good [1] ❏ Good [2] ❏ Satisfactory [3] ❏ Fair [4] ❏ Poor [5]

How I first heard about this book:

❏ Found in bookstore; name: [6]

❏ Advertisement: [8]

❏ Word of mouth; heard about book from friend, co-worker, etc.: [10]

❏ Book review: [7]

❏ Catalog: [9]

❏ Other: [11]

What I liked most about this book:

What I would change, add, delete, etc., in future editions of this book:

Other comments:

Number of computer books I purchase in a year: ❏ 1 [12] ❏ 2-5 [13] ❏ 6-10 [14] ❏ More than 10 [15]

I would characterize my computer skills as: ❏ Beginner [16] ❏ Intermediate [17] ❏ Advanced [18] ❏ Professional [19]

I use ❏ DOS [20] ❏ Windows [21] ❏ OS/2 [22] ❏ Unix [23] ❏ Macintosh [24] ❏ Other: [25]_____
(please specify)

I would be interested in new books on the following subjects:
(please check all that apply, and use the spaces provided to identify specific software)

❏ Word processing: [26]

❏ Data bases: [28]

❏ File Utilities: [30]

❏ Networking: [32]

❏ Other: [34]

❏ Spreadsheets: [27]

❏ Desktop publishing: [29]

❏ Money management: [31]

❏ Programming languages: [33]

I use a PC at (please check all that apply): ❏ home [35] ❏ work [36] ❏ school [37] ❏ other: [38] _____

The disks I prefer to use are ❏ 5.25 [39] ❏ 3.5 [40] ❏ other: [41]_____

I have a CD ROM: ❏ yes [42] ❏ no [43]

I plan to buy or upgrade computer hardware this year: ❏ yes [44] ❏ no [45]

I plan to buy or upgrade computer software this year: ❏ yes [46] ❏ no [47]

Name: _____ Business title: [48] _____ Type of Business: [49] _____

Address (❏ home [50] ❏ work [51] /Company name: _____)

Street/Suite# _____

City [52]/State [53]/Zipcode [54]: _____ Country [55] _____

❏ **I liked this book!** You may quote me by name in future
IDG Books Worldwide promotional materials.

My daytime phone number is _____

IDG BOOKS

THE WORLD OF
COMPUTER
KNOWLEDGE

 # YES!
Please keep me informed about IDG's World of Computer Knowledge.
Send me the latest IDG Books catalog.